THE ONTOLOGY OF

The nature of emotion is an important question in several philosophical and scientific domains, but little attention has so far been paid to identifying the general ontological category to which emotions belong. Given that they are short-lived, are they events? Since they often have components or stages, are they processes? Or does their close link with behaviour mean they are dispositions? In this volume, leading scholars investigate these basic ontological issues, contributing to current discussions about emotions and paving the way for new research into an underexplored area. With essays addressing issues including the temporal profile of emotions, the distinction between emotions and other affective states, and the epistemology of emotion, this original book will be valuable for students and scholars, and particularly for those working in the metaphysics of the mind and the affective sciences.

HICHEM NAAR is Visiting Assistant Professor of Philosophy at the University of Nebraska at Omaha. He has published a number of journal articles on the nature, value and normative significance of various attitudes, particularly emotions.

FABRICE TERONI is Associate Professor of Philosophy at the Universities of Geneva and Fribourg. His publications include *In Defense of Shame: The Faces of an Emotion* (2011) and *The Emotions: A Philosophical Introduction* (2012).

THE ONTOLOGY OF EMOTIONS

EDITED BY

HICHEM NAAR
University of Nebraska at Omaha

FABRICE TERONI
Universities of Geneva and Fribourg

CAMBRIDGE
UNIVERSITY PRESS

CAMBRIDGE
UNIVERSITY PRESS

University Printing House, Cambridge CB2 8BS, United Kingdom

One Liberty Plaza, 20th Floor, New York, NY 10006, USA

477 Williamstown Road, Port Melbourne, VIC 3207, Australia

314-321, 3rd Floor, Plot 3, Splendor Forum, Jasola District Centre, New Delhi - 110025, India

79 Anson Road, #06-04/06, Singapore 079906

Cambridge University Press is part of the University of Cambridge.

It furthers the University's mission by disseminating knowledge in the pursuit of education, learning and research at the highest international levels of excellence.

www.cambridge.org
Information on this title: www.cambridge.org/9781107527393
DOI: 10.1017/9781316275221

First published 2018
First paperback edition 2019

A catalogue record for this publication is available from the British Library

Library of Congress Cataloging in Publication data
NAMES: Naar, Hichem, 1985– editor, Teroni, Fabrice, 1974– editor.
TITLE: The ontology of emotions / edited by Hichem Naar, University of Nebraska at Omaha, Fabrice Teroni, Universities of Geneva and Fribourg.
DESCRIPTION: New York : Cambridge University Press, 2018. | Includes bibliographical references and index.
IDENTIFIERS: LCCN 2017030644 | ISBN 9781107110540
SUBJECTS: LCSH: Emotions (Philosophy) | Emotions.
CLASSIFICATION: LCC B105.E46 O58 2017 | DDC 128/.37–dc23
LC record available at https://lccn.loc.gov/2017030644

ISBN 978-1-107-11054-0 Hardback
ISBN 978-1-107-52739-3 Paperback

Contents

List of Contributors *page* vii

Introduction 1
Hichem Naar and Fabrice Teroni

1 Mind-Body Theories and the Emotions 14
William Jaworski

2 Dispositionality and Mentality 37
John Heil

3 Emotion as Process 51
Jenefer Robinson

4 The Ontology of Emotion 71
Matthew Soteriou

5 Phenomenal Commitments: A Puzzle for Experiential Theories of Emotion 90
Jona Vance

6 An Enactivist Theory of Emotional Content 110
Daniel Shargel and Jesse Prinz

7 The Perceptibility of Emotion 130
Joel Smith

8 Sentiments 149
Hichem Naar

9 The Metaphysics of Moods 169
Christine Tappolet

10 Night Fight 187
Clare Mac Cumhaill

Bibliography 209
Index 225

Contributors

CLARE MAC CUMHAILL is Lecturer in Philosophy at Durham University.

JOHN HEIL is Professor of Philosophy at Washington University in St. Louis and Honorary Research Associate at Monash University.

WILLIAM JAWORSKI is Associate Professor of Philosophy at Fordham University.

HICHEM NAAR is Visiting Assistant Professor of Philosophy at the University of Nebraska at Omaha.

JESSE PRINZ is Distinguished Professor of Philosophy at the City University of New York, Graduate Center.

JENEFER ROBINSON is Professor of Philosophy at the University of Cincinnati.

DANIEL SHARGEL is Associate Professor of Philosophy at Lawrence Technological University.

JOEL SMITH is Senior Lecturer in Philosophy at the University of Manchester.

MATTHEW SOTERIOU is Professor of Philosophy at King's College London.

CHRISTINE TAPPOLET is Professor of Philosophy at the University of Montreal.

FABRICE TERONI is Associate Professor of Philosophy at the Universities of Geneva and Fribourg.

JONA VANCE is Lecturer in Philosophy at Northern Arizona University.

Introduction

Hichem Naar and Fabrice Teroni

What is an emotion? No one will seriously doubt that it is a psychological entity of some sort. Rich and lively philosophical debates have failed to generate any stable picture regarding the nature of emotions that extends much beyond this platitude, however. At most, a bare majority of philosophers would agree that emotions exemplify the following features. First, emotions are characterized by a certain phenomenology: they are felt. Second, they are intentional phenomena and, as such, are in one way or another directed to various sorts of entities in the world (one is amused by the joke, sad at the death of a dear friend, or proud that one is a self-made man). Third, they are closely connected with evaluations of these entities – amusement connects with a positive evaluation of the joke, sadness with a negative evaluation of the death. Fourth, emotions are relatively short-lived: unlike other phenomena that are closely related to them, such as character traits and sentiments that may endure for substantial stretches of one's life, emotions endure at most for some hours. Beyond that, disagreement reigns and the debates, which have become increasingly important in the past two decades or so, have almost exclusively revolved around the identification of the necessary and sufficient conditions of the emotions.

Discussions of necessary conditions have tended to focus on the following issues, which mirror issues related to other types of psychological states or to psychological states in general:

a. Do emotions necessarily have an object, or should we acknowledge the possibility of objectless emotions? In the face of phenomena such as apparently objectless fear or shame, can we preserve the idea that all mental states are intentionally directed towards something (Crane 1998; Mendelovici 2014)?
b. Do emotions always feature an evaluation of their objects, or should we leave room for non-evaluative emotions? It is customary to distinguish the particular object of an emotion from its formal object

(Kenny 1963; Teroni 2007). The former roughly corresponds to the grammatical object of the relevant emotional verb: one is amused by the joke or sad at the death of a good friend. The latter corresponds to the sort of evaluation that is characteristic of emotions of a given kind. Sadness is related to an evaluation in terms of loss, amusement to one in terms of funniness. Many contemporary debates concern the nature of this evaluation and how it relates to emotions as psychological states. Do emotions feature an endorsement of the relevant evaluative contents (Roberts 1999)? Do they rely on the deployment of evaluative concepts (Tappolet 2000)? Is it mandatory to understand evaluation as an aspect of what emotions represent rather than as an aspect of a specific mode of presentation or a specific attitude (Deonna and Teroni 2012a)? Depending on how one answers these questions, the idea that there are non-evaluative emotions will take different shapes: it is one thing to claim that emotions need not represent evaluative properties, another to say that they are not evaluative attitudes.

c. Intimately related to, yet distinct from these issues regarding the intentional structure of emotions are *normative* issues. What does the fact that we readily ask why we undergo emotions show regarding their epistemological function (Goldie 2004; Brady 2013)? Should we understand these questions as concerned exclusively with the aetiology of emotions, or do they reveal that we conceive of emotions as states that, like judgements or beliefs, are justified or unjustified? If the latter, can emotions themselves function as reasons for evaluative judgements, or are they merely transmission belts for the good or bad reasons one has to emote in the first place (Deonna and Teroni 2012a and 2012b)? Is it necessary for emotions to be assessable as justified or rational? Or should we rather maintain that emotions are only indirectly assessable along these lines, i.e. when they are caused by justified or rational beliefs, or when they help produce actions that are justified or rational (Gordon 1987)? Answers to these questions have far-reaching consequences, having an impact on issues such as the nature of akrasia and rational agency.

d. What is the best account of emotional phenomenology, and how does this phenomenology relate to the representational aspect of emotions, if any (Tye 2008)? Is it necessary for an emotion to be felt in order to have an object and to evaluate it, or should we countenance the possibility of unfelt emotions that evaluate objects (Hatzimoysis 2007; Lacewing 2007)? Should we understand emotional phenomenology in terms of raw feels, of experiences of pleasure and displeasure, or in terms of feelings towards or quasi-perceptual experiences (Deonna and Teroni, forthcoming)?

e. Does being in a given emotional state imply having certain motivations, or is the relation between emotions and motivation more indirect (Tappolet 2010, 2016)? If we opt for the former claim, is this compatible with the idea that emotions sometimes explain action and may even provide the explanation for distinctive types of actions (Pacherie 2002)? And how can we reconcile this concept with the intuitively convincing claim that some emotions do not motivate in any way? Alternatively, if we endorse the claim that emotions relate more indirectly to motivation, should we conclude that emotions constitute (or, alternatively, make us aware of) reasons for action?

Related to each of these sets of issues about potential necessary conditions, parallel issues can be raised about potential sufficient conditions. Consider the following illustrations. Is it possible to develop a specific understanding of the object and evaluation dimension of emotions so that the resulting representation is apt to individuate emotions from other types of psychological states? Relatedly, should we conceive of moods as objectless emotions or as emotions with less determinate objects, or should we rather draw a fundamental distinction, based on their respective intentional structures, between these two types of affective phenomena (Fish 2005; Price 2006)? Is the epistemological profile of emotions exclusive to them? Is emotional phenomenology apt to individuate emotions from other types of affective states? More generally, one central subset of issues about sufficient conditions has been the demarcation of emotions from other types of affective phenomena such as moods, hedonic states (pleasure, displeasure), sentiments, character traits (Deonna and Teroni 2012a).

Topic of This Volume

While they are obviously important in their own right, these questions have been so prominent in recent debates that, regrettably, little attention has been devoted to more abstract questions about the nature of emotions and other affective phenomena.

More specifically, we might wonder about the ontological category to which emotions belong. Are emotions kinds of *events*, i.e. do they belong to the same ontological category as explosions, births, and walks? Their being typically short-lived happenings may suggest so. Relatedly, does it make sense to think that (some) emotions are instantaneous, or should emotions be categorized as events that necessarily have a non-null duration (Naar and Tappolet, ms.)? Alternatively, emotions are perhaps kinds of *processes* (Robinson 2005). Saying so would at least allow us to do justice to the idea that emotions have components or stages. The idea that emotions are processes will, for instance, help make sense of the fact that they typically unfold through time in a characteristic manner (they wax, wane, and then disappear), something that is reminiscent of paradigmatic processes such as the writing of a check (Goldie 2011). Yet another possible position is that emotions are *dispositions* of some sort (Ryle 1949; Wollheim 1999). There are after all grounds for assimilating emotions to dispositions: are not a person's anger, pride, and fear, like an object's brittleness, to be understood as conditions having to do with the (probability of) reacting in a given way if put in specific sorts of circumstances? That would, for instance, suggest a specific understanding of the link between emotions and behaviour.

Relatedly, we might wonder about the most general features we should attribute to emotions. Rather than ask about the typical temporal duration of emotions, we may ask how emotions occupy time and persist through time. We may also ask how emotions relate, in the most general ways, to other things, including other psychological phenomena. How do emotions relate to affective phenomena, such as love, hate, or being in a bad mood, which do not obviously count as emotions as usually construed? Can we ground such phenomena in emotions? Or should we posit them as additional phenomena whose relationship to emotions is to be further explained (Naar 2013; forthcoming)? Are emotions the sort of thing that we can experience only when we are awake?

These are *ontological* issues about emotions, not in the sense that they ask us whether emotions and other affective phenomena should be part of our ontology of the mind (all the contributors presuppose a broadly realist account of affective phenomena), but in the sense that they ask us about the most general features these phenomena exemplify and how they relate to each other in the metaphysically most general ways.[1]

The present volume is predicated on the conviction that investigating these basic ontological issues – which have begun to arouse the interest of philosophers of mind – can bring new considerations to the fore and positively inform the debates about the nature and roles of emotions with which philosophers working in the field are more accustomed to grapple. The various ways in which an ontological investigation into the emotions can inform these debates are evidenced in most of the

[1] We owe this characterization of ontology to Hofweber (2014).

contributions. We shall rest content here with illustrating how rich these interactions can be by three examples relating to the intentional structure of emotions.

First, Peter Geach (1969) has famously claimed that it makes no sense to conceive of thoughts or judgements as entities that occupy time – the question 'How much time did you spend thinking that thought?' hardly makes sense. But consider parallel questions about the emotions. 'For how long have you been afraid?' and 'How much time did it take to overcome your anger at John?' clearly do make sense, and we are often in a position to provide informative answers. This is a substantial, yet rarely emphasized reason for rejecting any account of the emotions in terms of thoughts or judgements. The latter simply do not occupy time in the way emotions do.

Second, many contemporary philosophers adopt perceptual models of the emotions – i.e. models according to which emotional experience constitutes a perceptual mode of awareness of significant aspects of the environment (de Sousa 1987; Deonna 2006; Tappolet 2016). In the context of the issues raised in the present volume, this should lead us to consider perceptual phenomena from an ontologically informed perspective. Some of these – such as Dretske's (1969, 1979) famed 'simple seeings' (seeing the bush, noticing a humming sound) – seem to be punctual events or achievements. Phenomena involving sensory attention (watching a bird, listening to a melody) occupy time in a different way (Vendler 1957; Steward 1997). Moreover, the nature of perceptual states is susceptible to being modulated by the nature of what they are about. The perception of a tree, the perception of a melody, and the perception of the scoring of a goal differ in their respective temporal shapes.[2] So, the prospects of a perceptual model of the emotions will change dramatically depending both on which perceptual phenomena the model appeals to and on one's own conception of the ontology of emotions and their objects.

Third, many of the debates sketched at the outset of our discussion are premised on the idea that emotions 'in the wild' are associated extrinsically and contingently with a variety of other phenomena. Here are two illustrations. First, on a view according to which emotions are perception-like evaluative experiences, emotions provide reasons to desire and act, but do not themselves motivate (Tappolet 2010, 2016). The desire to retaliate, say, is not part of anger: anger rather *represents* the situation as offensive and this provides the agent with a reason to retaliate. Second, on a Jamesian view according to which emotions are bodily feelings (James 1884), emotions do

[2] We owe the expression 'temporal shape' to Helen Steward (1997).

not intentionally relate to the environment beyond the subject's own body. The perception of a threatening tiger, say, is not part of fear: the most that can be said is that fear represents a constellation of bodily changes that happen to be caused by that perception. This illustrates the more general fact that traditional debates about the emotions have typically been driven by the implicit or explicit goal of avoiding what Prinz (2004) has described as the 'Problem of Plenty', i.e. the problem of understanding how, if emotions include several components, these components hang together into a coherent whole. This problem may result from a questionable ontology of the emotional domain, however. If emotions are processes rather than episodic events, say, then the Problem of Plenty does not look any more like a substantial problem for emotion theory in particular. Rather, it transforms into a specific version of a general ontological question regarding the nature of processes and the link between their various stages. Alternatively, if emotions are states, then their relation with the phenomena under discussion may be one of essential dependence, which makes room for a very different kind of response to the Problem of Plenty.

The ten contributions gathered together in the present volume offer many opportunities to pursue these lines of thought, and many more besides.

Structure of This Volume and Individual Contributions

The first two chapters of this volume approach the ontology of emotions from a broader metaphysical perspective, showing how general ontological considerations can inform debates about the emotions.

William Jaworski's 'Mind-Body Theories and the Emotions' situates the issue of emotional ontology in the traditional 'mind-body' problem, viz. the problem of how psychological phenomena relate to physical phenomena. After introducing and rejecting various answers to this problem – including substance dualism, panpsychism, eliminativism, and reductive and nonreductive physicalism – Jaworski presents his preferred solution, hylomorphism, and argues that it provides an attractive approach to the ontology of emotions. Dating back to Aristotle, hylomorphism rejects the claim that the properties of composite wholes are determined solely by the properties of the particles composing them. Although we are composed of physical particles, some of our properties are determined not by these particles, but by the way they are organized or structured. On this view, we are not 'mere quantities of physical materials; we are quantities of physical materials *with a certain organization or structure*' (our emphasis). Structure,

Jaworski argues, should be conceived on a par with the physical particles studied by physics in being both ontologically and explanatory basic: it contributes irreducibly to an explanation of what composite entities are and what they can do. Those entities include individuals like us, and also events such as our activities. Walking, talking, running, and so forth are not mere physiological changes, but physiological changes that are coordinated or structured in the right kinds of ways. Thinking, feeling, and experiencing emotions are activities as well. Experiencing an emotion is thus like walking or talking: a complex event in which physiological mechanisms, together perhaps with things in the environment, are coordinated or structured in the right kind of way.

Psychological properties, including emotions, are thereby the product of various physiological mechanisms whose operations are coordinated or structured in a certain way. These structures, Jaworski suggests, confer our psychological states their causal powers.

In 'Dispositionality and Mentality', John Heil starts by asking whether psychological states are dispositional. Putting forward a two-category ontology comprising substances and properties, he argues that all properties – psychological or non-psychological – are dispositional. The task is then to spell out what a disposition is. On Heil's view, dispositions are not to be conceived of as mere potentialities to be contrasted with real or actual properties. Rather, dispositions are features substances *actually* have and which explain what they do. Heil goes further than this by claiming that *genuine* properties are dispositional; a property is genuine only if it is powerful. This thought, he is quick to point out, does not imply a denial of qualities, such as being round or red, which are not obviously dispositional. It does not imply either a commitment to the claim that there are two kinds of properties – dispositional and qualitative – which substances can have. Instead, Heil argues that dispositions and qualities are two aspects of the same properties; in fact qualities are what empower substances to do whatever they do. Genuine properties, therefore, are *powerful qualities*. This claim in turn allows him to suggest that qualia do not constitute a problem for functionalist accounts of psychological states, for (conscious) psychological states could simply be qualitative states which empower the subjects to behave the way they do. If Heil is right, we have no choice but to answer positively the question whether emotions are dispositional.

The next five chapters do not tackle ontological questions about emotions from the perspective of general metaphysics or philosophy of mind. They more directly examine ontological issues that arise from perennial philosophical debates about the emotions.

In 'Emotion as Process', Jenefer Robinson takes her cue from the widely accepted idea amongst psychologists that short-term emotions are processes in order to argue that emotions are specific types of causal processes. She argues that the majority of psychologists and philosophers – William James providing a notable exception on Robinson's understanding of his position – have wrongly assumed that emotions should be identified with some particular components of these processes (such as appraisals, facial expressions, action tendencies, or feeling). According to Robinson, this assumption is wrong. 'Emotions', she maintains, 'not only "tell" the person or animal that something significant is in the environment but also get the person or animal to act in an appropriate way'. Emotions are complex and dynamic entities, which should be identified with specific causal processes that, typically at least, involve all the components under discussion (and many others besides). In response to what we have characterized here, following Prinz, as 'the Problem of Plenty', i.e. the challenge of providing an account of the coherent unity of the complex psychological whole with which an emotion is identified, Robinson then explains that what gives emotions their coherence as wholes is the fact that these various components flow causally into one another in characteristic 'pre-organized' ways. Robinson develops her approach in a Jamesian spirit and reviews some of the accumulating evidence regarding the role of the felt body in emotion and the dispensability of cognitive appraisals. She then builds on James' account by offering detailed explanations regarding e.g. the idea that bodily changes in emotion are 'instinctively' generated, the function of these same bodily changes in preparing the organism to deal with specific challenges and the role of cognition within emotional processes. This allows her to take issue with several prominent accounts of the emotions, such as Prinz's alternative development of the Jamesian framework and rival perceptual accounts.

Matthew Soteriou's contribution, 'The Ontology of Emotion', is concerned with a problem facing views – such as Robinson's – according to which emotions are complex, that is, made up of several components. Soteriou suggests that the most significant problem facing component approaches is not the Problem of Plenty. The problem is, rather, that such approaches end up 'depriving emotions of their distinctive explanatory potential'. If an emotion is nothing but a collection of mental and bodily states and occurrences, then it seems that all the genuine explanatory work is done by these underlying states and occurrences. The emotion as a whole is thereby explanatorily redundant. This is a problem for component approaches because emotions do seem to be sometimes explanatorily prior to whatever components they may have. Indeed, it sometimes seems that the presence of an emotion can explain the presence of states and occurrences that the component theorist takes to be part of it. After surveying various solutions to this challenge, Soteriou puts forward his own solution. The strategy is to find a way to reconcile the claim that emotions have parts or constituents with the claim that emotions can be genuinely explanatory. Drawing from larger considerations in the philosophy of mind, he makes a case for the view that an emotion is a state (or 'way a subject is modified') whose obtaining constitutively depends on the occurrence of various events and processes. Insofar as this view accepts the claim that emotions have parts or constituents, it thereby qualifies as a component approach.

Jona Vance's 'Phenomenal Commitments: A Puzzle for Experiential Theories of Emotion' is structured around a puzzle for experiential theories. According to this important family of theories regarding the ontology of emotions, emotions are experiences. This is an example of what Robinson's contribution identifies as a wrongheaded identification of emotions with specific components. The puzzle on which Vance concentrates relates to the fact that subjects seem to be evaluable as rational or irrational in the light of the emotions they undergo. Someone feeling guilt for what he acknowledges as a wrongful deed will be perceived as rational. And, to take a less dramatic example, someone feeling afraid of a tiny mouse will be perceived as irrational. Vance explains that this is potentially damaging for experiential theories by observing that we do not consider experiences as generating such a form of rational assessability – subjects are not claimed to be irrational for seeing or failing to see, for instance. As Vance emphasizes, the problem is significant, as it could constitute a point in favour of component theories, which do not conceive of emotions as rationally evaluable in virtue of their experiential component. His account, inspired by Helm's (2001) seminal discussion, is to defend experiential theories by arguing that the rational evaluability of subjects in light of their emotions presupposes rationally evaluable subjective commitments. These commitments generate rational evaluability in relation to emotional experiences and so qualify as 'phenomenal commitments'. Vance's account is distinctive in that the relevant commitments are non-constitutive, viz. they do not contribute to shaping the nature of emotional experiences. 'What makes one rationally evaluable for one's emotional experience', he writes, 'is not only that one commits to have (or not have) an emotional experience, but that the experience is appropriate given one's commitments and the norms that govern them' (p. 105). Thus, it is one's implicit commitment to preserve one's physical integrity that makes the fear one experiences in the presence of a threatening predator evaluable as rational. In putting forward his account, Vance argues that it compares favourably with views according to which the relevant commitments are constitutive in requiring less demanding conceptions of emotional experience.

In 'An Enactivist Theory of Emotional Content', Daniel Shargel and Jesse Prinz defend an approach to emotional content that has important ontological implications. They start by emphasizing that most prominent theories conceive of the emotions as contentful states that represent the world as being a certain way. As they observe, this is difficult to maintain within embodied theories of emotions, for which bodily experience is central. Shargel and Prinz next review strategies for reconciling embodied theories with the idea that emotions are contentful. Prinz's (2004) own embodied appraisal theory, which 'hooks up' the felt body and the meaningful aspects of the environment thanks to a teleosemantic account of representation, is a well-known strategy along these lines. Shargel and Prinz contend that this strategy cannot succeed. In particular, teleosemantics conceives of representation as an extrinsic relation between what represents and what is represented – the result being that the embodied appraisal theory 'tries to make bodily states the bearers of content, but, in the same gesture, it makes them irrelevant to content determination'. This provides Shargel and Prinz with the incentive to explore two alternative strategies. The first is Griffiths and Scarantino's account, according to which emotions represent affordances. Anger would, for instance, represent the fact that aggression is afforded. Shargel and Prinz think that, while promising, this account raises important worries. The most salient one is that, according to them, affordances are too objective and invariant to play the required role in emotion theory. This leads them to develop an *enactive* account of emotional content as an alternative strategy. In opposition to standard accounts of representation, enactivists insist on the ontological contribution of mental processes to what features in the environment. According to Shargel and Prinz's specific enactive account of emotional content, 'instead of representing core relational themes such as danger, loss, and offensiveness, emotions bring in new possibilities of action, and introduce a kind of to-be-doneness that temporarily alters affordance space'. They then explore the impact of this account on some central aspects of the emotions, such as their intensity, the contrast between their particular and formal objects, their rationality, and the nature of the representation they contain.

Joel Smith's 'The Perceptibility of Emotion' is concerned to defend a version of what he calls *Perceptibility*, the view that 'suitably placed and endowed observers can perceive others' emotions' (p. 130). After having distinguished this view from other views with which we might conflate it, Smith sets out three constraints on an adequate account of the perception of others' emotions. First, we do not perceive others' emotions 'directly', but by perceiving some distinct entity, chiefly one of their expressions. The question is not, according to Smith, *whether* the perception of emotion is indirect, but *how* it is. Second, emotions explain emotional expressions rather than the other way around, a claim which then allows Smith to suggest that if emotions can be perceived, it is in virtue of the perceptibility of their expressions. The question, then, is what relation holding between emotions and their expressions could explain this fact. This leads Smith to formulate the third constraint on *Perceptibility*: it should be sensitive to the *ontology* of emotions and their expressions. More generally, says Smith, 'a claim that we perceive entities of a certain sort must cohere with the most plausible account of the ontological category that such entities fall into' (p. 135). He goes on to develop his own account of the ontology of emotions and their expressions. On his view, emotions are *states* while their expressions are *processes*. This shows, Smith argues, that the latter cannot be parts of the former, and should therefore be conceived of as distinct. At this point, we might wonder what the relationship between emotions and their expressions is such that one can perceive emotions in virtue of perceiving their expressions, if expressions are not to be conceived of as parts of emotions. Fleshing out his account of the ontology of emotions, Smith finally argues that emotions are dispositions and their expressions are their manifestations.

The last three chapters explore the ontological relationships between emotions and other mental phenomena such as sentiments, moods, and wakeful consciousness.

In 'Sentiments', Hichem Naar distinguishes between emotions, which are typically attributed for short periods of time, and sentiments, which are often attributed for long periods of time. He then asks whether this linguistic/conceptual distinction between two kinds of affective states marks a genuine ontological distinction. First, he considers the most popular approach to this question, which reduces sentiments to patterns of emotions. Against this view, Naar argues both that a pattern of emotions is neither necessary nor sufficient for the presence of a given sentiment and that the view raises a number of worries. These worries motivate an alternative view, according to which sentiments and emotions are different kinds of mental states. According to Naar, the latter view – which he calls the 'distinctness' view – should be conceived of as the default account of the distinction between sentiments and emotions. A difficulty facing the account, however, is that there seems to be a conceptual or intuitive connection between sentiments and emotions, a connection that the account may not accommodate. Naar's rejoinder consists in examining how the idea that there is a necessary connection between sentiments and emotions can be accommodated by the distinctness view. In a way reminiscent of several other contributions, he suggests that we should understand the link between sentiments and emotions in dispositional terms: sentiments are powers that are essentially manifested in emotions.

Christine Tappolet's 'The Metaphysics of Moods' investigates the nature of moods and their relation to emotions. After laying down characteristics of moods which can act as pre-theoretical constraints, Tappolet discusses dispositional and functionalist accounts of moods. She argues that all fail to do justice to the phenomenology of moods. She then considers accounts according to which moods are emotions with a 'general' object, such as the world as a whole or one's entire life. It is instructive to notice that, in contrast with the dispositional account, this account does not take the difference between moods and emotions to cut much ontological ice – moods and emotions are claimed to differ only in their respective objects. This would therefore give us an ontologically parsimonious explanation of the distinction between moods and emotions. Tappolet, however, rejects this account on the ground that emotions can take general objects as well and that such an account implies that all moods are inappropriate. The view Tappolet puts forward as an alternative is comparable as far as ontological parsimony is concerned, as it does not draw a deep ontological distinction between moods and emotions. Indeed, she agrees with the 'large object' account that moods and emotions differ in their object, but proposes another way to cast the difference. On her view, while emotions concern actual evaluative states of affairs, moods concern only possible states of affairs, in particular possible evaluative states of affairs that are taken to be likely. She finally argues that this kind of object is not something towards which emotions can be directed and that moods are sometimes appropriate responses to their object.

The last chapter, Clare Mac Cumhaill's 'Night Fight', investigates the relation between the emotion of regret, the state of wakeful consciousness, and insomnia. Mac Cumhaill starts by emphasizing the striking fact that, in the literature on regret, the issue of its proper object has been very much disputed. She then explains why this multiplicity of candidate objects relates to the ontology of regret, and in particular to the often-mentioned but not fully understood relation between regret and insomnia. 'That regret may be variously theorised as having very different proper objects', she writes, 'is symptomatic of the fact that the state of wakeful consciousness is itself complex, a complexity that reflection on the nature of regret reveals and . . .

replicates' (p. 188). According to Mac Cumhaill, regret has an essential relation to wakeful consciousness and so cannot occur while dreaming. Borrowing from key insights in O'Shaughnessy's account of wakeful consciousness, she then explains why the sort of temporal orientation characteristic of regret, viz. its having an object that lies in the past, cannot by itself explain the distinctive relation between regret, wakeful consciousness, and insomnia. Next, using some worries raised by Williams' account of regret as a springboard, she suggests that regret is characterized first and foremost by a certain kind of mental activity, which is sometimes expressive. According to Mac Cumhaill, the mental activity is more specifically expressive of a wish that things had been otherwise – a wish that disposes the subject to engage in the higher-order mental activity of imagining its satisfaction. These imaginings and the thoughts that accompany them are, she claims, 'constitutively regretful in the sense that they may be understood not as productive of, nor as produced by regret, but rather as expressions of regret' (p. 189). This, she submits, not only supports the conclusion that regret is incompatible with sleep, but also suggests that it precludes falling asleep because the distinctive self-conscious character of these imaginings and thoughts is missing in dream.

CHAPTER I

Mind-Body Theories and the Emotions

William Jaworski

Problems for an Ontology of Emotions

Emotions are reckoned to have a variety of characteristics (Goldie 2000). Among other things we feel them, and our feelings have intentionality or directedness: I am afraid *of* something; I am angry *about* something; I long *for* something. But what exactly are the states that have these characteristics? When an individual experiences an emotion, what is that emotional state? Is it a physical occurrence or not? If it is, how is the psychological description of it related to the physical description of it? Does 'anger' always refer to the same type of physical state, or can it refer to different types of physical states under different circumstances? Is it possible to give an exhaustive account of the emotion in purely physical terms? If not, if the experience is not a physical occurrence, how is it related to the physical occurrences that seem to accompany it – to events in the limbic system of the brain, for instance? In what follows I'll survey some representative answers.

One way to understand various positions on the ontology of emotions is to see them as responses to mind-body problems – persistent problems in understanding how thought, feeling, perception, and other mental phenomena fit into the universe as described by our best science. To many philosophers and scientists it seems plausible that the behavior of everything in the universe can be described and explained exhaustively by physics. Yet we evidently have capacities, such as our capacities to think, feel, and perceive, that it is difficult to imagine could ever be described and explained by physics alone. Mind-body problems are expressions of this difficulty. One example is the problem of emergence.

The problem of emergence is the problem of explaining how lower-level physical or physiological occurrences can generate or produce higher-level mental phenomena such as conscious emotional experiences. Consciousness did not always exist in the physical universe. Neither does consciousness exist in all parts of the universe. Many philosophers and scientists take these observations to indicate that very specific physical conditions must be in place in order to cause or produce conscious phenomena. But what conditions are those, and how do they do it? How is it that, say, the movements of tiny particles in my brain can give rise to the rich emotional experiences I have? The following claims make it difficult to see how:

(1) We have conscious emotional experiences.
(2) We are composed of physical particles.
(3) The properties of a composite whole are determined by the properties of the particles that compose it.
(4) Physical particles do not have conscious emotional experiences.
(5) No number of nonconscious particles could combine to produce conscious emotional experiences.

Each of these claims is plausible on its face. It seems obvious that we have conscious emotional experiences as claim (1) says. Claim (2), moreover, seems well supported empirically; we seem to be composed of the same materials as everything else in the physical universe, and our best physics suggests that those materials are microscopic particles. Many examples seem to illustrate claim (3). I have the mass I have, for instance, because I am composed of physical particles with smaller masses that collectively add up to my bigger mass. Likewise, I have the position and velocity I do because the particles composing me are located in such-and-such a place and are moving with such-and-such a velocity. Change their position and velocity and you succeed in changing mine. Given the range of properties that are like this, it's not implausible to suppose that all the properties of composite wholes are determined by the properties of the particles composing them. It seems, moreover, that the behavior of those particles can be described and explained exhaustively by physics. We don't need to invoke a psychological or even a biological vocabulary to describe and explain what they are and what they can do. This lends some support to claim (4). There are also, it seems, good reasons to endorse claim (5). One particle by itself does not have the power to produce conscious experiences. If it did, then consciousness would have emerged much earlier in the universe's history than we think it did, and it would also be more widespread – even rocks and tables could be conscious. But if one particle by itself does not have the power to produce conscious experiences, then it is difficult to see how any number of nonconscious particles could combine to produce conscious experiences.

Each of the foregoing claims (1)–(5) is therefore plausible. Yet claims (1)–(5) are jointly inconsistent. Claim (1) implies that we have conscious emotional experiences, yet claims (2)–(5) imply that we do not. The claims cannot all be true; at least one of them must be false, but it is not clear which.

Eliminative Physicalism, Substance Dualism, and Panpsychism

Mind-body theories offer to solve mind-body problems in various ways. Eliminative physicalists, for instance, look to resolve the problem of emergence by rejecting claim (1). A psychological vocabulary is the by-product of a defective way of trying to describe and explain human behavior, one that will eventually be displaced by a complete physical description of that behavior. As a result, it is false to say that we have conscious emotional experiences. There are no such things. Substance dualists, on the other hand, look to reject claim (2). According to them, we are nonphysical beings that are only contingently attached to bodies; we are not bodies ourselves. Hence, we are not composed of physical particles or stuffs. Panpsychists, for their part, reject claim (4). They claim that fundamental physical particles are endowed with thoughts and feelings just as we are. As a result, there is no question of how those particles might come together to produce conscious emotional experiences. Conscious emotional experiences exist everywhere in the universe, right down to the fundamental physical level.

Eliminativism, substance dualism, and panpsychism are nevertheless marginal positions. Eliminativism is marginalized because it denies what seems to many people to be the manifest fact that we experience anger, joy, sadness, and other emotions. Substance dualism, on the other hand, is marginalized because it doesn't do justice to the phenomenology of emotional experience – its visceral character in particular. William James described that character in a well-known passage:

> What kind of an emotion of fear would be left, if the feelings neither of quickened heart-beats nor of shallow breathing, neither of trembling lips nor of weakened limbs, neither of goose-flesh nor of visceral stirrings, were present, it is quite impossible to think. (1884: 193–4)

If James is right, then emotions are essentially embodied; it is impossible for us to experience them apart from particular bodily changes, and if that is the case, then one of substance dualism's central claims about mental phenomena cannot be true of the emotions: they cannot exist apart from a body. Descartes himself, it seems, felt the pressure of this observation, and posited a third class of properties to try to account for the visceral phenomenology of emotional experience. In addition to mental properties and physical properties, he said, there were also properties pertaining to the union of mind and body – properties that included the emotions (Cottingham 1985).

Panpsychism is marginalized for its part because it is so counterintuitive to think that quarks, leptons, and other fundamental physical particles might have mental lives as rich as our own. Our best empirical accounts of these particles do not invoke a psychological vocabulary; we can describe, explain, and predict their behavior without positing thoughts or feelings.

In what follows I will focus on views that deny either claim (3) or claim (5). Views that deny (5) can be divided into three categories: physicalist theories, dual-attribute theories, and neutral monist theories. Views that reject (3) include hylomorphism.

Reductive and Nonreductive Physicalism

Physicalism claims that everything is physical; everything can be exhaustively described and explained by the most empirically adequate theories in current or future physics (Lewis 1983; Jaworski 2011, 2016). Physicalism has been the most popular framework for addressing mind-body problems since the mid-twentieth century. If we put to one side eliminativist theories, physicalist accounts of the emotions fall into two categories: reductive and nonreductive. The paradigmatic reductivist theory is the psychophysical identity theory.[1] It claims that mental states are identical to physical states and that we will discover these identities empirically in something analogous to the way we discovered that water is H_2O (Lewis 1966, 1972; Armstrong 1968, 1970; Jaworski 2011). Water might initially have been defined as, say, the drinkable stuff that filled rivers and lakes. By studying that stuff empirically, scientists were able to discover that it was H_2O. They were thus able to conclude that water was identical to H_2O. According to identity theorists, something analogous will be true of the emotions. Mental states in general might be defined initially by their typical causes and effects. Anger, for instance, might be defined as the state that is typically caused by suffering injustice and that typically causes such-and-such feelings and physiological changes. According to identity theorists, it is possible in principle to discover what the state with these typical causes and effects is. It is thus possible in principle to identify anger and any other emotion with some type of physical state.

One influential challenge to the identity theory has been the multiple realizability argument (Putnam 1967; Block and Fodor 1972; Fodor 1974;

[1] Behaviorism is the other kind of reductive physicalism (Jaworski 2011: 103–11).

for discussion see Jaworski 2011: 131–3).[2] The argument claims that it is possible for a mental state, such as anger, to be correlated with more than one type of physical state. If anger can be correlated with brain state B in humans and with a different type of physical state in Martians, then anger cannot be identical to brain state B. A thing cannot exist without itself, so if anger can exist in a Martian who doesn't have brain state B, then anger cannot be identical to brain state B. Identity theorists have responded to this argument in a number of ways (Kim 1972; Lewis 1980; for discussion see Jaworski 2011: 134–6). The most popular line of response claims that our current taxonomy of mental and physical states will undergo a revision in the future. Even though our current taxonomy posits a single type of state that goes by the name 'anger', that term instead can refer to multiple different types of states: anger-in-humans, anger-in-Martians, anger-in-robots, and so on. By analogy, people once took 'jade' to refer to a single type of mineral, but over time they came to recognize that it referred to multiple different types of minerals such as jadeite and nephrite. It is thus a mistake to speak of jade in general, and in the same way it is a mistake to speak of anger in general. There are instead many different types of states which have been grouped under the one confused heading of anger, and each of these species- or kind-specific types of states is identical to a physical state: anger-in-humans = physical state A, anger-in-Martians = physical state B, anger-in-robots = physical state C, and so on.

Far and away the most popular way of accommodating multiple realizability, however, has not been to rehabilitate the identity theory, but to abandon it in favor of some kind of nonreductive physicalism. The most popular theories of this sort combine physicalism with functionalism (Putnam 1967; Block and Fodor 1972; Fodor 1974; for discussion see Jaworski 2011: 136–49). Functionalism claims that psychological descriptions are abstract descriptions that ignore the physical details of a system and focus simply on inputs to it, outputs from it, and internal states that correlate the two. When we say that Eleanor is enjoying the play, we are saying that she is in some internal state that correlates certain sensory inputs to her with certain behavioral outputs from her. The psychological description does not specify what that internal state is; that's what makes the description abstract. This abstractness allows functionalists to accommodate the possibility that a single kind of mental state might be correlated with different kinds of physical

[2] For a detailed survey of the literature on multiple realizability and reductionist responses to it, see my 'Mind and Multiple Realizability' in the Internet Encyclopedia of Philosophy (www.iep.utm.edu/mult-rea/).

states. A human like Eleanor might differ physically from a Martian like Gabriel, but the physical differences between them needn't appear at an abstract psychological level of description. At that level, Eleanor and Gabriel might be indistinguishable; both might correlate inputs with outputs in a way we would describe as enjoying the play. Consequently, the same type of emotional state, enjoying the play, could be correlated with different types of physical states: one type of physical state in a human, and a different type of physical state in a Martian.

Nonreductive physicalism of the aforementioned sort has faced several challenges (Jaworski 2011: 149–64). Some of these have targeted physicalism, others functionalism, and yet others the combination of the two. When it comes to the emotions specifically, physicalist theories have faced challenges accommodating both the intentionality of emotional states and their felt qualities. Physicalists have typically tried to account for intentionality in terms of theories of mental representation (Fodor 1987; Dretske 1988; Jaworski 2011: 90–1). The simplest theories of this sort claim that mental representation consists in causal covariation between features of the environment and internal states of the organism or representing system. Suppose that my nervous system has a component, *c*, that is capable of being in two states, ON and OFF, and that these states covary with the presence of something red: *c* turns ON when it encounters something red, and it is OFF otherwise. Because *c*'s ON/OFF state covaries with the presence of redness, it indicates the presence of redness in something analogous to the way smoke indicates the presence of fire. Because fire reliably causes smoke, the presence of smoke typically conveys the information that there is fire. Similarly, because redness reliably causes *c* to be ON, *c*'s being ON typically conveys the information that something in the environment is red. To have an internal representation of redness is thus to have an internal component that is activated if and only if something in the environment is red.

Simple covariation theories nevertheless have difficulties accounting for the specificity of intentional content – for what makes a representation of or about this particular object, property, or event as opposed to some other (Fodor 1987). This is especially clear in the case of more sophisticated mental states such as emotions. Anger, let us suppose, is typically triggered by something insulting. According to a simple covariation theory, my anger should be reliably caused by insulting episodes. If I'm an irascible person, however, my anger might also be reliably caused by episodes that aren't insulting at all. What is it, then, that makes my anger a state that is about insults instead of a state that is about insults-or-non-insults? Simple covariation theories do not provide a satisfactory answer to this question. As a result most physicalists endorse more sophisticated theories of mental representation such as Fred Dretske's (1988).

Dretske's theory of mental representation combines causal covariation with designed or naturally selected functions. On Dretske's view, the components of a system perform various jobs or functions within it. In the case of artifacts, those functions are determined by a designer, someone who constructs the system with an eye to having its components contribute to an overall task. In the case of natural systems such as human organisms, the functions performed by various components are determined by natural selection. It plays a role in the development of organisms analogous to the role of a designer in the production of artifacts. Natural selection has assigned to various sensory organs or subsystems the functions of supplying organisms with information about the external environment and their other internal states – functions they perform by having internal states that covary with features of the environment and with other internal states.[3] Physicalists argue that the causal relations connecting states of the nervous system to features of the environment, as well as the natural selective mechanisms that determine something's function, can all be given an exhaustive physical description and explanation. If they are right, then mental representation can be exhaustively described and explained in principle by physics, and if intentionality can be understood in terms of mental representation, then it too can be accommodated within a physicalist framework.

Qualia-based objections to physicalism argue that physicalism cannot account for the qualitative aspects of experience, or qualia (Jackson 1986; Chalmers 1996, 2002; Jaworski 2011: 83–8). According to qualia theorists, there is something it's like to feel anger or fear or jealousy, and what it's like to experience one of these emotions is different from what it's like to experience another.[4] This what-it's-likeness, say qualia theorists, cannot be physical. One reason, they say, is that it seems possible for two physically indistinguishable individuals to have different qualia. What it's like for you to experience anger might be different from what it's like for an exact physical duplicate of you to experience anger. When your duplicate experiences anger, it might feel to him or her the way enjoyment feels to you. Or possibly when your duplicate experiences anger it might feel like nothing;

[3] Prinz (2004) defends a theory of the emotions along these lines.

[4] Not all theories of emotions agree on this. Theories like James Russell's (2003) claim that feelings are not intrinsically emotional. Feelings are instead neutral episodes that can be mere moods or that can be components of emotions if suitably directed.

your duplicate's anger might not have any qualitative dimension at all. If qualia were physical, qualia theorists argue, then necessarily you and your duplicate would have to have the same qualia, for you and your duplicate have all the same physical characteristics. But since it is possible for you and your duplicate to have different qualia, it follows that qualia must not be physical; they cannot be accommodated within a physicalist framework.[5]

A different challenge to providing a physicalist account of the emotions targets the combination of physicalism and functionalism. It claims that a theory of this sort ends up evacuating psychological discourse of any real explanatory content (Kim 1998; Jaworski 2011: 161–4, 169–76). If this is true, nonreductive physicalism implies that the real reasons why we behave as we do have nothing to do with our emotional states. To appreciate the argument, consider an analogy. Let us suppose that the behavior of fundamental physical particles can be exhaustively described and explained by physics. Suppose, however, that we decide to call particles 'J-particles' exactly if I'm giving a thumbs-up. In an instant I can transform every particle into a J-particle simply by raising my thumb, and conversely, I can transform every J-particle into a non-J-particle simply by putting my thumb down. These so-called transformations, however, are not real. In bringing it about that every particle is a J-particle, I do not alter in any way how those particles behave or the reasons why they behave as they do. The exhaustive account of their behavior and the reasons for it continue to belong to physics alone; it has nothing to do with J-particle discourse. The worry about nonreductive physicalism is that it implies something analogous about psychological discourse: if it is true, psychological discourse has no bearing on what things do and why they do it. If physicalism is true, then everything can be exhaustively described and explained using the vocabulary of physics. It is possible to describe the same physical things using a different vocabulary, including an abstract psychological one, just as it is possible to call the same particles 'J-particles'. But whatever vocabulary one chooses to describe physical things, if physicalism is true, the exhaustive account of what those things do and why they do it is still given

[5] Physicalists have responded to the qualia challenge in several ways. Some deny that qualia exist. Dennett (1992), for instance, argues that the very concept of qualia is incoherent (Jaworski 2011: 219–28). Others, such as Heil (Chapter 2, this volume), argue against the possibility of physical duplicates having different qualitative experiences. Yet others argue that even though qualia theorists insist that qualia constitute the raw data of experience, qualia are in fact posits of a dubious theoretical framework that fails to capture the phenomenology of lived perceptual experience (Noë and O'Regan 2002; Noë 2004). Other physicalists have challenged the claim that qualia cannot be accommodated within a physicalist framework. Dretske (1995), for instance, argues that it is possible to give an account of qualia in terms of mental representation.

by physics alone. Psychological discourse thus seems to be as irrelevant to that account as J-particle discourse; it is bereft of any real description or explanatory value. In fact, the problem looks even worse for nonreductive physicalists. They insist, after all, that the categories of psychological discourse do not correspond in a straightforward way to the categories of physical theory. A type of psychological state like anger could correspond to many different types of physical states. But if the physical categories are the ones that give us an exhaustive account of reality, and psychological categories don't correspond to those, then it is difficult to see how psychological categories could correspond to reality at all. If nonreductive physicalism is true, therefore, it is difficult to see how talk of thoughts, feelings, perceptions, and the like could provide any kind of explanation for human behavior.

Dual-Attribute Theories and Neutral Monism

Like most physicalist theories, dual-attribute theories claim that nonconscious particles could combine to produce conscious emotional experiences, but unlike physicalist theories, they deny that the account of how the production happens can be given exhaustively in physical terms. Rather, when conditions are right, physical things produce nonphysical attributes or properties, ones that cannot be described purely in terms of physics.[6]

The most popular dual-attribute theories are varieties of emergentism or epiphenomenalism. Both claim that physical states produce nonphysical mental ones; they differ over whether those nonphysical states can exert any causal influence over physical states in turn. Emergentists say they can; epiphenomenalists say they can't. What concerns us here, however, is the claim they share, namely that physical states produce nonphysical mental ones. How exactly is this supposed to happen? Critics argue that dual-attribute theorists have no satisfactory answer.

Some dual-attribute theorists, for instance, posit brute psychophysical laws. There are laws of emergence, they say, that are every bit as basic as the

[6] Dual-attribute theories are sometimes called forms of property dualism to contrast them with forms of substance dualism. But this use of the term 'property dualism' can be misleading since substance dualists are committed to property dualism as well (Armstrong 1968: 11). Likewise, the label 'dual-aspect' has also been used instead of 'dual-attribute', but this too can be misleading since 'aspect' suggests that, according to dual-attribute theories, the mental-physical distinction is merely a matter of how things appear to us. The term 'attribute' expresses more clearly the ontological nature of the dualism that dual-attribute theorists endorse.

laws governing purely physical interactions. Consequently, the world just is a place in which physical events produce mental events in accordance with basic laws. Critics argue, however, that psychophysical laws do not really address the problem (Strawson 2006; Jaworski 2011: 224–33). Knowing that there is a psychophysical law linking pain to brain state B might explain why this or that instance of pain is correlated with this or that instance of B, but it does not explain why there is a correlation between instances of pain and instances of B in the first place. It does not explain how the rapid vibrations of countless tiny physical particles can generate the felt qualities of fear or anger; it simply says that the generating happens in a regular, lawlike way. According to critics, however, some explanation is needed for why there would be laws connecting things as different as brain states and qualitative experiences. Without such an explanation psychophysical laws are every bit as mysterious as the psychophysical correlations they are introduced to explain.

Dual-attribute theorists are also free to endorse panpsychism: mental phenomena such as conscious emotional experiences are present at every level of reality, including the fundamental physical level. As we've seen, however, panpsychism is a marginal position because it is so counterintuitive to think that fundamental physical particles have mental states like our own. To soften the counterintuitive implications of panpsychism, some dual-attribute theorists endorse panprotopsychism, the claim that fundamental physical particles do not have mental states like ours, but rather protomental states – simpler precursors of the mental states we have (Chalmers 1996: 153–5; 2002: 265–7). According to panprotopsychists, when fundamental physical particles combine to form atoms or molecules, they give rise to protomental states that are more sophisticated, and when atoms and molecules combine to form neural tissues or different parts of the brain, they give rise to mental states that are more sophisticated still, and so the combinatorial process goes until combinations of lower-level items eventually give rise to the rich, sophisticated mental states that constitute our own mental lives.

Critics argue, however, that panprotopsychism only solves the problem of emergence by replacing it with a different problem: the problem of saying what protomental states are and how they combine to produce more sophisticated mental states. We know what thoughts, emotions, and perceptions are, but what are protothoughts, protoemotions, and protoperceptions supposed to be? Panprotopsychists can respond that protomental states are theoretical postulates, that they are precisely the states of lower-level things that in combination produce familiar mental states. But how exactly is any such combination supposed to work? Panprotopsychism assumes that protomental properties are aggregative properties like mass (Wimsatt 1985). Clearly if x has a mass of 1 kg and y has a mass of 1 kg, then x and y have a collective mass of 2 kg, but it is unclear how mental properties – or protomental properties – can manage to be aggregative in this way. Unless the foregoing issues are resolved, say critics, panprotopsychism does not really offer a solution to the problem of emergence.

A similar problem confronts neutral monist theories (Popper and Eccles 1977: 199; Strawson 1994: 97; Nagel 2000: 210; for discussion, see Jaworski 2011: 257–62). Neutral monism claims that the fundamental entities are in themselves neither mental nor physical but neutral; they can be accurately described as mental or physical if they satisfy certain extrinsic conditions. Some of these conditions qualify neutral events as mental, others qualify them as physical, and it is possible for the same neutral event to satisfy conditions of both sorts. But events needn't be described in either mentalistic or physicalistic terms at all since they can all be exhaustively described and explained in terms of a neutral conceptual framework, one that is neither mentalistic nor physicalistic (Russell 1921).

Perhaps the biggest challenge facing neutral monists is to provide a clear account of what neutral entities are. They are supposed to be entities that are in themselves neither mental nor physical but that qualify as mental or physical if they satisfy certain conditions. Some neutral monists say little more than this. They say, for instance, that neutral entities are the ones that can factor into both physical and psychological laws. The problem with definitions like these is that they fail to provide an adequate means of identifying which entities in the world the neutral entities are, or of determining whether neutral entities even exist. By analogy, imagine that we arrive together at a meeting of an organization, and you want to know from me which person in the room is the organization's president. I respond: 'Obviously the president is the person in the room who sets the meeting's agenda, who organizes the annual fundraiser, who was elected by the membership last January, who . . .' I might give an exhaustive description of the relations that define the role of the president, but I would still fall short of telling you what you want to know. The reason is that nothing I've told you enables you to pick out which person in the room actually occupies the presidential role, and that's what you want. Attempts to define neutral entities simply in terms of their relations to mental and physical entities seem to have an analogous shortcoming: they describe the role neutral entities are supposed to play within neutral monism, but they do not enable us to pick out which entities in the world, if any, actually play that role. If neutral monists cannot supply a definition that enables us to do this, then neutral monism does not offer a clear solution to the problem of emergence.

A final way that dual-attribute theorists can approach the problem of emergence appeals to the notion of spatial organization or arrangement. There is more to emergence than physical particles themselves. A tree trunk and a human brain are composed of the same kinds of fundamental physical particles; the reason one gives rise to conscious states and the other doesn't is that in one but not the other the particles are organized or arranged in the right kind of way. Spatial arrangement is thus the key to emergence. Critics nevertheless insist that this appeal to spatial organization does no better than the appeal to brute psychophysical laws. How, after all, is spatial arrangement supposed to explain the emergence of mental states? Suppose a certain number of fundamental physical particles do not generate any mental states. We then reposition the particles in space. How is this repositioning supposed to explain the emergence of mental states? If the particles do not give rise to consciousness in the first place, how could changing their spatial relations make any difference? Why should one spatial arrangement be more apt for producing mental states than another? There doesn't seem to be any principled answer. According to critics, then, both the appeal to spatial arrangement and the appeal to psychophysical laws attach a label to a mystery without doing anything to solve it.

Hylomorphism

So far I've focused on some popular ways of understanding how mental phenomena in general, and emotions in particular, are related to physical phenomena. I now want to focus on a different approach to the ontology of emotions, one based on hylomorphism, a metaphysical framework that Aristotle used to articulate an account of the emotions in antiquity and that has gained an increasing amount of attention from metaphysicians over the past decade (Fine 1999, 2008; Johnston 2006; Oderberg 2007; Koslicki 2008; Jaworski 2011, 2012, 2014, 2016; Rea 2011; Marmodoro 2013; Koons 2014).

Aristotle's approach to the emotions is encapsulated in the following passage:

> In fact, the affections of the soul all seem to be with a body: excitement, calmness, fear, pity, courage, also joy, and both loving and hating, for whenever we have them the body is in some way affected ... If this is the

> case, then clearly the affections are enmattered forms (*logoi enhuloi*). Hence, their definitions will be for instance, 'anger is a certain movement of such-and-such a body (or a part or power of it) by this for the sake of that' . . . [T] he affections of soul are inseparable from the natural matter of animals. (*De Anima* book I, chapter 1: 403a16–19, 24–7; 403b17–18)[7]

According to Aristotle, when we experience an emotion, the activities of our physical components are coordinated in a way that unifies them into a single event. The upshot is a view that is both antireductive and naturalistic. Because the coordination or form is not something inherent in the physical components, the emotion cannot be identified with the sum of the activities of those components. As a result, it is not possible to give an exhaustive account of the emotions by appeal to the activities of our physical parts; we cannot reduce our descriptions and explanations of emotions to descriptions and explanations in neuroscience or biology or chemistry. Form, however, cannot exist apart from something that's informed. A form must be the form of something. Consequently, an emotion cannot exist apart from the physical components whose activities it unifies. Emotions are thus essentially embodied in the physical components we have; they are all 'with a body,' as Aristotle says, 'inseparable from the natural matter of animals,' yet it is not possible to give a reductive explanation of them.

A hylomorphic account of emotion is what Prinz (2004: 10) categorizes as a hybrid theory, one that takes emotions to comprise a range of contributing factors: some felt, some cognitive, some physiological. To appreciate what makes the hylomorphic account distinctive we need to consider the hylomorphic framework in greater detail. Since this chapter concerns mind-body theories, I will focus on the way hylomorphism understands the relation between emotions and the physiological states that embody them.

At its core, hylomorphism claims that form or structure, as I'll typically refer to it (or organization, order, coordination, or configuration) is a basic ontological and explanatory principle. Some individuals, paradigmatically living things, are composed of materials that are structured or organized in various ways. You and I are not mere quantities of physical materials; we are quantities of physical materials with a certain organization or structure. That structure is responsible for us being and persisting as humans, and it is responsible for us having the particular developmental, metabolic, reproductive, perceptive, and cognitive capacities we have.

[7] See also *De Anima* 413a4–6.

We can illustrate the hylomorphic notion of structure with a simple example. Suppose we put Howard in a very strong bag – strong enough to ensure that nothing leaks out when we squash him with several tons of force. Before squashing, the contents of the bag include one human being; after squashing, they include none. In addition, before squashing, the contents of the bag can think, feel, and act, but after squashing, they can't. What explains these differences in the contents of the bag pre-squashing and post-squashing? It cannot be the physical materials, for those remain the same – none of them leaked out. What changed was rather the way those materials were organized or structured. That structure was responsible for there being a human before squashing, and for that human having the capacities it had. Once that structure was destroyed, there was no longer a human with those capacities. Structure is thus a basic ontological principle (it concerns what things there are) and a basic explanatory principle (it concerns what things can do). Structure also operates as a principle of composition and unity. It unifies diverse things in a single thing. Paradigmatically, it unifies diverse physical materials into a single composite whole.

We can express the theoretical roles hylomorphic structure is supposed to play using some slogans:

> **Structure matters:** it operates as an irreducible ontological principle, one that accounts at least in part for what things essentially are.
>
> **Structure makes a difference:** it operates as an irreducible explanatory principle, one that accounts at least in part for what things can do, the powers they have.
>
> **Structure counts:** it explains the unity of composite things, including the persistence of one and the same living individual through the dynamic influx and efflux of matter and energy that characterize many of its interactions with the wider world.

These theoretical roles serve to define hylomorphic structure,[8] which in turn underwrites a general account of composition encompassing both composite individuals and composite events. Emotional experiences are included among the latter, so understanding a hylomorphic account of emotion requires understanding hylomorphic composition. We can start by saying more about exactly what structures are.

[8] This is not the only account of hylomorphic structure on offer. Other accounts that have appeared in the literature include Kit Fine (1999), Mark Johnston (2006), David Oderberg (2007), Kathrin Koslicki (2008), and Michael Rea (2011). The account I develop here and in greater detail elsewhere (Jaworski 2012, 2016) differs from theirs in ways that will become evident as I proceed.

According to traditional hylomorphists like Aristotle as well as some contemporary hylomorphists such as Mike Rea (2011) and myself (2012, 2014, 2016), structures are powers.[9] There are several competing theories of powers in the literature. One is defended by C. B. Martin (1996a–b, 1997, 2007), John Heil (2003, 2005, Chapter 2, this volume), and Martin and Heil (1998, 1999). We can call it the *identity theory of powers*. It claims that every property is essentially dispositional; each essentially empowers its individual possessor to interact with other individuals in various kinds of ways. A diamond's hardness empowers the diamond to do a variety of things – to scratch glass, for instance. It is essential to the hardness that it empowers the diamond to do these things; it plays this power-conferring role in every possible world in which it exists. We describe this role in a variety of ways. We say that the diamond is able (or has the power or potential or capacity) to scratch glass, or that the diamond would scratch that mirror if raked across its surface, but we also say that the diamond has a tetrahedral arrangement of carbon atoms. According to the identity theory of powers, these descriptions are of numerically one and the same property. The diamond's hardness = the diamond's power to scratch glass = the diamond's having a tetrahedral arrangement of carbon atoms. These descriptions simply bring out different theoretical roles that the one property plays. Dispositional descriptions such as 'The diamond would scratch that mirror if raked across its surface' bring out the roles it plays as a power. Nondispositional descriptions such as 'The diamond has a tetrahedral arrangement of carbon atoms' bring out its role as a stable manifestation of a power possessed by the carbon atoms, namely the power to be arranged tetrahedrally. The one property is thus simultaneously both a stable manifestation of a power and a power itself, both an actuality and a potentiality.

One important feature of powers is that they are essentially directed toward their manifestations. This directedness has led some philosophers to draw analogies between dispositionality and intentionality (Martin and Pfeifer 1986; Place 1996a–b; Molnar 2003). Just as my desire is essentially a desire *for* something, and my fear is essentially a fear *of* something, so too a power is essentially *for* various exercises or manifestations. Moreover, just as my desire can remain unfulfilled and my fear unrealized, so too a typical

[9] The hylomorphic framework I describe here is committed to a substance-attribute ontology in which properties are sparse, not abundant in Lewis' (1983) sense (Jaworski 2014, 2016). The only properties that exist are ones that empower individuals to enter into causal relations. The framework also comprises events or states of affairs, which are individuals having properties or standing in relations at times.

power can remain unmanifested. A quantity of table salt has the power to dissolve in water, yet that power might never actually manifest itself. It is possible that the salt might remain forever undissolved (Martin 1996a).

Hylomorphic structures are powers to configure (or organize, order, or coordinate) things. What sets structures apart from other powers is that they cannot exist unmanifested; they are manifested essentially. Structured individuals are essentially and continuously engaged in configuring the materials that compose them. I essentially and continuously configure the materials that compose me, and you essentially and continuously configure the materials that compose you. Biologist J. Z. Young describes organization in similar terms as a complex activity in which living things engage:

> The essence of a living thing is that it consists of atoms . . . caught up into the living system and made part of it for a while. The living activity takes them up and organizes them in its characteristic way. The life of a man consists essentially in the activity he imposes upon that stuff. (Young 1971: 86–7)

Consider likewise neurophysiologist Jonathan Miller:

> [T]he physical universe tends towards a state of uniform disorder . . . [T]he survival of form depends on . . . [either] the intrinsic stability of the materials from which the object is made, or the energetic replenishment and reorganisation of the material . . . The configuration of a fountain . . . is intrinsically unstable, and it can retain its shape only by endlessly renewing the material which constitutes it; that is, by organising and imposing structure on the unremitting flow of its own substance . . . The persistence of a living organism is an achievement of the same order as that of a fountain . . . it can maintain its configuration only by flowing through a system which is capable of reorganising and renewing the configuration from one moment to the next. (Miller 1978: 140–1)

The foregoing remarks should make evident that hylomorphic structure is not a mere set of static spatial relations among something's parts. In this sense the hylomorphic notion of structure differs from the notion of mere spatial arrangement discussed in connection with dual-attribute theories. The structures that distinguish living things from nonliving ones are dynamic patterns of environmental interaction – what Mark Johnston (2006) calls 'dynamic principles of unity,' or what Kit Fine (1999: 68–9) calls 'principles of variable embodiment'. They comprise programmatic sequences of changes over time, and often involve different kinds of changes under different kinds of conditions. It is because of their dynamic structures, their ability to 'impose' those structures on incoming matter and energy, as Miller puts it, that complex individuals (paradigmatically living things) persist through the constant influx and efflux of matter and energy that characterize their interactions with the wider world.[10] Describing the characteristic way each structured individual configures the materials composing it is something that hylomorphists say is an empirical undertaking – in the human case, one left largely to biology, biochemistry, neuroscience, and other biological subdisciplines.

According to hylomorphists, composition occurs when and only when an individual configures materials. Composite individuals are *emergent* individuals on the hylomorphic view. There are empirically describable conditions that are sufficient to bring into existence new structured individuals where previously no such individuals existed. Once a structured individual comes into existence, it is essentially and continuously engaged in configuring materials. The materials it configures are precisely those that compose it. An individual living thing does not configure exactly the same materials for very long since those materials are in constant flux, yet despite this, the individual maintains itself one and the same through all the changes on account of its ongoing configuring activity. That activity is what unifies various materials into a single individual, both synchronically and diachronically.

But individuals are not the only composite entities on the hylomorphic view; there are composite events as well. The structures discussed so far are *individual-making structures*, the kinds of things medieval hylomorphists called 'substantial forms'; they make individuals what they are. But the activities in which structured individuals engage have structures as well – *activity-making structures*.

The idea that there are activity-making structures is based on the observation that the activities of structured individuals involve coordinated manifestations of the powers of the parts that compose them. When we walk, talk, sing, dance, run, jump, and engage in the various other activities we do, we impose an order on the ways our parts manifest their powers. My parts needn't manifest their powers in an ordered way. It is possible for my neurons to fire or my muscles to contract in ways that do not compose an activity of throwing a baseball or playing an instrument. Fatigue, injury, insufficient training, and many other factors can result in uncoordinated manifestations of the powers of my parts. But when I succeed in throwing

[10] Hylomorphic structures are similar to what Peter van Inwagen (1990) calls 'lives'. By 'a life' van Inwagen takes himself to mean what biologists do: the lives of concrete organisms (van Inwagen 1990: 83).

or playing, I succeed in imposing a structure on the way my parts manifest their powers; I structure their manifestations throwing- or playing-wise. In some cases the structuring is conscious and intentional as in throwing a baseball or producing the precise limb movements in a dance. But in many cases the structuring is neither conscious nor intentional as in digesting food or increasing blood flow to the legs in response to something fearful. In whatever way it occurs, whether consciously and intentionally or not, the result of this structuring is not a new individual but rather an activity, another manifestation of the power structured individuals have of imposing order on things.

Activity-making structures unify diverse events in something analogous to the way individual-making structures unify the physical materials composing individuals. My parts and the surrounding materials needn't manifest their powers throwing-a-baseball-wise. The very same muscle fibers that contract in my shoulder when I throw a baseball might also contract when I experience an uncontrolled muscle spasm, or when a physical therapist stimulates them electrically. What unifies the contractions of the muscle fibers, what coordinates the manifestations of their powers, is what I do when I try to make an out, or try to knock down cans at the county fair, or try to accomplish whatever I try to do when I throw a baseball. In undertaking these activities I impose a unified order on the way my parts and the surrounding materials manifest their powers.

On the hylomorphic view, structured activities include emotional experiences. When I experience an emotion I am engaging in an activity in which various parts of my nervous system and various objects in the environment manifest their powers in a coordinated way that unifies them into a single event. It is possible to describe the unifying role of activity-making structures in terms of a notion of activity composition analogous to the notion of composition for individuals. Just as physical materials compose an individual exactly if they have the right kind of individual-making structure, likewise various events compose an activity exactly if they have the right kind of activity-making structure. Suppose that a is a structured individual with the power to engage in activity F. Suppose, moreover, that $b_1, b_2, \ldots, b_n$ are individuals, and that a subset of the *b*s are proper parts of a. Suppose, finally, that each b_i has the power to engage in an activity, G_i: b_1 has the power to G_1, b_2 has the power to G_2, and so on. We can then define a notion of activity composition as follows:

> **Activity composition:** Necessarily, a's F-ing at t is composed of b_1's G_1-ing at t_1, b_2's G_2-ing at t_2, . . . and b_n's G_n-ing at t_n exactly if b_1's G_1-ing at t_1, b_2's

G_2-ing at t_2, ... and b_n's G_n-ing at t_n are structured *F*-wise, where time *t* includes the times t_1, t_2, ...,t_n.

In other words, *a* engages in the activity of *F*-ing exactly if *a*'s parts and surrounding materials manifest their powers *F*-wise. I throw a baseball exactly if my parts and surrounding materials manifest their powers throwing-a-baseball-wise. Similarly, I experience anger or enjoyment exactly if my parts and surrounding materials manifest their powers anger- or enjoyment-wise.

Given reasonable assumptions, activity composition implies that the behaviors of structured individuals never violate the laws governing their fundamental physical constituents. According to hylomorphism, the activities of structured wholes are composed of the structured manifestations of the powers of their lower-level constituents and surrounding materials. If those constituents or materials were to lose their powers, or were to become incapable of manifesting them, they would become incapable of composing the activities of structured wholes. Those activities depend on lower-level items retaining and manifesting the powers they have. By analogy, it is only because bricks and timbers retain their shapes under compression that they can be recruited as components of buildings. Similarly, it is only because lower-level materials retain their distinctive powers that structured individuals can recruit them as components for their own activities. This is one thing that sets the hylomorphic view apart from many emergentist theories that claim that higher-level powers trump or nullify the powers of lower-level things (Sperry 1984).

This definition also makes it clear that a structured individual has the power to engage in various activities on account of its parts. Those parts form a subset of the individuals with powers whose coordinated manifestations compose its activities. We can express this idea by saying that a structured individual's parts *embody* its powers. My visual system embodies my power to see; your circulatory system embodies your power to bring oxygenated blood to various parts of yourself; Gabriel's limbic system embodies his power to experience emotions, and so on.

According to the hylomorphic theory I've been describing, all the powers of structured individuals are essentially embodied in their parts; the activities in which they engage are essentially composed of the coordinated manifestations of the powers of their parts and surrounding materials. It is impossible, not just nomologically but metaphysically, for me to engage in the activity of throwing a baseball unless my parts manifest their powers in the right coordinated way. Likewise, it is impossible, not just nomologically but metaphysically, for Gabriel to experience anger or enjoyment unless his parts manifest their powers in the right coordinated way.[11]

On the hylomorphic view, then, emotions are essentially embodied in the physiological mechanisms that compose us, yet it is not possible to reduce descriptions and explanations of them to descriptions and explanations of physiological mechanisms.[12] The reason is that there is more to these activities on the hylomorphic view than the operations of physiological mechanisms; there is also the way those operations are coordinated or structured, and structure in general is something different from things that are structured. It is possible for parts of our nervous systems to be activated in the ways they are when we are experiencing a particular emotion even though we are not experiencing the emotion in fact. Patients with pseudobulbar affect, for instance, suddenly and unpredictably cry or laugh in ways that are indistinguishable from the ways they would if they were experiencing sadness or mirth, and yet they do not feel sad or amused (Parvisi et al. 2006). Parts of their nervous systems are activated in the ways they would be during a real emotional episode, and yet their activation fails to be coordinated in the way necessary to compose an emotion. The hylomorphic view is thus robustly antireductive despite its commitment to essential physical embodiment.

Based on what's been said, it's possible to appreciate how hylomorphists approach mind-body problems, including the problem of emergence. Hylomorphic structure carves out distinctive individuals from the otherwise undifferentiated sea of matter and energy described by our best physics, and it confers on those individuals distinctive powers. If hylomorphic structure exists, then the physical universe is punctuated with pockets of organized change and stability – composite physical objects (paradigmatically living things) whose structures are powers that distinguish what they can do from what unstructured materials can do. Those

11 Many hylomorphists of the past have denied that all our powers are essentially embodied in the powers of our parts. Aristotle himself appears to deny it in *De Anima* III.4 where he appears to argue that understanding or *nous*, the power to grasp the essences of things, has no organ and is in general unmixed (*amigēs*) with a body (429a10–27). A commitment to the essential embodiment of our capacities is nevertheless the default position for hylomorphists. In fact, Aristotle treats embodiment as the default position as well (403a16–19, 24–7; 403b17–18), and as we have seen, even he claims that the emotions are essentially embodied (403a16–19, 24–7; 403b17–18; cf. 413a4–6).

12 The term 'reduction' is used in a variety of ways in philosophy and the sciences. The notion of reduction that interests us here is inter-theoretic reduction (Churchland 1986: 278–9). Inter-theoretic reduction is a synchronic relation between theories or conceptual frameworks in which one of them, the reducing theory or framework, is able to take over the descriptive and explanatory roles played by the other, the reduced theory or framework.

powers include the powers to think, feel, perceive, and act. The other approaches to mental phenomena we've considered reject hylomorphic structure. As a result, they are committed to a worldview that lacks a basic principle that distinguishes the parts of the physical universe that can think, feel, perceive, and act from those that can't. As a result, the existence of those powers in the natural world can begin to look inexplicable and mysterious in a way that was highlighted by the problem of emergence.

If there is nothing built into the basic fabric of the universe that explains why Zone A has powers that Zone B lacks – if nothing explains why you, say, have the power to think, feel, and perceive, while the materials surrounding you do not – then the options for understanding the existence of those powers in the natural world become constrained: either those powers must be identified with the powers of physical materials taken by themselves or in combination (as panpsychists and many physicalists claim), or their existence must be taken as an inexplicable matter of fact (as many emergentists and epiphenomenalists claim), or their existence in the natural world must be denied altogether (as substance dualists and eliminative physicalists claim).

With hylomorphic structure, however, the options are no longer constrained in the foregoing way. Distinctive powers like yours and mine exist in the natural world because structure exists in the natural world. Moreover, because structure is a basic principle on the hylomorphic view, this does not simply push the demand for an explanation back a step. A framework's basic principles stand in need of no further explanation. Structures and things that get structured are both basic on the hylomorphic view. Nothing must explain why the former exist any more than something must explain why the latter do. As a result, the view leaves it unmysterious why and how thought, feeling, and perception exist in the natural world.

Consider now how hylomorphists solve the problem of emergence in particular. They target claim (3); they deny that all of our properties are determined by the properties of our parts. Although properties like the mass, location, and position of a complex whole may be determined by the masses, locations, and positions of the particles composing it, this is not true of all properties, for some of them depend on structure. In addition, hylomorphists spot an ambiguity in claim (5). It is true that no number of particles can produce conscious experiences by themselves, but if those particles compose something with the right structure, if they manifest their powers in the right coordinated way, then there is a sense in which a number of nonconscious particles can combine to produce a conscious whole. For on the hylomorphic view, a conscious experience is composed of the coordinated manifestation of the powers of something's parts and surrounding materials. Consequently, there is a sense in which hylomorphists can reject claim (5) as well.

Critics might still demand that hylomorphists explain exactly how the movements of tiny particles in my brain can give rise to the rich qualitative experiences I have. But hylomorphists argue that this demand is illegitimate. It is legitimate to demand an explanation of how *p* happens only if *p* happens in fact. Yet according to hylomorphists, lower-level physical occurrences do not produce thoughts, feelings, and perceptions. The latter are instead ways in which lower-level occurrences are structured, and structures in general are not generated or produced by the things they structure. The structure that makes something a piano is not produced by pieces of wood and metal; it is instead something imposed on the wood and metal by the piano maker. Likewise, say hylomorphists, brains do not generate or produce thoughts, feelings, and perceptions. The latter are instead manifestations of the powers of brains and other organic subsystems that are coordinated by us, sometimes consciously as when we imagine or remember, sometimes unconsciously as when we feel fear, surprise, or disgust. Our powers to think, feel, and perceive might be embodied in muscular contractions, neural firings, and other physiological occurrences, but they are not generated or produced by those occurrences, for structured things are not in general causal by-products of the lower-level things they structure. Consequently, demanding an explanation for how brains produce consciousness implicitly begs the question against hylomorphists, for it assumes the existence of a kind of occurrence that hylomorphists deny exists. On hylomorphists' own terms, it is not legitimate to demand an explanation of lower-level generation any more than it is legitimate to demand that a meteorologist explain how the will of Zeus produces rain.

Critics might persist and demand an explanation for the emergence of structure itself on the hylomorphic view. Structural phenomena did not always exist in the universe. What, then, were the lower-level physical conditions that were responsible for bringing them about? Hylomorphists do not deny that we can ask how particular structures came to be in place. My distinctively human structure came to inform various biotic materials on account of the reproductive activity of my parents. Likewise, we can ask how the first living things emerged, how the first living structures came to inform prebiotic materials. What we cannot ask, according to hylomorphists, is what is responsible for continually generating the structures that I and other living things have. My structure is not something continually generated by some external source or by the materials that compose me; it is instead a self-maintaining configuring activity in which I continuously and essentially engage. There is no sense, then, in which hylomorphists' refusal to answer a demand to explain the emergence of structure can count as a strike against their view, at least not without begging the question and assuming from the outset that the hylomorphic view is false. It is possible to reject the hylomorphic worldview and with it the claim that structure is basic. But to demand that hylomorphists explain how structure emerges is to request something that hylomorphism implies cannot be done.

Conclusion

Mind-body problems place constraints on the shape that an ontology of the emotions can take. For the past fifty years, the theories that have occupied center stage in discussions of mind-body problems have been antireductive and naturalistic. They claim, on the one hand, that we are physical beings whose emotional capacities are essentially tied to, realized by, or embodied in the physical materials that compose us. On the other hand, they claim that this essential dependence on physical materials does not sanction psychophysical reduction; it does not imply that physical theory can in principle take over the descriptive and explanatory roles that psychological discourse currently plays. The most popular theories of this sort have been forms of nonreductive physicalism, emergentism, and epiphenomenalism. They face a variety of well-rehearsed difficulties. Hylomorphism provides a framework that promises to avoid these difficulties. It posits structures as basic powers on a par with those of fundamental physical materials. Whether it provides a workable alternative to standard approaches to the emotions in the long run depends on the workability of its underlying metaphysics.

CHAPTER 2

Dispositionality and Mentality

John Heil

"Dispositional statements are neither reports of observed or observable states of affairs, nor yet reports of unobserved or unobservable states of affairs" (Ryle 1949: 125).

"A dispositional state is *there* in the most simple or complex physical instances or psychological instances. It is there to provide the relevant richness of alternative manifestations with its multiple alternative reciprocal disposition partners, some of which would be mutually exclusive in their actualization but *ready to go* for present, distant, non-existent, or even *never*-existent manifestation conditions, that is, reciprocal disposition partners" (Martin 1997: 204–5).

1 From Hume to Aristotle

As someone who has written extensively on the metaphysics of dispositions, I am often asked whether one or another category of psychological state is or might be dispositional. My first reaction is, How could it be otherwise? My second reaction is, It's a long story. I shall take the opportunity here to fill in the gaps, to say in detail why it is sensible to think of psychological states – including emotions – as dispositional, why, really, we have no choice.

I spent most of my early career working on topics in mainstream epistemology and philosophy of mind. Like many others, I became obsessed with the problem of mental causation that haunted – and still does haunt – nonreductive physicalist accounts of the mind. In tandem with many others, I tried my hand at a solution to the problem, which by the mid-1990s, had become the problem of the "causal relevance" of mental properties (see for example Heil 1992). Granted mental properties are distinct from, although dependent on, physical properties, granted mental properties have physical "realizers," how could mental properties *themselves* figure in causal relations? The properties on which mental properties depend, their realizers, would seem to preempt the influence of mental properties in the production of physical – and given the dependence of the mental on the physical – mental – effects.

The issues here will be familiar to most readers of this volume, so I shall forebear belaboring them (see Jaworski, Chapter 1, this volume). What I might note, however, is that the problem and the space of solutions to it is purely metaphysical. Getting the problem off the ground requires a particular approach to the nature of properties and the nature of causation. For years I attempted to finesse the metaphysics, preferring not to "take a stand" on the question what properties were or on the nature of causation. What gradually became clear, however, was that you cannot solve a metaphysical problem while finessing the metaphysics. Eventually I took a deep breath and turned from philosophy of mind to metaphysics. Now I am venturing back into the philosophy of mind.

In what follows I shall try to persuade you that an ontology that includes powers or dispositions – terms I shall use interchangeably – provides an assortment of resources not found in prevailing "Humean" ontologies. Today it is a commonplace that objects do what they do because they are governed by laws (see Heil 2012: chap. 6). This idea, aggressively promoted by Descartes, incorporates the rejection of an Aristotelian picture of the universe according to which things do what they do because they are as they are. Descartes removed powers from occupants of the universe and placed them in God. Material bodies obeyed God's injunctions. The job of the scientist is to discern principles on which God chooses to act: God's laws of nature.

On such a conception, the explanation for what things do or would do is determined by factors *extrinsic* to those things. But *what* factors? Although happy to invoke laws, few philosophers today would want to call on God as Descartes – and Newton after him – did. If you subtract God from the picture, however, what could it mean for laws to *govern* the behavior of objects? For some, this is not an issue. There are laws: ask the scientists! And laws govern objects' behavior; end of story (see Heil 2003: 34–6; 2012: chap. 6).

Such an attitude evinces a lack of candor, always a rare commodity in philosophy. Descartes stripped objects of their powers and relocated these in God. If you reject this scheme, then the natural move would seem to be to return the powers to the objects and look more closely at the Aristotelian idea that things do what they do because they are as they are. Electrons repel other electrons because they are a particular way: they are negatively charged. Laws reflect, not divine commands or contingent regularities, but powers accorded to objects by those objects' properties.

This move is widely regarded with suspicion. Powers are mysterious, governing laws, mother's milk. Although in some unfashionable quarters, philosophers are becoming more open to the Aristotelian picture, a deeply ingrained Humeanism still dominates the philosophical terrain, coloring attempts to understand the nature of powers.[1] As a result, philosophers have by and large failed to appreciate the richness afforded by an ontology that includes powers or dispositions.

My aim here is to make salient advantages accruing the philosophy of mind from a serious ontology of dispositions. Such an ontology is to be distinguished from one in which some notion of dispositionality is bolted onto an essentially Humean superstructure. This will require an initial excursion into fundamental ontology. My hope is that philosophers with an interest in the mind will see immediately the significance of dispositionality for our understanding of psychological states and processes including the emotions.

2 Ontological Preliminaries

One place to begin is with a general metaphysical picture according to which dispositionality serves as a mark of reality. The universe comprises substances standing in various relations to one another. Every substance is some way or other. Ways substances are, are properties. Although it does not matter much here, I take properties to be accidents or modes, not universals. Nowadays the term used most often to identify properties so considered – particularized properties – is "trope." Talk of tropes stems from the writings of D. C. Williams. Although Williams is one of my philosophical heroes, my modes or accidents differ importantly from Williams's tropes (see Williams 1953). For Williams, an object is constituted by tropes; objects are "bundles" of tropes. I embrace a more traditional two-category ontology of substances and properties.[2]

For some philosophers, denying that properties are universals is, if not incoherent, at least deeply controversial (for discussion and references, see Heil 2012: chap. 5). Such philosophers display an unbecoming ignorance of the history of philosophy. With few exceptions, philosophers from Plato and Aristotle through the medievals and early moderns accepted that properties were particulars. So I reject the suggestion that we are obliged to regard properties as universals until it is proved otherwise. It is not

[1] Nothing in philosophy is ever completely forgotten. See, for instance, Harré and Madden 1975.
[2] The ontology taken for granted here is defended in detail in Heil 2003, 2012.

modes or accidents, but universals, that appear to be ontologically unsavory, almost certainly the result of reading linguistic categories into ontology. There are general *terms*, but as countless philosophers have recognized, no reason whatever to think that these general terms stand for general *entities*.

I said that this will not matter much in the present context, but I want to make sure my cards are on the table. The conception of dispositionality I discuss here was not arrived at in the course of attempting to solve some high-level problem in philosophy of mind, but in working out what seems to me to be an utterly sensible, even lovable, fundamental ontology. That ontology turns out to have implications for the nature of whatever is, whether psychological or not.

So I begin with the idea that the universe comprises substances, and those substances are various ways, the ways being properties of the substances. But what are properties? What is their *nature*?

What a substance does or would do depends on its properties. A cricket ball rolls or would roll owing to its spherical shape. A vase shatters or would shatter owing to its fragility. You would be hard pressed to think of a property that does not make a difference to what its bearer does or would do. Such a property would be unobservable and apparently undetectable, at least it would be if the observation or detection of something requires that thing's affecting the observer – or affecting something else that affects the observer. For these and various other reasons, I regard all properties, all *genuine* properties, as dispositional. You could put this by saying that properties are powers possessed by objects.

Properties are not merely – or "purely" – powers, however. Objects are as they are *qualitatively* owing to their properties. Although any property can be considered as a quality and as a power of whatever possesses it, qualities and powers are not two kinds or classes of property. A ball's shape is a paradigmatic quality of the ball, but a ball's shape empowers the ball to roll. We have, I believe, excellent reasons to think that properties, *genuine* properties, are *powerful qualities*, the distinction between powers and qualities being what the scholastics and early moderns would have called a distinction of reason, not a real distinction.

I have twice used the phrase "genuine properties." This suggests a distinction between real and merely apparent properties. The important contrast, however, is that between predicates, and truthmakers for applications of predicates, on the one hand, and properties, on the other hand. A predicate can hold true of an object without designating a property possessed by that object. Determinable predicates, for instance, hold of an object because that object possesses some determinate property. An electron has mass by virtue of having some determinate mass and charge by virtue of possessing some determinate charge.

I believe, as well, that only simple substances, only objects that do not have parts that are substances, can be property bearers. So I am using "property" in a somewhat technical sense. What we would ordinarily call properties, familiar characteristics of complex objects – their colors and shapes, for instance – are rarely properties, rarely *genuine* properties in my sense. Although the restriction of properties to simples has momentous consequences, it plays no role in what I have to say here. I shall, then, speak freely of properties often meaning, not genuine properties, but what Keith Campbell (1990) calls *quasi*-properties, "properties-by-courtesy," and I have elsewhere called Episcopalian properties.[3]

3 The Psychological and the Dispositional

If properties are powerful qualities, if every property is a power or a disposition, then psychological states, to the extent that they involve properties, will be dispositional. Even if you had doubts about the austere ontology I have endorsed, however, you might arrive at this conclusion solely by considering the nature of ordinary psychological states.

Take beliefs, the philosopher's favorite. Beliefs are thought to explain what you do or would do. What you do is a manifestation of your beliefs in concert with your circumstances and with various features of your makeup, including your desires. This is even more clear in the case of emotions. Whatever emotions are, your being in a particular emotional state is a matter of your being in a state that, in addition to exhibiting a distinctive qualitative character, affects both your behavior and your psychology – your beliefs, desires, and mental imagery, for instance.

If you are attracted to functionalism, you are already thinking of psychological states dispositionally. Although functionalism is often described as characterizing states of mind causally, what is important is not that a given state stands in the right causal relations to other states, but that it *would* interact with those other states in the right way. The interactions, when they occur, are best understood as manifestations of dispositions.

[3] *The Book of Common Prayer* tells us that God is "a being whose property is always to have mercy," an evocative way of saying that God is by nature merciful; see Heil 2012: 152.

Many find functionalism wanting because it appears to leave out the *qualitative* nature of psychological states: the painfulness of pain, the scent of freshly mowed grass, the taste of anchovies. This qualitative nature is taken to be altogether separate from the dispositionality that drives psychological mechanisms and issues in behavior.

Philosophers speak of *qualia* in these contexts, and worry that functionalism excludes *qualia*, qualities of conscious experiences, the very essence of consciousness. Some philosophers grant that *qualia* regularly, even lawfully, *accompany* physical states that are responsible for behavior. But *qualia* are distinct from those states – obviously! – and bear at most a contingent relation to them. Although it seems true of terrestrial creatures that their physical condition is responsible for their undergoing qualitatively saturated experiences, it might have failed to be so. You can imagine "zombies," creatures like us physically down to the last detail, but who altogether lack conscious qualities (Kirk 1974, 2005; Chalmers 1996).

Thoughts of this kind give rise to theories that attempt to explain the connection between non-qualitative, causally efficacious physical goings-on and qualitatively imbued conscious experiences. But perhaps this is just another case of philosophers' beginning with gratuitous assumptions that culminate in disaster. If you start with the idea that the qualitative is non-dispositional and the dispositional non-qualitative, you will be left with the seemingly impossible task of understanding how the one could be related to the other without rendering qualities epiphenomenal.

As noted already, I endorse the commonsense idea that properties are powerful qualities. Every property is a quality the possession of which disposes its possessor to behave in particular ways in particular circumstances. Suppose color and shape are uncontroversially qualities of objects. The red cricket ball rolls (rather than tumbles) across the ground because it is spherical; it reflects light so as to look red owing to its color.

Once you move beyond the tired idea that qualities and dispositions are different species of property, or that dispositions require a non-dispositional, "categorical" "ground" or "base," functionalism takes on a new look. As originally conceived, functionalism regards the identity of a particular state of mind as depending on its "causal role" within the system. Something is a pain (or a pain "realizer") because it plays the pain role. But pains are *painful*. How do you get painfulness out of a causal role? And what of the distinctive aura associated with ordinary emotions? How could this be extracted from qualitatively bereft causal profiles?

Substituting dispositionality for causality, functionalism can be understood as the thesis that psychological states are dispositionally characterizable: it is not simply what a state *does*, but what it *would* do in concert with other states that determines its identity. Psychological states are distinguished by their dispositional profiles. If a state is something's being a particular way, and something's being a particular way is its possessing a particular property, you can replace talk of states with talk of properties.

Suppose, now, I am right in regarding properties as powerful qualities. It would follow that psychological states are qualitative states embodying particular dispositional profiles. Further, they have these profiles – pains are apt to play the "pain role," feelings of anger or frustration have the effects they have – *because* they are as they are qualitatively. Functionalism as standardly conceived has the order of explanation backward. Pains, for instance, are not painful because they "play the pain role"; they play the pain role because they are painful. Similarly, the qualitative character of emotions is what equips them to contribute as they do to agents' thoughts and actions.

This means that you can accept a broadly functionalist picture of the mind without jettisoning *qualia*, without relegating the qualitative dimensions of the mind to a second-class status, without denigrating the "causal relevance" of the qualitative. Qualities are not inert add-ons, not epiphenomena. Qualities are in at the ground level. Qualities are muscular, qualities throw their weight around, qualities get things done.

I believe this idea is perfectly compatible with everyday views of qualities. Philosophers who have insisted that qualitativity and dispositionality must be metaphysically diverse have buzzed their way into the fly bottle.[4]

In fact, philosophers who believe that qualities are non-dispositional and dispositions are non-qualitative rarely argue for the thesis explicitly. It is rather taken as obvious. It seems obvious, however, only when you start with a substantive, nonnegotiable metaphysical conception of properties as dispositional (hence non-qualitative) or qualitative (hence non-dispositional). Although the popularity of this conception is incontestable, I believe it rests ultimately on a conflation of predicates and properties. You start with the idea that qualitative and dispositional predicates are not analyzable or definable in terms of one another, and move from this linguistic fact to an ontological conclusion: qualitative and dispositional predicates must designate different species of property.

[4] This is a natural outcome of distinguishing "dispositional" *if-then* properties and "categorical" *here and now* properties. The *locus classicus* is Ryle 1949, but see also Prior, Pargetter, and Jackson 1982. For discussion, see Heil 2003: chap. 9; 2005.

A move of this kind will seem plausible if you think that every predicate that applies truly to objects designates a property possessed by those objects. If you have distinct predicates then, predicates not analyzable or definable in terms of one another, these must designate distinct properties if they designate anything. You have "is red," "would reflect light so as to look red," on the one hand and, "is spherical," "would roll," on the other. If these predicate pairs lack appropriate analytic connections, does this mean that they must designate different properties? I do not see why.

Think about truthmakers for such predicates. It could well turn out that "is red" and "would reflect light so as to look red" as applied to the cricket ball have a single truthmaker: the property of being red. Similarly, the truthmaker for "the ball is spherical" and "the ball would roll" could be the ball's spherical shape. Indeed this seems to be how it is with the ball: where there is one property, there can be more than one truly applicable predicate. And in this regard, the cricket ball is in no way special.

You might find the thought that properties are powerful qualities surprising, even dubious. But, if you do, I invite you to reflect on your reasons for this reaction. And, while you are doing that, you might reflect as well on the myriad philosophical problems arising from the idea that qualities and powers are metaphysically incommensurable. These problems range from the *qualia* problem that plagues functionalism to the problem of the causal relevance of consciousness, the latter-day problem of mental causation we have inherited from Descartes. We scoff at Descartes' dualism of substances, while happily accepting Descartes' bifurcation of the mental and the physical. We then associate qualities with the mental and powers – dispositionality – with the physical. Having prized the two apart, we then inflict on one another scores of books and articles endeavoring to put them back together again or assigning to the one or the other an attenuated degree of reality. But the mistake was in our prizing them apart in the first place; the mistake was in following Descartes in his bifurcation of the universe.

4 The Nature of Dispositions

I have focused on the idea that properties are powerful qualities, and the implications of this idea for the philosophy of mind. I now turn to the nature of dispositionality.

Dispositions are most naturally characterized conditionally. If salt is soluble in water, then, were the salt placed in water, it would dissolve. If a particular vase is fragile, it would shatter were it dropped. The conditional nature of dispositional ascriptions is what led Ryle to distinguish dispositions from categorical states (Ryle 1949). To ascribe a disposition to an object is to describe the object conditionally. Categorical states, in contrast, are ascribed categorically, that is unconditionally.

Ryle is notorious for holding that *all there was* to a vase's being fragile is for the conditional to hold of it.[5] If the vase is fragile, there is no categorical – unconditional – state of the vase that makes it true that the vase is fragile. Ryle's successors rightly balked at this idea, preferring to think that, when dispositional ascriptions are true, they are true by virtue of objects' possession of various categorical "grounds." This is the conception of dispositionality I have tried to persuade you to abandon. The dispositional–categorical distinction is a linguistic artifact that cuts no ice ontologically.

Although today many philosophers are prepared to take dispositions ontologically seriously, Ryle's conditional (that is, "non-categorical") characterization of dispositions has continued to be influential. The practice – in itself unobjectionable – of using conditionals to refer to dispositions, can, in the wrong hands, breed ontological confusion. Seeing why this is so will take us in the direction of a more sensible conception of dispositionality.

Start with an idea on which all sides agree, namely that the identity of a disposition is determined by what it is a disposition *for*. Solubility is a disposition to dissolve, fragility is a disposition to break. Often this is put in terms of stimuli and manifestations. Solubility, for instance, is naturally characterized as a disposition to dissolve when placed in a liquid, or a liquid of the right kind. And this characterization is typically spelled out in terms of a "stimulus" or "trigger" and a manifestation. A stimulus, S, causes a disposition, D, to manifest itself in manner M:

$$\text{(D)} \quad S \rightarrow D \rightarrow M$$

Such a formulation is unperspicuous and potentially misleading, however. First, as well-known counterexamples to attempts to produce conditional analyses of dispositional predicates attest, it is easy to think of cases in which you have both S and D, without having M, you can have the disposition and the stimulus, but not the manifestation. A particular poison would be lethal if ingested, but not if you take an antidote. The antidote might work by inhibiting the action of the poison or, a different case, by changing the chemical makeup of the poison so that it ceases to be lethal. A wire is live if, were it touched by a conductor, electrical current

[5] Ryle, at least, was commendably candid about this; see his 1949: 125, quoted at the outset of this chapter.

would flow from the wire to the conductor. Let the wire's being live be *D*, *S* be the wire's being touched by a conductor, and *M* be electricity's flowing from the wire to the conductor. C. B. Martin's Electro-Fink shuts the power off when the wire is touched by a conductor, so the conditional – if the wire were touched by a conductor, electricity would flow from the wire to the conductor – is false, yet the wire is live (Martin 1994).

Philosophers have tried in various ways to circumvent such cases and preserve the conditional analysis, or a version of it, and the simple $S \rightarrow D \rightarrow M$ model (Lewis 1997). But, even if these difficulties could be overcome, the model is unsatisfactory in other ways. The model invokes causality to explicate dispositionality, but there are excellent reasons to regard dispositionality as fundamental and to explicate causation in terms of the manifesting of dispositions. If that is right, the simple model has the order of explanation backward. I shall not defend this claim here, but its plausibility should become evident in what follows (see Heil 2005, 2012: chap. 6).

Let us agree that the identity of a disposition is determined by what it is a disposition for, but not *simply* this. A disposition's identity depends on what it is a disposition for *with* particular kinds of reciprocal disposition partner. The manifesting of a disposition is a cooperative, reciprocal affair. When salt dissolves in water, dispositions present in the salt and in the water work together – perhaps with the help of other "background" elements such as the gravitational field and atmospheric pressure – to yield a particular manifestation: a saline solution.

I believe that, quite generally, the manifesting of dispositions is like this: manifestations of dispositions are mutual manifestations of reciprocal disposition partners. Dispositions cooperate to yield manifestations. Dispositions mutually manifesting themselves in this way *are* instances of causation. Just as it is misleading to think of the manifesting of dispositions as a linear $S \rightarrow D \rightarrow M$ affair, so it is misleading to think of causation in terms of chains. These models result from our regarding particular components of a dispositional system as especially noteworthy. We say that the burning match caused the fire, when in fact the fire was a mutual manifestation of the burning match, oxygen, various flammable materials on hand, and undoubtedly much else besides.

I have said that causation is best understood as the mutual manifestings of dispositions. Do all dispositions require reciprocal partners for their manifestation? Are all manifestings *mutual* manifestings?

Physicists tell us that, when a radium atom decays yielding a radon atom and an alpha particle, it does so spontaneously. Its decaying appears to be the manifestation of a disposition the manifestation of which requires no reciprocal partner, no "hidden variable." As Schrödinger's cat and the atomic bomb make clear, such spontaneous manifestings can have momentous consequences, consequences that are themselves mutual manifestations of reciprocal partners.

Although I regard spontaneous manifestings as ontologically important, indeed as the wellspring of contingency (see Heil 2013), I shall ignore such cases here, and focus on dispositions the manifestations of which require the cooperation of other complimentary dispositions.

I have identified dispositions with properties, ways objects are. Once you make this move, however, you will want to embrace the following principle, the significance of which cannot be overstated:

> (P) One and the same disposition can manifest itself in different ways with different kinds of reciprocal disposition partner.

A grasp of (P) is crucial to understanding the nature of dispositionality.

Consider a particular cricket ball, and, more to the point, consider the cricket ball's spherical shape. The ball's shape is a powerful quality. But if the ball's shape is dispositional, what is it dispositional *for*? Well, by virtue of being spherical the ball would roll (rather than tumble) down an incline. But it is also true that, by virtue of being spherical, the ball would make a circular concave impression in the carpet, would fit smoothly through a circular opening the circumference of which matches the diameter of the ball, would look spherical, would feel spherical. One property, the ball's sphericality, one disposition, many different kinds of manifestation with many different kinds of reciprocal partner. So it is with dispositions generally. By virtue of its charge, an electron would repel other electrons, would attract positrons, would cooperatively interact with protons.

This feature of dispositionality is what undermines attempts to explicate dispositions in the linear $S \rightarrow D \rightarrow M$ manner, and attempts to analyze dispositional predicates conditionally. Failure to see this point results in over-counting dispositions. Although the cricket ball's shape disposes it to behave in very different ways in different circumstances – that is, in concert with different kinds of reciprocal partner – there is but a single disposition, a single property responsible for its so behaving. As will become clear, this crucial feature of dispositionality has important implications for attempts to understand psychological states dispositionally. Before turning to psychological states, however, let me head off one potential objection.

Return once more to the cricket ball. I said that the ball would roll down an incline owing to its spherical shape. But it takes more than sphericality to roll. The ball must, in addition, be rigid and possess sufficient mass. The ball's rolling is a complex manifestation of an ensemble of dispositions possessed by the ball and by everything with which the ball is interacting.

Right. The ball's spherical shape is but one of many dispositions required for its rolling. What I said originally, however, was that the ball's spherical shape was responsible for its rolling *rather than tumbling* down an incline. This manifestation itself is a complex, multifaceted affair. Holding the ball's other properties and properties of the ball's circumstances fixed, the ball's spherical shape is responsible for one of these facets. This is how it is quite generally when complex objects interact with a complex environment.

Locke was fond of noting that, in describing and explaining what goes on around us, we engage in *abstraction*, focusing on aspects of the situation that are, for one reason or another, salient (see for example *Essay*, II, xii). Newton provides a systematic account of how objects behave *qua* possessors of mass, *qua massy*. Newton's laws spell out the contribution mass makes to the behavior of objects with mass. Objects with mass possess other properties that can affect their behavior, however. An oak leaf and a lead pellet with the same mass do not fall at the same rate near the surface of the Earth. It is rarely the case that an object's behavior is exclusively a manifestation of its mass in concert with the masses of other objects.

This is how we should understand familiar laws of nature. Laws do not tell us how "ideal" objects would behave under "ideal" circumstances. Why should anyone care? Laws provide an insight to the contribution various properties make to the behavior of their possessors.

Let me offer one final comment on the metaphysics of dispositionality before returning to psychology. I have enthusiastically promoted the idea that properties are powerful qualities. One and the same property endows its possessor with a particular quality and a particular dispositionality. Although I believe this way of thinking about properties is supported by common sense and was taken for granted by many philosophers in the past, nowadays it is likely to be greeted with an incredulous stare. It appears easy to prize dispositions or powers and qualities apart. The relation seems at best contingent.

Peter Unger, who vigorously defends the need for qualities, nevertheless argues that powers and qualities are related only contingently (Unger 2006). It is contingent that a spherical object rolls, rather than tumbles as a cube might, down an incline.

The plausibility of this kind of quasi-Humean picture rests on a failure to appreciate (P), however, a failure to recognize that a disposition is a disposition for various different kinds of manifestation with various kinds of manifestation partner. Suppose that, by virtue of being spherical, the ball would roll (rather than tumble) down an incline, would make a circular (rather than square) convex impression in the carpet, would pass with ease through a circular hole the diameter of which matches the ball's, would look spherical and feel spherical (rather than cubical). Now *is* it so easy to conceive of something spherical that tumbles down an incline, makes a square-shaped impression in the carpet, cannot pass smoothly through a circular hole of the right diameter, looks cubical, and feels cubical?

For some philosophers, such considerations carry little weight. Unless you are a committed Humean, however, unless you *start* with the idea that "all events seem entirely loose and separate" (*Enquiry*, VII, II) and that dispositions and qualities must be distinct kinds of property, you might begin to feel the attraction of the idea that properties are powerful qualities. In any case, I shall assume that this is so and now ask what bearing it might have on the ontology of psychological states.

5 Psychological States as Dispositional

My hope is that I have said enough to make the thought that psychological states are dispositional less surprising than it is often thought to be. Again, start with belief. Suppose you believe that a can of soup rests on the shelf in front of you. In concert with a desire for soup, you might be moved to reach for the can. Your reaching is a mutual manifestation of your belief and desire (and doubtless much else, a consideration I omit in what follows for the sake of simplicity). The same belief in concert with other beliefs might lead you to form the belief that you would need to turn on the stove to heat the soup. This new belief is a mutual manifestation of assorted beliefs and probably other, non-doxastic states as well.

Beliefs are central to functionalist accounts of the mind, but what of emotions? To the extent that your undergoing an emotion is a matter of your being in a particular psychological state that could influence other psychological states and your behavior, emotions are through and through dispositional. This will be so regardless of differences among conceptions of emotion, provided only that what makes it the case that a particular ascription of emotion holds of an agent at least in part because of some way that agent is.

Although I have not mentioned it, a disposition can be a disposition for the acquisition of a disposition.[6] A steel blank has the disposition to be

[6] C. B. Martin and I have argued that this feature of dispositionality can be exploited to accommodate the phenomenon of rule following (Martin and Heil 1998). I shall not repeat our arguments here, but merely note in passing that dispositions for the acquisition of dispositions are psychologically important.

shaped in the form of a key that would have the disposition to open locks of a particular kind. Similarly for beliefs and emotions. Do you believe that the moon is larger than a walnut? Well, you were, prior to reading the previous sentence, disposed to form this belief in concert with other beliefs. If you are the sporting type, then you are disposed to jubilation when your home team wins an important game and to desolation when it loses.

Suppose that your being angry on a particular occasion is a matter of your being in a particular kind of psychological state. This state, together with particular kinds of disposition partner, can yield many different kinds of manifestation. Thus, in combination with thoughts about the consequences of an angry outburst, it might lead to the recruitment of mechanisms of self-control. In other circumstances, your anger might lead you to an act of violence, a mutual manifestation of your anger and assorted other psychological and non-psychological states.

None of this requires a decision on the question whether anger or emotions generally are "natural kinds."[7] Emotional predicates apply truly to agents and truthmakers for these applications, whatever their deep nature, are going to be dispositional. This will be so even if the truthmakers vary across, or even within, agents. Psychological kinds are almost certainly orthogonal to, and unanalyzable in terms of, physical kinds, kinds at home in fundamental physics, but the deep story about truthmakers for terms expressing psychological kinds is the story you get in fundamental physics.

I realize that this last claim is likely to set off alarms in some quarters. In a way, nothing I have said requires its adoption. Nevertheless I have argued elsewhere that there are excellent reasons to accept it – and that it poses no threat to psychology or any other "higher-level" endeavor (Heil 2003, 2012). Like it or not, metaphysics, and in particular, ontology, cannot be done piecemeal. Ontology is a package deal: one thing leads to another. When you get on the bus, you must ride it to the end of the line.

Despite these ominous-sounding remarks, I believe that the idea that psychological states generally and emotions in particular are dispositional is unavoidable and unexceptionable. Dispositionality is everywhere. Dispositionality is the engine that holds things together and drives the mechanisms that populate the universe as we find it. It is completely unsurprising, then, that our psychology is a reflection of our dispositional makeup.

[7] See, for instance, Griffiths 1997 and Roberts 2003. You might think it mattered if you thought that causation requires subsumption under causal laws and laws concern natural kinds. In contrast, I have argued that causation is to be explicated in terms of manifestings of dispositions, and laws reflect the contributions particular kinds of dispositions make to their bearers. If emotions are dispositional, then any particular emotional state will be causally – that is, dispositionally – loaded.

CHAPTER 3

Emotion as Process

Jenefer Robinson

1 Introduction

Most philosophers and psychologists of emotion have distinguished between emotions as long-term states or dispositions such as enduring love or lifelong resentment, and emotions as relatively short episodes, such as flashes of anger, bouts of fear, surges of affection, fits of gloom, or spasms of contempt. Philosophers have a tendency to identify these emotional episodes with some other type of mental state or event, such as appraisals (Solomon 1976, 1988; Nussbaum 2001), perceptions (Döring 2007; Tappolet 2010), "feelings towards" (Goldie 2000, 2002), "felt bodily attitudes" (Deonna and Teroni 2012a), or "gut reactions" (Prinz 2004). In this chapter I will argue that even the shortest emotional episode (henceforth "emotion") is in fact a *process*, which includes a number of different states that are causally linked together.

The idea that even short-term emotions are processes is widely accepted among psychologists. But usually psychologists have focused mostly on some particular constituent of the emotion process. Thus some psychologists work on the "appraisals" that they think are the most important components of emotion (Lazarus 1991a; Roseman 2001; Smith and Kirby 2001; Ellsworth 2013). Philosophers emphasize that appraisals are what distinguish one emotion from another, especially closely related emotions such as shame and remorse or anger and indignation (Solomon 1976). Other psychologists study the bodily components of emotion, with some focusing on facial expressions (Tomkins 1984; Ekman 1992, 2003), vocal expressions or intonations signifying a particular emotion (Scherer et al. 2001; Juslin and Laukka 2003), states of action readiness or action tendencies (Frijda 1986), or autonomic nervous system changes (Cacioppo et al. 2000; Levenson 2003; Kreibig 2010). Other psychologists and philosophers think that the crucial component of emotions must be feeling states with "broad dimensions of positive and negative activation, or pleasure-displeasure (valence) and feelings of activation or arousal" (Barrett 2006: 35). (See also Russell 2003.)

In this chapter I will argue that emotions are causal processes that typically involve all of the components listed, and that are "pre-organized" in characteristic ways. I take my cue from philosopher-psychologist William James, who emphasized the order of events in emotion and who implicitly recognized that emotions are complex and dynamic. Emotions are not instantaneous but take time, and different components in the emotion process are typically on different timelines. In my view, when philosophers claim that emotions *are* appraisals or attitudes or whatever, they are simply focusing on what they take to be the *essential feature* of an emotion. But this is a mistake. Emotions are *essentially* processes involving a number of components, as I hope to show in this chapter.[1]

2 William James's Theory of Emotion

According to cognitivists about emotion (e.g., Solomon 1976, 1988; Lazarus 1991a; Deigh 1994), the essential element in emotion is a *cognitive appraisal* or *evaluative judgment* of a situation or event as a threat (in fear), a loss (in sadness), something repulsive (in disgust), or, more generally, in terms of what neuroscientist Joseph LeDoux (1996) has called a "fundamental adaptational encounter" and psychologist Richard Lazarus (1991a) refers to as a "core relational theme." Weaker versions of cognitivism claim that the relevant appraisal is a "concern-based construal" (Roberts 2003) or a "feeling towards" something, i.e., thinking of something "with feeling" (Goldie 2000, 2002). Some cognitivists acknowledge a role for bodily changes. Among philosophers, William Lyons argues that emotions are "abnormal bodily changes" caused by a cognitive appraisal of a situation (1980: 57–8). However, Lyons never explains why the very same cognitive appraisal sometimes produces "abnormal physiological changes," and sometimes does not, nor does he explain what an "abnormal" physiological change consists in (see Robinson 1983).

There has been much discussion of what exactly counts as a *cognitive* evaluation. Social psychologist Robert Zajonc says that cognition occurs when there is "some form of transformation of a present or past sensory input" (1980: 154), but this is an overly broad definition, which, as Jesse Prinz points out, would allow even "the reflection on the retina" sending a signal through the optic nerve to count as a cognitive process (2004: 43).

[1] I first defended the view of emotion as process in Robinson 2005: chapters 1–3. Although the basic idea remains the same, the details are considerably different in the present chapter. For example, I would now reject my attempt to rehabilitate Schachter and Singer.

Prinz himself proposes that cognitive states are those "that exploit representations that are under the control of an organism rather than under the control of the environment" (45). But this suggestion implies that there is a clear distinction between what the organism controls and what the environment controls, whereas in emotion there is always *interaction* between organism and environment, neither one of which wholly controls the interaction. In this chapter I will assume that "cognition" is a "higher" process, to be distinguished from instinctual responses and bodily habits, and which is probably mediated via the prefrontal cortices of the neocortex.

In opposition to the cognitivists, William James famously claimed that the essential component in emotion is *a feeling of bodily changes.* James explicitly questions the common-sense view about the order of events in an emotion process, arguing that common sense about emotions gets things back to front: common sense suggests that we "lose our fortune, are sorry and weep; we meet a bear, are frightened and run." In fact, however, "*the bodily changes follow directly the perception of the exciting fact, and . . . our feeling of the same changes as they occur* IS *the emotion*" (1981: 1065).[2] James gives a three-stage argument in favor of this conclusion. First, in light of his study of instincts, James says that it is well established that "objects do excite bodily changes by a preorganized mechanism" (1066). Second, he claims that every one of these bodily changes "is FELT, acutely or obscurely, the moment it occurs." Finally, "the vital point" of his theory is that if we try to imagine some strong emotion without the presence of feelings of bodily change, "we find we have nothing left behind, no 'mind-stuff' out of which the emotion can be constituted, and that a cold and neutral state of intellectual perception is all that remains" (1067).

Now, as Phoebe Ellsworth (1994) explains, this argument leads to the conclusion not that emotions *are* feelings of bodily change, but that feelings of bodily change are a *necessary condition* for emotion. What James seems to want to emphasize is that even if there is a "cold and neutral state of intellectual perception" present in the emotion process, that cannot be what makes the situation emotional. After all, what Robert Solomon has called "the standard objection" to cognitivism about the emotions asserts that the very same appraisal – e.g., "I am in danger" – can sometimes lead to emotion and sometimes not (Solomon 1988). I can judge that I am in danger, for example, without turning a hair. For James,

[2] Very similar theories were developed almost simultaneously by James and by Danish physiologist Carl Lange. The theory is therefore known as the James-Lange theory of the emotions.

what makes a situation emotional is the presence of bodily changes, including autonomic changes and other physiological reactions. In general, it is felt bodily changes that put the *emotionality* into a situation.

Moreover, even if there is an appraisal in emotion, it does not seem to be a *cognitive* appraisal à la Lyons. Rather, "the perception of the exciting fact" immediately and automatically unleashes some *instinctive* bodily responses. Significantly, the chapter on emotion in James's *Principles of Psychology* follows immediately the chapter on instincts. James says: "Instinctive reactions and emotional expressions ... shade imperceptibly into each other. Every object that excites an instinct excites an emotion as well" (1981: 1058). An "instinctive" reaction is one that occurs immediately and automatically. Hence even if there is an appraisal interposed between perception and response, the appraisal itself must be swift and crude, "quick and dirty," having as its main function to register something in the environment as requiring immediate attention and possible action. By definition instincts do not require cognitive intervention.

James also suggests that cognition is not essential to emotion by pointing out that one route to emotional experience does not require appraisal at all. Deliberately adopting a set of bodily changes characteristic of a particular emotion – such as a sad or cheerful posture, gestures, facial and vocal expressions – can lead to an experience of sadness or cheerfulness (1077–8): the feelings of the bodily changes are experienced as *feelings* of sadness or cheerfulness. Typically, however, for James, emotions have three stages in a "preorganized" sequence, the perception of the exciting fact, bodily changes, and the consciousness of those bodily changes as emotional feelings. In short, "the emotion" is the whole sequence of events rather than simply the last stage, the feeling of bodily changes (James 1994).

3 Empirical Confirmation of the Jamesian Hypothesis

Much of what James suggested has since received empirical confirmation. (1) He was right to say that the "perception of the exciting fact" *immediately* and *automatically* causes bodily changes and that an "intellectual perception" or "cognitive appraisal" is not even necessary for emotion, let alone the main causal factor in emotion (although, as we will see later, it may often be present). (2) He was right to treat sorrow at the loss of a fortune – an apparently "cognitively complex" emotion – in the same way as "primitive" emotions such as fear at encountering a bear. (3) He was right to emphasize the importance of bodily changes to emotion. (4) He was right that emotional feelings are feelings or perceptions of bodily changes. And

(5) he was right to stress the order of events in emotion. In this section I will review the evidence in favor of each of these claims. In the next section I will discuss some of the problems raised by this approach and suggest some useful modifications to the emotion process view.

(1) There is a great deal of evidence that we respond "instinctively" to threats, offenses, pleasant events, and so on, and that either we are born with such responses or with a predisposition to acquire them. This claim is confirmed by Robert Zajonc's ground breaking research (1980, 1984) showing that "affect" can precede cognition, as in the mere exposure effect, the subception experiments, and affective priming. For example, people prefer stimuli to which they have been exposed more often, even though they cannot recognize the stimuli in question, and people who have been conditioned by electric shocks to fear certain nonsense words produce a skin conductance response when they encounter those words, even though, again, they do not recognize them. Similarly, Watson's notorious experiments on newborn babies showed that newborns universally exhibited rage at head restraint, fear at sudden loss of support, and pleasure (or "love," according to Watson) at gentle caresses (Watson 1924). Moreover, although babies are not born with fear of snakes and spiders, it is very much easier to condition a person to fear snakes and spiders than flowers and mushrooms (Öhman et al. 2001). In short, human beings are born with a predisposition to respond emotionally to certain sorts of stimuli, such as the threatening, the offensive, and the pleasant. For many "primitive" emotions, no cognitive appraisal is needed; the emotional reaction is simply "instinctive," i.e., preprogrammed or very readily acquired.

Zajonc's mere exposure, subception, and priming experiments have been given strong support by LeDoux's discovery of a fear circuit in the rat brain, which bypasses the cortex and goes directly from the thalamus to the amygdala, which is responsible for setting off autonomic and motor effects. It seems likely that the responses in the subception experiments, for example, are the result of subcortical circuitry and do not require any *cognitive* mediation. Exposure to an instance of some "core relational theme" in this case, a threat or something unpleasant, automatically results in an "instinctive" bodily response. Moreover, Zajonc argued that emotion and cognition involve distinct neuroanatomical structures, and LeDoux showed that there is a distinctive emotion pathway through the amygdala, at least for fear (1996).

(2) Interestingly, however, James treats sorrow at the loss of a fortune – an apparently "cognitively complex" emotion – in the same way as the more "primitive" emotion of fear at encountering a bear. He suggests that

"bodily changes follow directly" not only the sight of a bear, a response that could well be preprogrammed in humans, but also the realization of losing one's fortune or being insulted by a rival, which would seem to be events requiring cognitive interpretation (1981: 1065). In other words, we respond *instinctively* in the same way to *any* loss or *any* offense (whether we are preprogrammed to respond to it or whether its significance has to be figured out and learned). This would explain why an angry reaction takes much the same form – increased flow of adrenaline and heart rate, clenched fists, grim gaze, and so on – whatever the offending object may be, and whether or not some kind of cognitive activity precedes the perception of offense.

Neuroscientist Antonio Damasio (1994) distinguishes between "primary" emotions, i.e., relatively "primitive" emotions that can be explained by James's "preorganized mechanism," and "secondary" emotions, i.e., emotions that rely on learning and individual experience, which are built upon the mechanisms for primary emotions. Whereas *primary* emotions are pre-wired, *secondary* emotions are the result of learning and individual experience; they depend on learned associations between certain types of individual experience and certain emotional responses, connections which are underpinned by circuits in the prefrontal cortex. As a result of these learned associations, a cognitively complex thought or memory can set off the very same reactions in the amygdala (and elsewhere) as primitive emotional triggers.

Damasio's evidence for this hypothesis is largely drawn from studying patients with damage to the ventromedial sectors of the prefrontal cortices, who are unable to "generate emotions relative to the images conjured up by certain categories of situation and stimuli" (1994: 138), and thus cannot *mark* these situations and stimuli *somatically*. Such people can tell you that a particular picture of a horrific road accident is "disturbing," but they are not disturbed by it; their bodies do not react to it. They show no change in skin conductance, for example (209–10).

Interestingly, although these patients have intact primary emotions and also intact intelligence and powers of abstract thinking, they show marked deficiencies in everyday reasoning tasks. In the famous gambling experiments developed in Damasio's lab, patients with damaged frontal lobes recognized "intellectually" that two of the four packs of cards in the game were untrustworthy or "dangerous" (giving larger payouts but also demanding much larger payments than the other two packs), but they continued to take from these two packs, despite mounting losses as a result of this strategy. Normal subjects, by contrast, learned to mark these packs *somatically* as "dangerous" and took from them only occasionally. Significantly, normal subjects gradually began to show a (bigger and bigger) response *before* turning over a card from one of the "dangerous" packs, whereas the damaged subjects "*showed no anticipatory responses whatsoever*" (221). Damasio concludes that normal people classify classes of scenario as "dangerous" or "safe" in a way that is *marked somatically*, i.e., registered in the body, and that these "bodily classifications" can be made in response to stimuli whose significance has to be *learned*. In short, cognitively complex emotions such as "fear of the bad pack of cards" piggy-back on more primitive emotions, such as fear of the bear, using "cognitive evaluation" *plus* somatic markers.

(3) James stresses the importance of bodily changes to emotion. A "cold and neutral state of intellectual perception" all by itself will not affect my autonomic nervous system or my action tendencies, posture, or facial or vocal expressions. Recall Charles Darwin's account of his reaction to the puff adder, which was safely behind glass at the zoo. Darwin was examining it unemotionally, presumably as an interesting biological specimen, when it suddenly uncoiled and reared its head. Darwin reports that he instinctively jumped back; no doubt he was sweating, his heart rate increased, and his facial expression changed (Darwin 1998: 43–4) In short, emotional episodes are episodes of bodily change. Indeed, as in the subception experiments, Darwin's body "knew" how to react before he himself had had time to give a cognitive evaluation of the situation as dangerous.

Now, it might be objected that a person can be envious or angry even though not currently in an emotional state. In such cases, the terms "envious" and "angry" perhaps refer to dispositional emotional states, i.e., states in which one is *disposed* to become emotionally aroused in some way. But sometimes such emotion terms are used when one is not disposed to become emotional at all but is simply making a certain kind of purely cognitive appraisal. What appears to be *the same* appraisal – e.g., "this is dangerous" – can be simply a "cold and neutral state of intellectual perception" or it can be the cause of an instinctive bodily disturbance, i.e., an emotional response. *Emotionality* is provided by bodily changes, but not every case of "anger," "fear," or "envy" is emotional. Of course this is puzzling: why does the same appraisal sometimes evoke bodily changes and emotion, and sometimes not? Later we will see that there is something different, not about the content of these appraisals, but about the *type* of appraisals they are.

(4) James was right to say that emotional feelings are feelings or perceptions of bodily changes. Damasio has found good evidence that the *feeling*

of emotion is indeed a "mapping" by the brain of a pattern of bodily changes that occurs in emotion. In experiments in which subjects were asked to think about an emotional episode from their lives while being given a PET scan, "all the body-sensing areas under scrutiny – the cingulate cortex, the somatosensory cortices of insula and SII, the nuclei in the brain stem tegmentum – showed a statistically significant pattern of activation or deactivation," indicating that "the mapping of body states had been significantly modified during the process of feeling" (2003: 99–100). Moreover, *"changes in skin conductance always preceded the signal that a feeling was being felt"* (101), suggesting that a bodily response to emotional thoughts really was occurring.

According to Damasio, a somatic marker is not just a bodily change that marks some scenario emotionally; it is the *feeling* of this bodily response that "tells" me that the pack is bad, that my boyfriend is a disaster waiting to happen, or that the stocks I want to buy are risky. It is the feeling that gives me greater flexibility in my decision-making not only by helping me to weed out undesirable alternatives and favor desirable ones, but also by serving as a "*booster for continued working memory and attention*" (1994: 198). Hence the prefrontal patients in the gambling experiments fail to act rationally because they do not *feel* bad or good when faced with the bad and good packs.

Damasio's view of emotion is clearly Jamesian in spirit, but he does not endorse James entirely. Thus he points out that James was wrong to say that every bodily change is *felt* as soon as it occurs: the brain can register changes in bodily state without these changes reaching conscious awareness. In Damasio's terminology, I can be in an emotional state without *feeling* anything. Second, Damasio recognizes the possibility of "as-if loops," i.e., cases where the brain is activated *as if* bodily changes have occurred, and we feel *as if* we are in some emotional state, but in the absence of actual bodily changes (1994: 156). Third, Damasio criticizes James for undervaluing the role of cognition in emotion. Here, however, I think he is misinterpreting James, whose examples of anger at insults and of sorrow at losing one's fortune suggest that he is quite aware that some stimuli need to be cognitively categorized before they are responded to "instinctively" as to be avoided or embraced or whatever. Moreover, as we have seen, James suggests that if you abstract from an emotion all feeling of bodily changes, what is left is often a state of "intellectual perception." Consequently, I think Damasio is speaking very much in the spirit of James when he concludes that emotion is normally the "combination" of a "mental evaluative process" with changes in bodily states and mental processing (such as attention and memory). He also agrees with James that the "essential content" of *feelings* of emotion is "the mapping of a particular body state" (2003: 88).

James noted that if his theory were correct, then voluntarily changing one's posture, gestures, facial expressions, etc. ought to produce a change in one's emotional feelings. James Laird has devoted years of research to establishing this conclusion. In *Feelings: The Perception of Self*, Laird summarizes the large number of studies confirming this hypothesis for facial and vocal expressions, autonomic changes, gaze, and posture. Although there are individual differences in how susceptible people are to these manipulations, the results he cites confirm the importance of bodily change to emotions and underline the fact that cognitive appraisals are not essential to emotions.

(5) Finally, James was right to stress the order of events in emotion. For James emotions are *processes*, in which one event causes another in a "preorganized" sequence, beginning with "perception" of a threat, an offense, or some other "adaptational encounter" that automatically produces bodily changes that in turn may (at least in human beings) be experienced as emotional feelings.

4 Emotions as Processes: A Modified Jamesian Account

James gives us a useful framework for a theory of emotion as process, but there are still some puzzles that need to be addressed. First, James claims that the bodily changes in emotion are "instinctively" generated, but does not explain exactly what this means. Second, James has little to say about the *function* of the bodily changes that he thinks are so crucial to emotion, and how they might relate to actions motivated by emotions. Third, there is some dispute about the extent to which distinct emotions have distinct bodily profiles. And finally, the role of cognition in James's theory is unclear. James acknowledges that we can change our emotional states by manipulating our behavior, but largely ignores the role of cognition in emotional management or what I call "cognitive monitoring" of our emotional responses.

4.1 "The Perception of the Exciting Fact"

For James, emotions are not "absolutely individual things" (1981: 1065), but either are or are embedded in *processes* in which there is *an interaction between an organism and its environment.* In passage after passage in the

Mind article, "What Is an Emotion?" James defends and illustrates this Darwinian theme.

> The neural machinery is but a hyphen between determinate arrangements of matter outside the body and determinate impulses to inhibition or discharge within its organs. When the hen sees a white oval object on the ground, she cannot leave it; she must keep upon it and return to it, until at last its transformation into a little mass of moving chirping down elicits from her machinery an entirely new set of performances. The love of man for woman, or of the human mother for her babe, our wrath at snakes and our fear of precipices, may all be described similarly, as instances of the way in which peculiarly conformed pieces of the world's furniture will fatally call forth most particular mental and bodily reactions, in advance of, and often in direct opposition to, the verdict of our deliberate reason concerning them. (1884: 190)

He then explains that:

> the most important part of my environment is my fellow-man. The consciousness of his attitude towards me is the perception that normally unlocks most of my shames and indignations and fears. The extraordinary sensitiveness of this consciousness is shown by the bodily modifications wrought in us by the awareness that our fellow-man is noticing us at all . . . This being so, it is not surprising that the additional persuasion that my fellow-man's attitude means either well or ill for me, should awaken stronger emotions still. In primitive societies "Well" may mean handing me a piece of beef, and "Ill" may mean aiming a blow at my skull. In our "cultured age," "Ill" may mean cutting me in the street, and "Well," giving me an honorary degree. What the action itself may be is quite insignificant, so long as I can perceive in it intent or *animus*. *That* is the emotion-arousing perception; and may give rise to as strong bodily convulsions in me, a civilised man experiencing the treatment of an artificial society, as in any savage prisoner of war, learning whether his captors are about to eat him or to make him a member of their tribe. (195–6)

According to James, I respond instinctively with "bodily convulsions" to *any* danger or offense or loss, as well as to any display of hostility and friendliness in a fellow human being. Human beings may have to reflect in order to figure out what the "animus" of some human action is, but once we have detected what it is, the response is immediate and "instinctive," and, importantly, we often respond instinctively to the animus of a person or action *before* we have recognized or realized what exactly constitutes the animus. In claiming that emotional reactions are "reflexive," I think James is emphasizing how much of our emotional life consists in reactions that are either preprogrammed in us simply by virtue of our being the kinds of creatures that we are, or reactions that have developed by learning and experience into bodily habits. Just as the subception experiments suggest that even the unconscious perception of something dangerous or unpleasant is enough to unleash skin conductance responses, so the mere perception of a hostile or friendly act, or of something offensive or disgusting to us, is enough to set off a bodily reaction. Sometimes, of course, we need a cognitive evaluation before we realize that we are in fact being threatened or offended, but once the threat or offense has been registered, bodily changes are automatically induced. Either way, it is not a "cognitive evaluation" that directly causes the bodily changes.

How, then, should we think of "the perception of the exciting fact'? In "Startle" I argued – somewhat quixotically – that emotional episodes in general have the same structure and function as the startle response:

> an emotional response is distinguished as having three main features. It is (1) a bodily response that (2) makes something salient to the organism (focuses the organism on something), and (3) what it makes salient or focuses on is something registered as significant to its well-being. (1995: 62)

As for the function of an emotional response, I suggested that it is "to pick out from the mass of information available to the organism in its environment those things which the body registers as significant to the organism's well-being" (62), whether that is something perceived and instantaneously responded to (like being injured by a bus), or it is something that requires cognition in order to be classified as unpleasant, such as the lengthy calculations I make before discovering that I have lost my life savings. Whether I am reacting to a sudden injury or to the result of a long calculation, as soon as I register that I have suffered an offense or a loss, a characteristic bodily response is unleashed. Emotions *focus attention* on important "adaptational encounters" or "core relational themes" – threats, offenses, pleasant occurrences, unpleasant occurrences, and so on – by marking them in a bodily way.

What triggers the emotional response need not be a perception but could be something remembered or imagined or merely thought about. I followed James in claiming that the instinctive response to an offense or danger is very similar regardless of what kind of offense or danger is in question and how much reflection needs to go on before the offense or the danger is recognized as such. Whether responding to a perception, a thought, or an image, however, if I respond emotionally, then "my body alerts me" to the significance of what I am perceiving, thinking about, or imagining and reacts accordingly (65).

Critics reasonably questioned how *bodily changes* could register complex information such as the fact that my life savings have vanished. Jesse Prinz implicitly answered that question with an elegant theory according to which emotions are a species of *perception*, "gut reactions," that "use our bodies to tell us how we are faring in the world" (2004: 69). Emotions *represent* core relational themes, such as threats and losses, by means of *registering* particular patterns of bodily change. Lazarus's "core relational themes" are not inner judgments; they are external conditions that elicit emotions. Drawing on Fred Dretske's theory of mental representation, Prinz claims that emotions are perceptions of patterns of bodily change that *represent* core relational themes, by virtue of the fact that they are *reliably caused* by these things. Emotions are perceptions of bodily changes that have the function of detecting offenses, losses, threats, and so on. From a neuroscientific perspective, all emotions are "neural responses to patterned bodily states" (158).[3] Prinz also endorses James's view that "emotional consciousness is consciousness of changes in bodily states" (206), but he agrees with Damasio that emotions do not have to be conscious in order to fulfill their primary function, which is to "carry information about core relational themes" (202).

But on another issue he disagrees with Damasio (and with me), arguing that so-called higher cognitive emotions, such as jealousy or resentment, are either blends of basic emotions (as contempt is said to be a blend of anger and disgust), or they are basic emotions or blends that have cognitions as "prior conditions" (98), but never as constituent parts of emotions. Higher cognitive emotions, in his view, are "embodied appraisals that have been recalibrated by judgments to represent somewhat different relations to the environment" (99). For example, the core relational theme for jealousy is something like "spousal infidelity." This produces bodily symptoms of anger or sadness (say), which are registered in the brain. The perception of these bodily changes has been *recalibrated* to represent not just an injury (as in anger) or a loss (as in sadness), but the particular kind of injury or loss that occurs in spousal infidelity. The "calibration file" for jealousy may contain judgments about one's spouse's infidelity, but it may also contain the unfamiliar smell of perfume on the spouse's clothes, the perception that one's spouse is distracted, and so on. Prinz is keen to argue that there is no particular *cognitive appraisal* that always sets off jealousy;

[3] Notice that Prinz is using the word "emotion" for what Damasio calls "feeling," i.e., the "perception" of body states by the brain.

what jealousy *really is*, is a perception of a pattern of bodily changes that represents infidelity.

I think it's fair to say that Prinz and I both agree with James that our bodies react instinctively to threats, losses, and other core relational themes, and that different patterns of bodily change are characteristic of different emotional states. We also agree with James that cognitively complex emotions work in essentially the same way as more primitive emotions. Prinz has provided a clever way of understanding how, as I put it in "Startle," bodily changes can *register* cognitively complex information, such as the fact that my life savings have vanished. But there is a significant difference between us in that, for Prinz, emotions simply *are* "embodied appraisals" (or, as we shall see shortly, "valent embodied appraisals"), namely interoceptions – perceptions of the body's internal states – and the registration of bodily changes simply *is* what represents whatever we love, fear, or resent.

Recall that, for James, emotions are not "absolutely individual things" (1981: 1065). Prinz, like other philosophers, wants a simple definition of something that is essentially complex. True, he and I agree that it is "the perception of the exciting fact" that sets off the instinctive emotional response, and "marks" the offense or loss or whatever *somatically*, as Damasio explains, but in my view, there is no reason to deny that the identification of a particular offense, or loss, or whatever – especially if it is cognitively complex – may require cognitive activity *before* an instinctive emotional response can be generated. As Karen Jones (2006) argues, the smell of perfume on the beloved's clothes will not all by itself produce a jealous response; it is only if the jealous person already suspects or believes that the spouse might be unfaithful that the smell of perfume gives rise automatically to a sad or angry emotional response.

In the context of this chapter, the big difference between Prinz's view and my own is that in my view, emotions are *processes*, and some emotion processes will include cognitions as components, whereas in Prinz's view, emotions simply *are* "valent embodied appraisals" and cognitions as such are never constituents of emotions. Although we agree that in emotion the bodily changes mark somatically both simple and cognitively complex instances of core relational themes, I think there is no good reason to deny that cognitively complex instances can be recognized as such before they set off the relevant changes.[4] In short, I would claim that my view is

[4] In Robinson 2005 I called the "perception of the exciting fact" that sets off the instinctive emotional response the "affective appraisal," an expression that serves as a placeholder for whatever it is that generates the quick and dirty bodily registration of DANGER, OFFENSE, or whatever. I suggested

closer to Damasio's than Prinz's in that it maintains that cognitively complex emotions piggy-back on more primitive emotions by using "cognitive evaluations" *plus* somatic markers.

4.2 *Bodily Changes as Preparation for Action*

We have seen that, for Prinz, emotions have the function of detecting core relational themes via the registration of bodily changes in the way he describes, but emotions do not seem designed solely to *track* offenses and losses and so on. They also ready the organism to *cope with* these things. Indeed, the main function of emotion seems to be to focus attention on core relational themes, i.e., events, people, or situations that are highly significant to our survival and/or well-being (or that of our "group"), and simultaneously *to act so as to deal with* those events, people, or situations. Given that emotional responses are set off by a quick and dirty appraisal, our instinctive responses may not be very useful, although they might have been appropriate in the environment of evolutionary adaptation.

Prinz thinks his embodied appraisal view needs to be "supplemented" to take account of valence, which he thinks is what pushes and pulls us to act out of emotion. Emotions, he writes, are "compound" states "containing both an embodied appraisal and . . . 'an activation' that 'represents' the object of the appraisal as positive or negative" (2004: 163). Borrowing from Damasio's idea of "somatic markers," Prinz suggests that associated with certain stimuli are "valence markers," which "tell" us "More of this!" or "Less of this!" In jealousy, for example, the thought of the spouse's infidelity or the smell of unfamiliar perfume is marked "Less of this!" In joy, the experience of seeing one's beloved again after an absence is marked "More of this!" In general, "positive emotions are ones we want to sustain, and negative emotions are ones that we want to get rid of" (174). In choosing what to do on future occasions, these valence markers will influence us appropriately. Hence Prinz claims that emotions are not just embodied appraisals, but "valenced embodied appraisals."

However, there is no need for a separate account of valence in order to explain how emotions motivate behavior: the bodily changes that constitute the emotional response are themselves preparing the person or other animal for appropriate action. In anger, for example, the bodily state is one of general tension or arousal and preparation for attack. Prinz's "embodied

different ways in which the affective appraisal could be construed. I agree with Prinz that even in cognitively complex emotions, what actually sets off the emotion is not some complex cognition.

appraisals" are embodied in bodily behavior that *constitutes* an action tendency, a way of dealing with the situation. As we have seen, in James's view, perceptions and actions are tightly coupled in the emotion process: a quick and dirty appraisal of "Offense!" or "Friend!" immediately sets off bodily changes appropriate to dealing with the situation.

Interestingly, focusing on emotions as motivations for quick behavioral reactions suggests an alternative view of whatever it is that sets off the instinctive emotional response (i.e., "the perception of the exciting fact"). According to a number of contemporary emotion theorists (e.g., Döring 2007; Tappolet 2010, 2016), emotions are *perceptions of value*, such as the hostile, the fearsome, or the funny. But, as I have just remarked, typically emotions are not only perceptions of the enemy as hostile or the bear as fearsome; they also get us ready to *deal with* the hostile or fearsome individual. In general, the most distinctive feature of emotions is that they *both* detect values relative to the animal concerned *and* prepare the animal or person to react to those values (with appropriate physiological changes and the behavior they support). Thus in fear one does not simply perceive a fearsome event or object; one acts to avoid getting hurt by it. Likewise, in maternal love, the mother not only perceives the child as needing nurture, but also acts so as to provide such nurture. Indeed, it may well be that the proper function of fear is to keep us away from the dangerous, the proper function of maternal love to nurture her young, and the proper function of disgust to keep us away from the poisonous or disease-ridden and contagious.[5]

On this way of thinking, if emotions are perceptions, they are perceptions not simply of "values" in the environment, but of the "actionability" of the environment, to borrow a term introduced by J. J. Gibson. We see the world as *affording* or inviting certain actions. We perceive not just a chair, but something sit-on-able, not just an apple or a spherical solid, but something munchable. Gibson famously argued that we do not need to form mental representations when we see the world. Animals that are incapable of conceptualizing the world are perfectly capable of perceiving affordances: indeed, that is precisely how animals negotiate their worlds. All animals, including human beings, perceive their environments not just by purely visual perception, but by haptic and kinesthetic exploration. We discover the environment by moving around in it and using the world itself as a prop.

[5] As Toronchuk and Ellis (2007: 1800–1) have suggested, fear keeps us away from external dangers and disgust from internal.

Gibson stresses that the term "affordances" "implies the complementarity of the animal and the environment." An ecological niche "implies a kind of animal, and the animal implies a kind of niche." *Affordances* are "relations between particular aspects of animals and particular aspects of situations" (Chemero 2003: 192). Like James, Gibson notes that one of the most important aspects of "the environment" consists in "other animals." Other animals afford social interaction, such as "sexual, maternal, competitive, cooperative" interaction, as well as "social grooming, play, and even human conversation" (1986: 42). Clearly, these social interactions have highly emotional implications. Affording nurturing is true of the beloved child, and affording attack of the offensive enemy. And affordances have *valence*: they can be positive or negative, like emotions.

Another way of conceiving of James's "perception of the exciting fact" – in my terms, whatever it is that sets off the emotion process – is therefore as a perception of an affordance.[6] We instinctively perceive a bear or a snake as something to be avoided, our newborn baby as someone to be caressed and nurtured, and our enemy as someone to attack or to defend against. On this interpretation the perception of the exciting fact automatically classifies that fact as "actionable" in Gibson's term, i.e., as inviting a particular kind of response: approach or withdrawal, dominating or submitting, accepting or rejecting. Indeed, psychologist Nico Frijda thinks that emotions should be identified with states of action readiness of exactly this sort.

Now, for Gibson, an object is always perceived as "actionable," as inviting a certain response. But not every response invited by an object is acted upon. Not all chairs perceived as sit-on-able are actually sat on. But what's special about emotions is that they not only perceive the world as affording actions; they prepare the body to act in response to the perceived affordance. Thus, the perception of the bear not only invites me to run away, but actually gets me moving: it gets my adrenaline going, and my heart rate increasing and in general *helps* me to run away.

If emotions are indeed initiated by perceptions of affordances, this would explain the link between "the perception of the exciting fact" and the motivation to act in a particular way. Emotions are not just mechanisms for *focusing attention* on something important to survival and/or well-being; they also immediately *generate responses* in an unthinking, speedy, and efficient way. In a state of maternal love, I see my baby as caressable and I am instinctively motivated to caress her. Emotions not only "tell" the

[6] I have developed this idea in Robinson 2017.

person or animal that something significant is in the environment, but also get the person or animal to act in an appropriate way.

Moreover, the facial, vocal, autonomic, and gestural or postural expressions that are *preparations for appropriate behavior* also function as signals that *communicate* the state of the animal or person to others. Indeed, communication of one's emotion in bodily gestures may be all a situation requires: showing a willingness to submit rather than to approach aggressively is likely to change the behavior of a potential foe, so that conflict can be avoided; and in response to my weeping, you recognize that I need succor and you provide it. But if action is required, the bodily states characteristic of emotion also prepare one for action, such as running away when threatened or clenching one's fist when angered (see Frijda 1986, 1994a).

4.3 *The Specificity of Bodily Responses*

Both Prinz and I assume that there is considerable commonality among the various bodily responses characteristic of emotions, especially "basic" emotions. Unfortunately, however, the evidence that there are uniquely identifying bodily profiles for each basic emotion is somewhat ambiguous, especially with regards to autonomic differences. Levenson (2003) has cited interesting differences in heart rate and skin conductance among anger, fear, sadness, and disgust, but these differences are far too gross to support the claim that there is uniquely identifying physiology for each of these emotions. Cacioppo and his colleagues (2000) in an influential review essay also cast doubt on autonomic specificity for each "basic" emotion. Kreibig's thorough study (2010) also finds considerable complexity in emotional responses.

As we have seen, Nico Frijda suggests that distinctive bodily changes do not correspond to specific emotions, but to states of action readiness that might be common to more than one emotion. Thus hiding behavior is characteristic of both shame and fear. Moreover, there is now good evidence that there is no one set of bodily reactions characteristic of an apparently specific emotion such as fear: Tappolet (2010: 232), for example, has documented how the marmot fear reaction varies depending on whether the eagle is seen circling above, or swooping closer, or actually clutching its prey. Similarly, Kreibig has found autonomic differences between disgust at contamination and disgust at mutilation (2010: 401). The best evidence for emotion-specific bodily changes has been thought to come from Ekman's pioneering studies of facial expression (see for example

2003), but even these classic studies have come under attack from, e.g., James Russell and Lisa Feldman Barrett, who think that bodily changes can be classified solely in terms of valence and arousal. Yet the search for specificity in bodily expression of emotion continues, and it seems to me that, within cultures at any rate, there must be distinguishing marks of either specific emotions or emotions in context or, more generally, states of action readiness. Unless we could relatively reliably read off other people's bodily expressions of emotion, emotions would not serve one of their most important roles: to communicate to others one's state of mind or perhaps the situation in which one finds oneself and thereby to facilitate social coordination. Exactly how emotions do this, however, is a matter for further research.

4.4 *Cognitive Monitoring*

James is clearly aware that cognitive activity may *precede* an emotional response as when I first have to figure out that I've been insulted before unleashing an angry response. But in the human case cognitive monitoring can also occur *after* the initial "perception" or "appraisal" and the automatic bodily response and its accompanying behavior.

This suggests that there is a further stage in the emotion process, *cognitive monitoring* of the situation, which typically occurs after the bodily response to "tell" me that the response is inappropriate or ineffective or both, and to modify or abort my behavior accordingly. I respond instinctively when I think I have been offended and my blood begins to boil, but then I realize (*cognitively*) that I have misheard an innocent remark. Or I see a blurry shape under the trees at dusk and react with fear before grasping cognitively that it is only the shadow of a bush. I may continue to tremble, but I no longer perceive the bush as dangerous.[7] Even in "lower" animals, an initial perception is sometimes succeeded by after-the-fact *cognitive monitoring*. Indeed, even the reflex startle response is followed by more "thoughtful" behavior: the startle response is generalized withdrawal behavior, but it is not directed away from the source of the loud sound. However, if I monitor my reaction, I may realize that a gun has fired and I should stay away from the place from which the sound apparently

[7] See Robinson (2005: 57–61, 75–83) for more on cognitive monitoring. See also Michael Brady: "the persistence of attention in emotional experience has a central or primary function of facilitating a reappraisal" of "our initial emotional response" (2013: 107).

originated, or that a car has backfired and no further action is required on my part.

Interestingly, in human beings cognitive monitoring also sometimes serves to label behavior in a more fine-grained way than rough-and-ready "appraisals" or perceptions of affordances permit: I'm not just sad but (on reflection) nostalgic, not just angry but (on reflection) indignant.

Finally, the various elements in the emotion process constantly feed back into the process: physiological changes help to *fix attention* on the stimulus, allowing for cognitive monitoring to kick in; cognitive monitoring can alter my assessment of a situation and my action tendencies and incipient behavior; and appropriate behavior may change the situation so that the emotion process is modified or aborted (your angry reaction to my threat persuades me to back down and become submissive). On the other hand, it is notoriously difficult to change or abort one's reactions, especially if they have become embedded in bodily habits. Cognitive-behavioral therapy is designed to combine the Jamesian strategy of changing one's behavior with the "intellectual" strategy of changing one's cognitions.

In summary, James was right to treat emotions as *processes*: emotional responses are bodily responses – including facial and vocal expressions, autonomic changes, and action tendencies – that result "instinctively" or automatically perhaps from perceptions of affordances or perhaps from some rough-and-ready bodily "appraisal" of the stimulus as instantiating a particular core relational theme. In the human case, these crude appraisals or perceptions of affordances may be preceded by cognitive evaluations of various sorts and they are invariably succeeded by cognitive monitoring. The swift automatic bodily responses can thus be modulated or aborted, to some extent, by cognitive intervention.

As we have seen, "[There is considerable dispute about the distinctiveness of the bodily responses characteristic of emotions, and it may turn out that only broad action tendencies – such as approach and withdrawal – can be identified in terms of specific bodily changes, or perhaps specific emotions in specific contexts. However this dispute is resolved, it is clear that bodily changes are crucial to emotions, and that feelings of bodily changes can be experienced as feelings of emotion.]"

It remains to add that *each of these elements in the emotion process feeds back on the others*, so that the process is a dynamic one. When I realize that the shadow under the trees is not a mugger, but a blameless bush, my fear – although still present for a while in physiological symptoms and corresponding feelings of bodily change – mutates into relief. I now perceive the situation as harmless and my physiological reactions change accordingly.

Sometimes when fear gives way to joy or relief, the result may be simultaneous crying and laughing. As Phoebe Ellsworth (1994) nicely puts the point, our emotional life occurs in "streams," and there are constant transitions from one emotion process to another. Moreover, the streams have somewhat different time courses: for example, when physiological changes persist even after cognitive monitoring has "told" me that they are no longer useful.

My account of emotion has a number of advantages. It explains why emotions are not entirely under our control. Emotional responses are the result of instinctive processes, so we are to some extent passive before them. Similarly, emotions are recalcitrant: once our instinctive responses have become embedded in bodily habits, it is very hard to dislodge them, despite the efforts of cognitive monitoring. The account demonstrates that animal emotions have basically the same structure and function as our own (except that cognitive monitoring will not take a linguistic turn in nonlinguistic creatures). It maintains the centrality of bodily response to emotion: emotional responses *are* bodily responses that have a certain sort of cause. It shows in what sense emotions can be described as *modular*: whether it is "bodily appraisals" or perceptions of affordances that initiate the emotion process, they immediately result in instinctive behaviors. And finally, it shows why emotions are by and large adaptive: emotional responses focus attention on matters of importance to us and help us to deal with them.

CHAPTER 4

The Ontology of Emotion

Matthew Soteriou

To which ontological category do emotions belong?[1] Are they states? Are they events or processes? In the philosophical literature on emotions, one finds associated with any given emotion a variety of different mental and bodily phenomena, of different ontological categories – e.g. cognitive states, conative states, affective states, evaluative judgements, phenomenal feelings, bodily sensations, episodes and conditions of bodily arousal, physiological expression and behavioural tendencies. So it seems that before one can address any such question about the ontology of emotions, one has to answer a more basic, preliminary, but nonetheless difficult question: which of these phenomena *is* the emotion?

When faced with that challenge, one might be tempted to adopt the following approach: to prune back this complex constellation of mental and bodily states and occurrences until one has uncovered what is *essential* to the emotion in question. At which point one can then consign the remainder to one or more of the following categories: cause of the emotion, effect of the emotion, occurrence which is a manifestation of the emotion. If all goes well, having singled out an aspect of mind that is the emotion, one can then provide an account of its distinctive features (e.g. perhaps its phenomenology, its intentional content and its attitudinal component). One might also address questions concerned with the justification and rationality of the emotion.[2] And if one also happens to have an interest in matters ontological, then one will be in a position to address the question of ontological category too. The ontological category of the emotion will be determined by the manner in which the relevant aspect of mind fills time – e.g. whether it

[1] Although I do not explicitly discuss Brian O'Shaughnessy's work in what follows, my thinking on these issues has been greatly influenced by remarks O'Shaughnessy makes in *Consciousness and the World*, and in particular his discussion of 'The Anatomy of Consciousness' in chapter 2 of that book.

[2] For this issue, see for example de Sousa 1987, Damasio 1994, Elster 1999, D'Arms and Jacobson 2000, and Deonna and Teroni 2012a: chs. 8–10.

obtains over and throughout intervals of time, occurs over intervals of time and/or continues to occur throughout intervals of time.[3]

This approach suggests a view on which the interesting and difficult questions about emotions are prior to, and independent of, what appear to be more esoteric concerns with their ontological category – the latter being fringe issues that may be of concern to those with a specialist interest in the ontology of mind, but which don't really add anything of substance to an account of the emotions. However, questions about the ontology of the emotions may become more pressing, and may be of more immediate concern, if this approach doesn't proceed as smoothly as anticipated. For instance, if one begins to doubt that there is a *single* aspect of mind with which any given emotion is to be identified – if one begins to suspect that some *set* of mental phenomena may well be essential to any given emotion, and no single ingredient is sufficient. For the latter suspicion is suggestive of a view on which an emotion is a complex mental phenomenon that has constituent parts or ingredients, where these constituent ingredients are elements of mind (perhaps also bodily[4] and agential phenomena) that are not of the same psychological kind as the mental phenomenon (the emotion) which together they constitute. And if that conception of the emotions turns out to be well grounded, then a host of ontological questions about the relations between this psychological whole (the emotion) and its constituent parts can be raised.

Peter Goldie expresses a suspicion of this kind in his discussion of the emotion of grief. There he notes the tendency of philosophers 'to simplify the contents of our minds, to tidy up the mess inside, and, whenever the opportunity for ontological parsimony seems to arise, to apply Occam's razor: the maxim not to multiply entities beyond necessity'. Goldie remarks, 'Instead, perhaps there should be a reverse maxim, not to eliminate entities beyond necessity, and perhaps we have one that expresses that sentiment very nicely, namely Bishop Butler's wisdom, that everything is what it is and not another thing.' Applying Butler's wisdom, Goldie suggests that grief is an emotion that is not to be identified with any individual mental state or event of a particular kind. It is not to be identified with some cognitive or conative state, and it is not to be identified with some non-cognitive feeling. For any such state or feeling won't be sufficient to determine that grieving is

[3] For the importance of such temporal considerations to questions of ontological category, see especially Steward 1997.

[4] For the suggestion that certain emotions have significantly different bodily profiles, see for example Panksepp 1998. See also Kreibig 2010, Stephens, Christie and Friedman 2010, and Laird and Lacasse 2014.

taking place (2012: 64). He proposes instead that there are different parts, or ingredients, to the emotion (characteristic thoughts, judgements, feelings, imaginings, memories, expressive and habitual actions), and the emotion is not to be identified with any one of them.[5]

My aim in this chapter is to examine the cogency of this sort of 'component' approach to emotions, as it is sometimes called. I suggested that this sort of approach to the emotions raises ontological questions about the relations between this posited psychological whole (the emotion) and its constituent parts; and here we might distinguish the following four general areas of concern: (i) What account should be given of the unity of this complex psychological whole? (ii) What sort of dependency relations obtain between the constituent parts of the emotion and the emotion itself? (iii) Is there a respect in which this complex psychological whole is explanatorily prior to its constituent parts? (iv) Finally, in what ways might our answers to these questions depend on, and/or affect, the account we give of the ontological category of the constituted complex psychological whole which is the emotion? I shall make some general remarks about the first three of these areas of concern in Section 1. That will serve as a prelude to a discussion and a critical assessment of Goldie's version of a component view (in Section 2), where I shall make some remarks on the relevance of the fourth area of concern that I listed: the question of the ontological category.

I shall be suggesting that it isn't clear that Goldie's own preferred 'process' view of emotion adequately accommodates some of the claims that he wants to make about the relation between an emotion and its constituents – in particular, the claim that the emotion is ontologically and explanatorily prior to its constituting ingredients. This will lead me to propose an alternative account of the ontology of emotion that a component theorist might adopt, one which identifies the emotion with a conscious state, rather than a process or an event. I'll introduce that account of the ontology by first proposing a model of the ontology of more basic conscious affective phenomena – such as being in pain, being hungry and being thirsty (Section 3). And finally (in Section 4), I shall suggest how we might apply that general model of the ontology to emotions.

5 See also Oakley 1992 for the suggestion that emotions are complexes of belief, desire and feelings. And for discussion appraisal theories of emotion that are componential and processive, see Ellsworth and Scherer 2003 and Robinson 2005, ch. 3.

I

A challenge that Jesse Prinz (2004) presents to those tempted by a component view of the emotions is to answer the following question. If all these constituent parts/ingredients of a given emotion are really essential to it, then 'how do they hang together into a coherent whole'? (2004: 18). If one isn't able to provide an adequate answer to that question, he argues, then one can be charged with introducing a 'gratuitous complexity' into an account of the emotions. Prinz's challenge might appear to fall under the first general area of concern that I listed. For it appears to be directed at the problem of providing an account of the *unity* of the complex whole with which we are supposed to identify an emotion. However, if one is at all sympathetic to a component view of the emotions, one might not find that sort of challenge particularly worrying. For there is a respect in which all unity is coherent unity, and unity is pretty cheap. For instance, the proposal that there is a complex, unified, coherent, psychological whole that is the emotion appears to be consistent with the view that the relation between the constituent parts and that complex psychological whole is additive in nature, insofar as it appears to be consistent with a picture on which emotions are somewhat arbitrary mental constructs – psychological wholes that we have cobbled together from distinct parts by mere convention.

Here it might be thought that this sort of response to the first of the questions I listed (i.e. the unity question) would leave unaddressed the real concern behind Prinz's challenge. For the assumption behind that challenge is that there must be a deeper story to be told about the relations between the various mental and bodily events and states that are associated with any given emotion. That is to say, it's implausible to think that when any given emotion occurs/obtains the unity that lies behind the different mental, bodily and behavioural phenomena associated with that emotion simply consists in the fact that they just so happen to accompany one another (or in the fact that they just so happen to occur successively), and that we just so happen to label such groupings using the vocabulary of the emotions. It should, rather, be possible to uncover dependency relations between the various mental, bodily and behavioural phenomena associated with any given emotion – e.g. relations of cause, effect and manifestation.

In response it could be said that a component approach to the emotions is perfectly consistent with the existence of such dependency relations between the constituent parts of the emotion. However, opponents of the approach may complain that if such relations of causal dependence do indeed obtain between the mental and bodily phenomena associated with an emotion, and we nonetheless persist in declining to identify the emotion with any one of them, then we thereby stand in danger of robbing the emotion of its distinctive explanatory potential. For any such phenomenon associated with a given emotion will either be a constituent of that emotion, or a mere cause/effect of some constituent of that emotion. In either case, any genuine causal explanation will need to be conducted at the level of the constituents of the emotion, rather than by citing the emotion itself.

The worry here is that advocates of a component view will find themselves in the unsatisfactory position of having to concede that any appeal we make to an emotion in the psychological explanations we offer will turn out to be one that obscures and masks the *genuine* explanations that are to be given at the level of its constituting phenomena.[6] However, whether that charge can be made to stick may depend on the answers given to the second and third of the general areas of concern that I listed: (ii) What sort of dependency relations obtain between the constituent parts of the emotion and the emotion itself? And (iii) is there a respect in which this complex psychological whole is explanatorily prior to its constituent parts? Let us briefly consider each in turn.

I suggested that a component approach to the emotions may be perfectly consistent with the existence of relations of causal dependence between the constituent parts of an emotion. However, saying that much leaves unaddressed questions about the respects, if any, in which these constituent parts may be dependent on the whole (i.e. the emotion) of which they are parts. For instance, is each psychological constituent of the emotion an independent existent – i.e. is each such constituent a psychological state or event that can obtain/occur in the absence of the emotion of which it is part? If the constituents of an emotion are independent existents, then one might think that while the existence of the whole (the emotion) is dependent on (and hence to be accounted for in terms of) the existence of such constituent parts, it cannot be the case that the existence of any constituent part is dependent on (and hence to be accounted for in terms of) the existence of the whole (i.e. the emotion). However, if, on the other hand, there are constituents of the emotion that are not independent existents – if there are constituent parts of the emotion that can only occur/obtain if they are constituents of an emotion – we may then have a case in which it is true to say both 'the whole because of the parts' *and* 'the parts because of the whole'. And that

[6] For example, if we appeal to a subject's grief when explaining her feelings, thoughts, memories and/or behaviour.

might disarm the concern that a component view of the emotions would rob emotions of their explanatory potential.

These questions about the ontological dependency relations that obtain between the psychological whole and its constituent parts are not entirely unrelated to the third area of concern that I listed – the question of whether there is a respect in which the complex psychological whole (the emotion) is explanatorily prior to its constituent parts. But it is worth distinguishing them. For one might envisage a component account of emotions that concedes that each constituent part of an emotion is an independent existent (i.e. a psychological state or event that can obtain/occur in the absence of the emotion of which it is part), but which nevertheless insists that we should explain the occurrence/obtaining of any such constituent by reference to the whole (i.e. the emotion) of which it is part. For example, one might envisage a components account of emotions according to which there is some end or goal towards which the *joint* occurrence and/or obtaining of the constituent parts of each emotion are directed. If some such story about the explanatory priority of the whole (i.e. the emotion) can be defended, then a proponent of a component view may be able to salvage and restore to emotions a distinctive and legitimate explanatory role.[7]

Clearly, much more will need to be said if one is going to be persuaded that any one of these ways of defending a component view of the emotions is a genuinely viable option. Until then, these rather abstract proposals will merely remain unrealised abstract possibilities. Goldie undertakes the task of offering a more detailed and positive proposal, and I'd like now to examine some of that detail, for doing so will serve to introduce the potential relevance of the fourth area of concern that I listed – the question of the account that is to be given of the ontological category of the constituted complex psychological whole that is the emotion.

2

Goldie proposes that grief is a kind of process. Other accounts, he writes, 'privilege a single mental state or event amongst a number of mental states and events as the emotion; whereas I privilege no particular mental state or

[7] Yet a further question we might ask of a components view is the following. Are there properties of the whole (i.e. the emotion) that cannot be accounted for by simply providing a conjunctive description of the constituents of the emotion and their properties? If there are (if the whole is, in that sense, greater than the sum of its parts), then again, this might help allay the worry about robbing the emotion of its explanatory potential. For the relevant properties of the whole may have some explanatory role to play that cannot be captured by simply providing a conjunctive list of the constituent elements and their properties.

event but rather the process, which is made up of mental states and events, and of much else besides, and which unfolds in a characteristic pattern' (2012: 64). The various ingredients that constitute the process (characteristic thoughts, judgements, feelings, imaginings, memories, expressive and habitual actions) together constitute 'a complex pattern of activity and passivity, inner and outer' (56), and that pattern is understandable as grief 'because it follows a characteristic shape' (62).[8] In particular, Goldie proposes that 'The pattern of a particular grieving is best understood and explained through a narrative, and not merely causal, account' (56).

Goldie suggests that the process with which the emotion is to be identified is structurally heterogeneous. It has different stages, and 'None of the stages continues throughout the process' (62). In response to Prinz's challenge to a component account of emotion (how do the components of the emotion hang together into a coherent whole?), he writes, 'The components of the emotion "hang together" in virtue of being stages of a structurally heterogeneous process' (63). More specifically, he suggests that 'the elements of this process can be seen to "hang together into a coherent whole", to use Prinz's phrase, through the coherence of a narrative of the process' (61).

These remarks appear to address the unity question that one might pose to an advocate of a component view – i.e. what account should be given of the unity of the complex psychological whole that is the emotion? They also address the question of the ontological category of the emotion – according to Goldie, the emotion of grief is a *process*, rather than a mental state or event. However, it isn't so clear that they address the concern that a component view may rob the emotion of its distinctive explanatory potential. And that is a worry that one might feel ought to be addressed. For don't we want to preserve the idea that at least some of the so-called ingredients of the emotion of grief (e.g. the subject's feelings, characteristic thoughts and memories, actions and behaviour, such as the subject's weeping) are to be explained by appeal to the subject's emotion – her grief?

At one point, Goldie suggests that the process with which the emotion of grief is to be identified is 'ontologically prior' to its parts (61). But it is not clear that he says enough to justify this claim. Indeed, it might be argued that if the emotion is a structurally heterogeneous process, and the constituents of the emotion are parts of this structurally heterogeneous process, then these constituents of the emotion must be independent

[8] Goldie adds that although the relevant pattern has a characteristic shape, it will nonetheless be 'individual and particular to the person, and will no doubt be significantly shaped by cultural as well as biological influences' (62).

existents – i.e. each such constituent must be a psychological state or event that can obtain/occur in the absence of the emotion of which it is part. For given that they are parts of a structurally heterogeneous process, they must occur/obtain *successively*. And if the constituents of the emotion occur/obtain successively, then that suggests a view on which there are parts of the emotion that are temporally prior, and hence ontologically prior, to the whole process (with its overall complex pattern) that they help to constitute. So on this process view, while it will be true to say 'the whole because of the parts', it isn't clear that it will be true to say 'the parts because of the whole'.

If Goldie's process account doesn't secure the ontological priority of the emotion over its constituent parts, does it nonetheless secure the explanatory priority of the whole? Goldie suggests that the 'unfolding pattern over time is explanatorily prior to what is the case at any particular time' (56). But what he says in defence of that idea is rather limited. He writes:

> Some mental phenomena are primarily processes, and only secondarily can we properly comprehend the mental states and events they are made up of: the parts do not even come into view *as* parts unless and until they are seen as parts of a particular kind of process. The process is thus ontologically and epistemically prior to the parts. (61)

It may well be true to say that the parts of a whole do not come into view *as parts* unless they are seen as parts of a whole, but this claim is not in itself enough to secure the ontological, explanatory or, indeed, epistemic priority of the whole over its parts. (That a tree is part of a forest is a fact that does not come into view unless the forest does too, but from this it doesn't follow that the forest has ontological, explanatory or epistemic priority over any of its constituent trees.)

I said earlier that one might envisage a component view of emotion according to which there is some end or goal towards which the joint occurrence and/or obtaining of the constituent parts of the emotion are directed, and that such an approach might be able to salvage and restore to emotions a distinctive explanatory role. When giving examples of other 'processes', Goldie sometimes cites telic accomplishments – e.g. baking a cake and writing a cheque. However, Goldie doesn't explicitly say that he has in mind any such teleological conception of the emotion of grief; and if he did have such an approach in mind, he doesn't tell us what the relevant telos is supposed to be.

What general conclusions can we draw from this about the prospects for a component view of the emotions? On the one hand, I have suggested that the task of providing some kind of account of the 'coherent unity' of the complex psychological whole with which we are supposed to identify the emotion may not be such a challenging undertaking. However, on the other hand, I've also suggested that a more serious challenge facing defenders of a component approach is that of avoiding the charge that their accounts end up depriving emotions of their distinctive explanatory potential. And it's not clear that endorsing a 'process' view of the ontology of emotions is the way to establish the kind of ontological and/or explanatory priority of the psychological whole over its constituent parts that might address such concerns. We can add, I think, that an appeal to the ontological category of 'event', rather than 'process', will fare no better in this regard. For none of the distinctions that are standardly drawn between events and processes seem to hold out the promise of resolving these particular concerns.[9]

One option open to the component theorist is to acquiesce in the face of this challenge, and concede that all genuine causal explanation of the bodily, mental and agential phenomena associated with a given emotion should ultimately be conducted at the level of the constituents of the emotion, rather than by citing the emotion itself. In granting that point one is not thereby conceding that emotions have no explanatory relevance at all. For after all, the mere addition of concepts of the emotions to our conceptual repertoire can have a significant impact on the way in which we respond to others, as well as to our own mental lives, and that is a point that a component view of the emotions is perfectly well placed to accommodate.[10]

A further option open to the component theorist may be to defend the proposal that there is some telos towards which the *joint* occurrence and/or obtaining of the constituent parts of any given emotion are directed.[11] As I explained earlier, that may be a way of assuring that the emotion can be attributed some form of explanatory priority. That particular proposal may

[9] Which is not to say that the question of how to mark the distinction between event and process isn't contested. For discussion of various ways of marking the distinction, see for example Mourelatos 1978, Stout 1997 and 2003, Crowther 2011, and Steward 2013 and 2015.

[10] Note that accommodating this point does not depend on endorsing a 'constructionist' view of emotion, for one might reject constructionism and yet still hold that a subject's ability to deploy concepts of emotions, and hence recognise such emotions in others, as well as herself, can have a significant impact on that subject's mental life. For discussion of the constructionist views, see for example Averill 1980 and Armon-Jones 1986.

[11] One might look to an evolutionary approach to emotions to defend that proposal. See for example Cosmides and Tooby 2000. Fabrice Teroni has also suggested to me that one might also be able to flesh out this proposal in a way that is not directly informed by evolution theory, by appealing to Frijda's action tendencies. See Frijda 1986.

be thought more plausible in the case of certain 'basic' emotions.[12] Perhaps it will also be felt to have some plausibility in the case of non-basic 'negative' emotions.[13] For one might think that the presence of the latter indicates that there is some concern that is to be addressed, or come to terms with, and one might speculate that the telos of the emotion is the achievement of that goal.

Whether that line of thought can be defended and plausibly applied to the so-called positive emotions is an issue I shall not be pursuing here. For in what remains I want to explore a further option that may be open to a proponent of a component view of the emotions. That is to adopt a view on which the emotion is regarded as a state, rather than an occurrence. If a component theorist is to adopt that position, and if she also wants to maintain that events and/or processes can be constituents of the emotion (e.g. occurrent phenomenal feelings, bodily sensations, episodes of physiological arousal and so on), then she will need to make cogent the proposal that a state can be constituted, at least in part, by events/processes. She will also need to explain how the relation between the relevant state and its constituents can successfully integrate the affect, phenomenology and intentionality associated with any given emotion. Can this be done in a way that manages to avoid the charge that a component view of the emotions will deprive emotions of their distinctive explanatory potential?

As a first step towards investigating that question, I shall start by making some remarks on the ontology of conscious affective phenomena that might be regarded as somewhat simpler than the emotions – e.g. pain, hunger and thirst. My remarks on these conscious affective phenomena will be rather cursory. I don't have the space to offer anything like a proper treatment of them. But I shall be suggesting that although such aspects of mind may, with some justification, be regarded as simpler than emotions, there is, nonetheless, a complexity to them; and uncovering that complexity can help point towards a model of the ontology of emotions – a model according to which our emotions are conscious states that are constituted, at least in part, by various events and/or processes.

3

We have various ways of talking about pain, and sometimes it seems that we are invoking states, sometimes occurrences. We talk in terms of (a) pain

[12] For discussion of 'basic' emotions, see Ekman 1997.

[13] How to mark the distinction between 'positive' and 'negative' emotions is, of course, a contested issue. For discussion, see for example Lazarus 1991b, McLean 1993, and Solomon and Stone 2002.

as an object of awareness (there is a throbbing pain in my toe), but we also talk in terms of (b) pain as an awareness of sensation (the feeling of a burning sensation in my hand), (c) pain as a condition of some part of one's body (my back hurts), and (d) we often talk of pain as a psychological state of the subject (I am in pain). How does the last of these relate to the other three? Is our talk of a subject *being in pain* simply a way of capturing the fact that the subject in question is feeling pain while leaving unspecified the details of what is felt – e.g. the felt location, quality and intensity of the subject's sensation of pain?

Nikola Grahek (2001) has argued that to regard matters in this way would be to oversimplify the complex structure of normal pain experience. For it is possible to feel pain without being in pain – a dissociation most drastically exemplified by those suffering from pain asymbolia. There is a respect in which the pain experience of such subjects successfully tracks objective physiological conditions of their bodies – such as actual damage to the body, or physiological conditions that are relevant to potential damage to the body. For when such physiological conditions obtain, the subject suffering from pain asymbolia will usually feel an appropriately located bodily sensation, the quality, intensity and extent of which varies with variations in relevant physiological conditions of the body part. The subject can report all of these features of such sensations, and also recognise them as 'pain' sensations. However, in their case, such experience does not induce any avoidance or protective reactions, nor does it induce the normal affective reactions. It doesn't bother them at all. In having such experience, Grahek argues, the subject is not *in pain*. In consequence, according to Grahek, such pain experience is 'no longer a signal of threat or damage and no longer moves one's mind or body in any way. It becomes a blunt, inert sensation, with no power to galvanize the mind or body for fight or flight. Such pain no longer serves its primary biological function' (2001: 73).

How should we characterise what is missing in the case of the subject suffering from pain asymbolia? Should our approach be that of identifying some motivational state of the subject that can be identified with the state of *being in pain*? One might well regard with scepticism the suggestion that the state of being in pain is simply to be identified with some desire that is present when someone is in pain but absent when they are not. It's not clear that the condition of being in pain is reducible to some desire, or a belief/desire pair. Indeed, it's not clear that we should think of ourselves as being in the business of identifying any particular propositional attitude upon which we can pin that condition. However, when explaining what is missing in the case of the subject with pain asymbolia, it seems highly likely that one will need to advert to the sorts of motivational states and behavioural tendencies that are present when pain is felt by those who do not suffer from that dissociation.

So how then should we characterise the condition of being in pain? Should we adopt any one of the following proposals?

(i) The condition of being in pain is to be identified with some motivational state or some set of motivational states (and perhaps behavioural tendencies) that are distinct from the experience of feeling pain.

(ii) The condition of being in pain is to be identified with some complex condition that involves some motivational state or some set of motivational states (and perhaps behavioural tendencies) that are distinct from the experience of feeling pain, *and* the phenomenal occurrence of feeling pain.

(iii) The condition of being in pain is to be identified with the complex condition proposed in (ii), but we need to further stipulate that when this complex condition obtains, the relevant motivational state(s) (and behavioural tendencies) are *caused* by the phenomenal occurrence of feeling pain.

One might suspect that none of these proposals adequately captures the condition that obtains in the case of those who don't suffer from a pain dissociation. For in the case of such subjects, it seems that the relation between the components mentioned in (i)–(iii) will be more intimate than is suggested by any of the proposals. One way of expressing that thought is to say that one cannot help but surmise that there must be a *phenomenal* difference between the feelings of pain that are experienced by those suffering from pain asymbolia, and the feelings of pain experienced by those of us who don't suffer from that dissociation; and it seems likely that the relevant difference in the phenomenology will be crucially linked to the differences that such feelings have on the motivational states and behavioural tendencies of their subjects. The proposals do not in themselves suffice to capture this point.

The thought here is that we won't be able to specify adequately the phenomenology of a 'normal', excruciating feeling of pain *without* adverting to the impact that it has on its subject's motivational states and behavioural tendencies (and here one might include tendencies to inhibit as well as produce behaviour). One way of capturing this thought is to say that one cannot adequately specify the phenomenal properties of such an occurrence of feeling of pain without specifying how that occurrence modifies the subject undergoing it; and in specifying how the subject is modified by such occurrence one will need to specify states of the subject (including motivational states and perhaps behavioural tendencies) that obtain in virtue of (that is to say, because of and for the duration of) that phenomenal occurrence. In that respect, the nature of the phenomenal occurrence in question is *dependent* on states of the subject that obtain in virtue of its occurrence.

Moreover, I think that a case can be made for thinking that there may also be a relation of constitutive dependence in the other direction. At one level of abstraction one might type the kind of states that obtain when such a phenomenal event/process occurs without making any reference to the kind of phenomenal event/process in virtue of which such states obtain. For example, one might attempt a functional characterisation of the kind of psychological states that obtain when a subject is in pain without making any reference to the phenomenal events/processes in virtue of which those functionally specified states obtain.[14] But in the case of the kind of mental state that obtains when one undergoes an excruciating sensation of pain (i.e. the state of one's being in pain), if one doesn't make any reference to the kind of phenomenal event/process that occurs, then, in a crucial respect, one will have underspecified the nature of that state. For such states are conscious. They have a phenomenology. There is something it is like for a subject to be in pain. And what it is like for a subject to be in pain, on any given occasion, will be determined by phenomenal properties of the phenomenal occurrence she undergoes when she feels pain. So in order to specify the phenomenology of such a state (what it is like for the subject to be in pain), one will need to make reference to phenomenal properties of the phenomenal occurrences in virtue of which that state obtains. In that respect the nature of the phenomenally conscious state that obtains when a subject is in pain will be dependent on the phenomenal occurrence in virtue of which that state obtains. We might say, then, that there is an *inter*dependency between state and phenomenal occurrence when a subject is in pain.

On this view, the state of being in pain is not simply a distinct non-conscious effect of a phenomenal occurrence of feeling pain. For the obtaining of the state is *constitutively* dependent on such phenomenal occurrence. Although such a state, as a state, obtains over intervals of time, its obtaining constitutively depends on the occurrence of phenomenal

[14] For discussion of the question of how to square such functional characterisations of mental states with descriptions that make reference to phenomenology, see Heil's contribution in Chapter 2 of this volume, 'Dispositionality and Mentality'.

events/processes that unfold, or go on, during the interval of time over which it obtains. The state is not merely one that is caused by, or one that merely accompanies, conscious occurrence. For non-conscious states can satisfy that description.

The proposal, then, is that in the case of a subject who doesn't suffer from a pain dissociation, talk of their being in pain signifies a conscious state of that subject. There are various ways in which that kind of conscious state can be instantiated;[15] and fully specifying the way in which that conscious state is instantiated in any given case will involve specifying the nature of some conscious occurrence and the way in which the subject undergoing it is modified by that conscious occurrence. This in turn will involve specifying what one might think of as various aspects and *components* of that conscious state: e.g. phenomenal properties of a felt sensation, the apparent location of that sensation, the apparent condition of parts of the body, bodily sensations accompanying forms of physiological arousal that are induced (e.g. increased heart rate and respiratory rate), and the motivational states and behavioural tendencies that obtain in virtue of such phenomenal and physiological occurrences.

According to this view, talk of a subject being in pain signifies a state of the subject (a conscious state of the subject) that obtains over intervals of time, rather than some occurrence undergone by the subject. But it is a state the obtaining of which constitutively depends on the occurrence of phenomenally conscious events/processes. In consequence, although in any given case the obtaining of the state will involve an intentional component, there is a complexity to the obtaining of the state which would be masked if one simply sought to identify some intentional mental state which is the state of being in pain (even if one were to add that the posited intentional mental state possesses further non-intentional phenomenal properties).

Similar points can, I think, be made about the conscious affective states associated with hunger and thirst (and perhaps also tiredness, as well as more pleasant forms of bodily arousal). These are conscious states which, like pain, have an affective dimension and which are associated with conditions of one's body. Such conscious states involve the occurrence of phenomenal bodily sensations and feelings the nature of which cannot be fully specified without reference to the way in which the subject

[15] Consider variations in the phenomenology of the bodily sensations (as well as behavioural tendencies and motivational states) that are associated with the different kinds of experience of pain one can undergo – e.g. in cases of broken limbs, stomach cramps, headaches, burns, sciatica, the piercing and slicing of flesh.

undergoing them is modified by their occurrence. And a full and adequate specification of the way in which the occurrence of such feelings modifies the subject undergoing them will need to advert to motivational states of the subject that obtain in virtue of their occurrence – motivational states the intentionality of which may not be solely directed upon the subject's body.

Again, I suggest that although the obtaining of such conscious states may involve an intentional component, there is a complexity to the obtaining of these states which would be masked if one simply sought to identify, in any given case, some intentional mental state (the content and functional role of which one might try to specify) which is the state of being hungry or being thirsty (even if one were to add that the posited intentional mental state possesses further non-intentional phenomenal properties). That simplified approach would overlook and fail to accommodate the interdependencies between conscious state and conscious occurrence that one will need to track in order to fully specify what is involved in being in such states.

The proposals I've made in this section are to be taken only as an indicative sketch of an approach one might adopt in providing accounts of these conscious, affective aspects of mind. Clearly much more would need to be said in order to mount a proper defence of that approach, and there are many important details missing from the outline I've presented.[16] However, I want to note some general points about this model of the ontology of these aspects of mind – points that will have some bearing on the suggestions I shall be making about the ontology of emotions.

The first point to underline is that this model of the ontology of certain affective aspects of mind is one that appeals to a conscious *state* of a subject that obtains over and throughout intervals of time (e.g. the conscious state of the subject's being in pain). But, according to this model, in order to specify the nature of the relevant state, one will need to make reference to the nature of phenomenal and bodily events and processes – events and processes on which the obtaining of the conscious state *constitutively* depends. Moreover, the model is one which posits an *inter*dependency between the states and occurrences in question. So it wouldn't be right to say that the occurrences in question are ontologically prior to the states that constitutively depend on them. In consequence, while it's true to say 'the state because of the occurrence', there is a respect in which it's equally true to say 'the occurrence because of the state'.

[16] For some further details on pain, see Soteriou 2013: ch. 3.

For that reason it wouldn't be quite right to think of the occurrence as explanatorily prior to the state, and neither would it be right to think of the state as explanatorily prior to the occurrence. However, that is not say that it would be inappropriate to cite the occurrence when explaining the obtaining of the state, and there may be occasions when it is appropriate to cite the state when explaining its constituting occurrence. The order of explanation that it seems most natural to offer may vary from case to case (e.g. she's in pain because she is feeling pain, whereas she's feeling hungry because she is hungry).

Here are some further points to highlight. I noted that there are various ways in which the state of being in pain can be instantiated. Think, for instance, of the significant variations in the phenomenology of the bodily sensations (as well as behavioural tendencies and motivational states) that are associated with the different kinds of experience of pain one can undergo – e.g. in cases of broken limbs, stomach cramps, headaches, burns, sciatica, the piercing and slicing of flesh. Given such variation, it would be a mistake to assume that *all* of the features of any given instance of being in pain are *essential* to the state of being in pain. That is to say, it would be a mistake to assume that all such features will always be instantiated whenever a subject is in pain. For the same reason, it would be a mistake to assume that the conscious state of being in pain cannot have any *non*-essential constituents.

Having acknowledged that such conscious states may have non-essential constituents, we shouldn't be surprised if there is not always a clear dividing line to be drawn between constituent of the state on the one hand, and mere effect of the state (or mere effect of a constituent of the state) on the other. For there may be occasions when it is unclear whether the occurrence in question should be regarded as a non-essential constituent of the state, or simply a mere effect. For example, consider the bodily sensations accompanying forms of physiological arousal that can be induced when one is in pain, such as the bodily sensations associated with increased heart rate and respiratory rate. Should these occurrences be thought of as mere effects of being in pain, or should they be regarded as constituents of the state? We may not be able to settle on an answer to that question by simply determining whether or not they are *essential* to the state of being in pain.

In the next, and final, section of this chapter, I shall apply some of these ideas in outlining a proposal about the ontology of emotions. According to that proposal, our emotions are to be regarded as conscious states, rather than processes or events. But these are conscious states that constitutively depend for their obtaining on the occurrence of various events and/or processes. So this stative account of the ontology of the emotions can be thought of as a version of a component view.

4

Before considering how we might apply to the emotions the ontological model that I have just sketched, it's important to note some of the key differences between emotions and the sorts of conscious affective phenomena I mentioned in the previous section. Unlike pain, hunger and thirst, emotions can be induced by states and events that are psychological in nature – e.g. perceptions, conscious thoughts, judgements, memories and imaginings. The onset of an emotion is not dependent on a physiological condition of one's body in the same way that the aforementioned conscious affective phenomena are.

A further difference is this. In the case of being in pain, being hungry or being thirsty, it seems more obvious that we will be able to identify (and predict) singular goals to which felt urges will be directed when a subject is in such states. Whereas it is less obvious there will be any such common singular goal to be identified in the case of any given emotion.[17] The precise impact that any given emotion is likely to have on its subject's motivational states is less predictable and clear-cut. The first point of difference that I noted may not be entirely unrelated to this second difference. When a subject becomes, say, angry, the way in which she will be psychologically modified (both motivationally and cognitively) by the occurrence of events and processes that ensue (e.g. bodily sensations, phenomenal feelings) may depend on the nature of the eliciting psychological cause, and the nature of this cause can vary considerably from case to case. The most obvious differences may be in the intentional contents of such psychological causes.[18] And such differences in intentionality offer more determinate ways of characterising the emotion that is induced (anger with . . . /at . . . /that . . .).[19] Furthermore, the way in which the subject is psychologically modified will also depend on the bedrock of psychological states (both cognitive and motivational) upon which the eliciting cause and subsequent phenomenal events and processes occur; and again, this factor can also vary considerably from case to case.

17 For a recent philosophical discussion of the issue of the flexibility of emotion that is germane to this point, see Scarantino 2014.

18 There may be other significant differences too – e.g. further differences that may be relevant to what is distinctive of the responses elicited when one is reading or watching fiction.

19 It is often suggested that without such determinacy, what prevails should be classified as a mood, rather than an emotion. See for example Goldie 2000.

No doubt there are many more important differences to be noted between emotions, on the one hand, and conscious affective phenomena such as pain, hunger and thirst, on the other. However, these two differences alone ensure that in the case of emotions there will be a more complex and less predictable interplay between associated phenomenal and bodily occurrence, and the way in which the subject is psychologically modified by such occurrence. And an important point to underline is that on the model of the ontology of the emotions that I am sketching there will be an *interplay* between occurrence and the psychological states that obtain when a subject is so modified.

For example, the eliciting psychological cause may produce bodily sensations and/or phenomenal feelings[20] that modify their subject's cognitive and motivational set, as well as behavioural tendencies,[21] and the effect that this produces on the subject's motivational and cognitive set may in turn affect the way in which the subject deploys her agency. Here I have in mind not only the way in which the subject deploys her agency over her body, but also over her thinking and attention.[22] So the effect produced on the subject's motivational and cognitive set may affect what conscious thoughts, judgements, imaginings, memories etc. thereby occur. Given that emotions can be produced by (and also sustained by) psychological causes, the occurrence of such conscious thoughts, judgements, imaginings and so on can in turn have an effect on the phenomenal feelings and/or bodily sensations that subsequently occur. And such occurrences can in turn modify the subject's motivational and cognitive set. And so on.

Think, for instance, of the way in which anxiety can fuel anxiety. In such cases should we say that the prevailing conscious emotional state continues to obtain because various conscious episodes that are associated with that condition continue to occur (e.g. persistent one-track trains of thinking and imagining, as well as phenomenal feelings)? Or should we say that such episodes continue to occur because the subject continues to be in an anxious state? On the model of the ontology being proposed, our answer can be: both of the above.

In the previous section I noted that there are various ways in which the state of being in pain can be instantiated. Clearly the corresponding point applies in the case of the different emotions. That is to say, there are various ways in which any given emotion can be instantiated. The further points I

[20] Phenomenal feelings that we might characterise in terms of the vocabulary of the emotions.

[21] And here one might include Frijda's 'action readiness'. See Frijda 1986.

[22] Here one might compare de Sousa's (1987) discussion of the effect of emotions on 'patterns of salience' among objects of attention. See also Matthews and Wells 1994, and Brady 2013.

noted at the end of the previous section also apply to the emotions in corresponding ways: it would be a mistake to assume that any given conscious emotional state cannot have any non-essential constituents; and having acknowledged that such conscious emotional states may have non-essential constituents, we shouldn't be surprised if there is not always a clear dividing line to be drawn between constituent of an emotional state on the one hand, and mere effect of the emotional state (or mere effect of a constituent of the emotional state) on the other.

Acknowledging that there may be significant variation in the way any given emotional state can be instantiated is, however, consistent with thinking that for any given kind of emotional state we may be able to identify typifying features of the phenomenal, bodily and physiological events and processes that occur, as well as typifying features of the ways in which the subject of such events/processes is modified by their occurrence (e.g. both motivationally and cognitively). This model of the ontology is consistent with thinking that there are characteristic patterns to the inter-dependencies between occurrence and state that it invokes. In that respect it accommodates something that Goldie was keen to emphasise: the idea that there can be characteristic patterns to the unfolding of occurrences – events/processes which are to be thought of as *constituents* of the emotion, rather than simply effects of the emotion. However, it accommodates that idea without sacrificing the distinctive explanatory potential of the emotions. For on the model of the ontology of emotions that I am proposing, the occurrence of these constituent events/processes, and the pattern of their unfolding, can be explained by citing the prevailing conscious state that is the emotion – e.g. the subject's grief.

It should of course be conceded that this sketch of an ontology of the emotions does not in itself provide us with any answers to many of the most important and interesting questions about the emotions. But if it offers a cogent way of adopting a component view of the emotions, without us having to sacrifice any of the distinctive roles that our appeals to the emotions play in the psychological explanations that we offer, then it may help to temper what may be false hopes and expectations in a study of the emotions – the expectation or hope that we should be able to pare down the complex constellation of mental and bodily phenomena associated with any given emotion until we have identified *the* single mental event or state which *is* the emotion.[23]

[23] For very helpful comments on an earlier draft of this chapter, I am grateful to Fabrice Teroni, Hichem Naar, Guy Longworth and Hemdat Lerman.

CHAPTER 5

Phenomenal Commitments: A Puzzle for Experiential Theories of Emotion

Jona Vance

1 Introduction

This chapter raises and responds to a puzzle for experiential theories of emotion. Experiential theories entail that some emotions just are experiences. The puzzle is to explain how subjects could be rationally evaluable in virtue of their emotional experiences, as experiential theories entail in conjunction with the desideratum that subjects are rationally evaluable in virtue of their emotions. Component theories entail that no emotions just are experiences. On some component theories, the experience component of emotion is distinct from the rationally evaluable component. These theories do not face the puzzle. As a result, these component theories have a potential advantage over experiential theories. In response to the puzzle, I defend experiential theories of emotion. Like many others, I argue that the rational evaluability of subjects in virtue of their emotions requires rationally evaluable subjective commitments. Unlike many others, I argue that the commitments need not be even partly constitutive of emotions. Instead, I suggest that emotional experiences are rationally evaluable because of their relation to other commitments the subject makes and the norms that govern those commitments.

1.1 Experiential and Component Theories of Emotion

Some emotions have phenomenology; for at least some emotions, there is something it's like to be the subject of that emotion. Instances of fear, disgust, and anger provide examples. There is something it's like to feel afraid of a nearby dog. There's something it's like to feel angry at your neighbor.[1] In addition, at least some mental entities with emotional phenomenology are

[1] Arguably the phenomenology of these types of emotions is characteristic and distinct: what it's like to feel afraid of the dog is phenomenally different from what it's like to feel angry at the dog. However, nothing in this chapter turns on these points.

emotional experiences. One way to think of 'experience' is as a synonym for 'phenomenally conscious mental entity'. On that way of thinking of experience, mental entities with emotional phenomenology are experiences by definition. However, one could argue that experiences in general are a subset of phenomenally conscious mental entities. For example, one could hold that occurrent judgments have cognitive phenomenology and hold that phenomenally conscious judgments are not experiences. Regardless of whether one distinguishes between experiences and mental entities with phenomenology, it should be uncontroversial that at least some phenomenally conscious emotional feelings are experiences.

Some theories of emotion entail that each emotion has many components. The components may include evaluative appraisals, physiological changes, action tendencies, behavioral expressions, and experiences. Other emotion theories entail that emotions consist of only one component. In this chapter, I will be especially interested in theories of emotion on which some phenomenally conscious emotions have just one component: an emotional experience. Call these *experiential theories*. An experiential theory of emotion is true if and only if some emotions just are emotional experiences; that is, an experiential theory is true just in case some emotions have emotional experiences as their only (improper) part. A *component theory* of emotion is true if and only if no emotion just is an emotional experience; that is, a component theory is true just in case every emotion has as a part something other than an emotional experience. On this way of drawing the distinction, experiential and component theories are mutually exclusive and jointly exhaustive of the logical possibilities.

Experiential theories need not entail that all emotions are experiences. It is controversial whether there are phenomenally unconscious emotions. One could hold an experiential theory on which all emotions are experiences, or one could hold an experiential theory on which some emotions are experiences while others are not. Prominent experiential theories of emotion include theories on which emotions are conscious feelings (Hume 1739/1978), theories on which some emotions are perceptual experiences (James 1884; Lange 1885; Prinz 2004; Roberts 2003; Tappolet 2000, 2016), attitudinal theories on which emotions are felt bodily attitudes (Deonna and Teroni 2012a), and neo-judgmentalist theories on which some emotions are states of phenomenally conscious assent (Helm 2001).[2]

[2] Some theorists hold that all emotional experiences are mental *states* (Prinz 2004). Others hold that some emotional experiences are *processes* (Goldie 2012). As drawn here, the distinction between experiential theories and component theories is neutral on whether emotional experiences are states or processes. The experiential/component theory distinction crosscuts the state/process theory of

Component theories entail that no emotion just is an emotional experience. On component theories, if an emotion includes an experience as a part, the experience is a proper part of the emotion. The most familiar component theories in contemporary emotion research are dimensional appraisal theories. According to dimensional appraisal theories, emotions are processes with several components: an appraisal component in which evaluations of the environment are made along various dimensions, a motivation component in which action tendencies are initiated, a somatic component in which physiological responses occur, a motor component with expressive and instrumental behavior, and a subjective experience component (Moors et al. 2013).[3] Although process theories of emotion are currently the most prominent examples of component theories, non-process component theories are also available. On such a view, emotions consist of multiple, metaphysically distinct states. For example, on some views, emotions are combinations of beliefs and desires (Descartes 1649/1989; Green 1992; Searle 1983).

1.2 A Desideratum

It is a desideratum of emotion theorizing that at least some emotions with experiential phenomenology are rationally evaluable, and, moreover, that subjects are rationally evaluable in virtue of having these emotions.[4] Evaluating emotions for rational status is distinct from evaluating them for accuracy. A mental entity has accuracy conditions if it has representational content (Siegel 2011). But having representational content is not sufficient for a mental entity to be rationally evaluable (nor for subjects to be rationally evaluable in virtue of it). Emotions are mental entities for which we can have or fail to have adequate reasons. That we can have or fail to have adequate reasons for our emotions is at least part of why they are rationally evaluable (Deonna and Teroni 2012a; Vance 2014).

One common way to illustrate the rational evaluation of emotions is with recalcitrant emotions (Brady 2007, 2009; D'Arms and Jacobson 2003;

emotion distinction. States and processes can be distinguished in various ways. A common way to mark the distinction is that states persist through time by enduring whereas processes perdure (unfold) over time. It is controversial exactly how to characterize the difference between enduring and perduring (see other contributions to this volume for more on these issues). For our purposes, the details of these characterizations do not matter.

[3] For another component process view of emotion, see Robinson, Chapter 3, this volume.

[4] Relatedly, emotions are evaluable in terms of their justification, and subjects are evaluable as justified or unjustified in virtue of their emotions. My discussion in the main text is in terms of rationality, but I take it that similar points apply in terms of justification.

Greenspan 1988; Roberts 2003).[5] Suppose that you are afraid of heights and enter a virtual reality simulation in which it seems to you that you are standing atop a tall building. You feel tremendous fear even though you know that you are safely on the ground. In such a case, your fear is irrational. In addition, you are irrational for feeling so afraid in the circumstances.

Emotions might be evaluable for more than one kind of rationality. Emotions (and their subjects) might be evaluable in terms of *epistemic* rationality. If so, emotions are evaluable in a way that is related to the way in which beliefs, judgments, and credences are epistemically evaluable in light of one's evidence. In addition, emotions (and their subjects) might be evaluable in terms of *practical* rationality. If so, emotions are evaluable in way that is related to the way in which actions and activities are practically evaluable in light of one's goals or ends. In what follows, we will see that the puzzle of rationally evaluable emotional experiences can be raised independently of any particular conception of the kind of rational evaluability at issue, including whether it is epistemic, practical, both, or some further kind.

2 A Puzzle for Experiential Theories

2.1 *The Puzzle*

Given the desideratum that some phenomenally conscious emotions are rationally evaluable (and that subjects are evaluable in virtue of their emotions), experiential theories of emotion entail that there are rationally evaluable emotional experiences and that subjects are rationally evaluable in virtue of them. This raises a puzzle for experiential theories. The puzzle is to explain how subjects could be rationally evaluable in virtue of their emotional experiences – that is, in virtue of how things seem to them emotionally – as experiential theories entail in conjunction with the desideratum that subjects are rationally evaluable in virtue of their emotions. Call this the *puzzle of rationally evaluable emotional experiences* – or more succinctly, the puzzle of evaluable experience.

The puzzle arises because it sounds odd to say that emotional experiences are rationally evaluable, and it sounds odd to say that subjects are rationally evaluable in virtue of their emotional experiences. Experiences

[5] The puzzle at the center of this chapter is distinct from a familiar puzzle about the nature of the irrationality of recalcitrant emotions. I clarify this distinction later.

involve appearances, ways things seem to one. It is *prima facie* plausible that you are not rationally evaluable in virtue of how things seem to you.

In having things seem to you some way, you need not make any subjective commitments to their being that way. But, one might think, subjective commitments are necessary for rational evaluability of the subject. So, a subject is not rationally evaluable in virtue of how things seem to them. A subject may be rationally evaluable in virtue of various commitments they make in response to how things seem to them and in virtue of various commitments they make that shape their experiences. But the experiences themselves, one might think, are not rationally evaluable, nor are subjects rationally evaluable in virtue of their experiences.

Similar points have often been raised against perceptual theories of emotion according to which some emotions just are *perceptual* experiences. The objection is this: emotions are rationally evaluable. But perceptual experiences are not. So emotions are not perceptual experiences (Brady 2007; Deonna and Teroni 2012a; Helm 2001; Pitcher 1965). This objection is a special case of the puzzle of evaluable experience. However, the focus on perceptual experience alone is arguably too narrow. The objection is plausible for other kinds of experience – though perhaps not ultimately compelling for all kinds, as I will argue. For example, a phenomenally conscious autobiographical memory is an experience at least partly constituted by seeming awareness of one's past. A subject is rationally evaluable for how she responds to an autobiographical memory experience: e.g., she can be evaluated as irrational for which beliefs she forms in response. And a subject is rationally evaluable for activities she carries out that shape her memory experiences: e.g., she can be evaluated as irrational for forming irrational beliefs that then shape her memory. But, at least at first blush, it sounds odd to say that a subject is (ir)rational for having it seem to her in her memory as though she did such-and-such. Similarly, at least at first blush, it can sound odd to say that a subject is (ir)rational for how things emotionally seem to her. That is, it can sound odd to rationally evaluate a subject in virtue of her emotional experiences. Experiences – perceptual, memorial, emotional, and otherwise – may look to be poor candidates for entities in virtue of which we make rational evaluations.[6]

We can now sharpen the puzzle. In raising the puzzle, I suggested that rational evaluation requires subjective commitment. More precisely, for S to be rationally evaluable in virtue of *x*, S must make a subjective commitment

[6] Similar points can be made with respect to other kinds of experience, such as pain experience, intuitive experience, and religious experience, since all such experiences can be characterized in terms of how things seem to the subject.

that involves *x*. I will say more about why we should think that subjective commitment is required for rational evaluation, what it means for a commitment to 'involve' emotional experiences, and what such commitments are. For now, I note that the puzzle of rationally evaluable emotional experiences can be formulated as an argument against experiential theories utilizing the following claims:

> *Constitutive commitment requirement* S is rationally evaluable in virtue of x only if x is at least partly constituted by a rationally evaluable commitment by S.
> *Mere seeming conception of emotional experience* Every emotional experience is a mere seeming, such that no emotional experiences are even partly constituted by a rationally evaluable commitment by their subject.

Together the constitutive commitment requirement and mere seeming conception of emotional experience entail that no subject is rationally evaluable in virtue of her emotional experiences. To respond to the puzzle of rationally evaluable emotional experiences, defenders of experiential theories must deny at least one of these claims.

2.2 *Component Theories and the Puzzle*

Jesse Prinz (2004) defends an experiential theory of emotion. He identifies emotions with a certain kind of perceptual experience and opposes theories of emotion that include other things as parts, such as facial expressions, physiological changes, and action tendencies. Prinz calls these 'encompassing theories' of emotion. He writes,

> Encompassing theories are perhaps the ultimate aspiration of most emotion theorists. Researchers want to afford a place to every aspect of an emotional response. There is a preference for inclusion. This is perfectly reasonable. Emotion episodes are complex, and singling out one component as the emotion may obscure that complexity. We can honor complexity by defining emotions as complex states [or processes]. (Prinz 2004: 18)

In the quoted passage, Prinz identifies one potential motivation for component theories. On his suggestion, researchers want to 'honor' the complexity of emotion phenomena, and they do that by including a wide range of these phenomena as parts of the emotion.

The puzzle of rationally evaluable emotional experience suggests an independent motivation for component theories – one that is compatible with Prinz's suggestion, but is logically independent of it. On component theories, emotions could have the relevant phenomenology in virtue of their experience components, and they could be rationally evaluable in virtue of some other component. The puzzle does not arise for such views because there is no need to find a single mental entity that is both rationally evaluable and experiential.

Appraisal process theories illustrate how component theories can avoid the puzzle. On contemporary appraisal theories, emotions are processes with distinct stages, including dimensional appraisals, physiological changes, facial expressions, action tendencies, and experiences. Some of these stages are rationally evaluable, e.g., the upshots of appraisal processes are often thought to be assessments by the subject of a target object along various dimensions.[7] In component appraisal theories, the appraisal is distinct from the experience.

Similarly, component theories on which emotions are composites of multiple states can avoid the puzzle. Suppose that conscious emotions are constituted by a state of emotional assent and a distinct state with phenomenal character. These two states could be closely metaphysically related. For example, the assent state might metaphysically ground the phenomenal state, such that one is in the phenomenal state (metaphysically) because one is in the assent state. On such a view, one would not have to claim that subjects are rationally evaluable in virtue of how things emotionally seem to them. Rather, one could hold that (i) the emotion has phenomenology in virtue of the phenomenal state and (ii) the emotion is rationally evaluable solely in virtue of the assent state.[8]

The fact that component theories can avoid the puzzle puts pressure on proponents of experiential theories to explain why we should think that emotional phenomenology and rational evaluability apply to a single state or process. Experiential theories might have other advantages over component theories.[9] But they would be in a better dialectical position compared

[7] Dimensional appraisal processes are not parts of canonical emotions. All processes are homogeneous in terms of predication (Steward 2013). That is, at every moment at which the process is occurring, the process can be said to occur. If dimensional appraisal processes were stages in emotion, then, even at the earliest stages of dimensional appraisal processes, the emotion could be said to occur. For example, even during the initial goal relevance check, fear could be said to occur. But this is implausible. Still, the *upshots* of dimensional appraisal processes could be parts of emotions (Cf. Moors 2013).

[8] For discussion of the claim that non-phenomenal states metaphysically ground phenomenal states, see Chudnoff (2015: 14–17). Chudnoff's focus is on cognitive states such as judgment and intuition, which he claims ground distinct phenomenal states with cognitive phenomenology. But, as noted in the main text here, similar points can be made about non-phenomenal emotional states grounding phenomenal emotional states.

[9] For example, Prinz (2004) presents what he calls the Problem of Plenty for component theories: the problem of explaining how all the alleged components of emotions hang together. Experiential

to component theories if they also had a solution to the puzzle of rationally evaluable emotional experience.

2.3 *A Distinct, but Related Puzzle*

It is worth noting a related puzzle in the philosophy of emotion concerning rational evaluation. The puzzle centers on recalcitrant emotions. When an emotion is recalcitrant, one feels the emotion despite believing or even knowing that it is inappropriate in the circumstances. For example, as we saw earlier, if you feel afraid of falling, while knowing you're safely on the ground, your fear is an irrational, recalcitrant emotion.

The puzzle of rationally evaluable emotional experience is distinct from the puzzle of recalcitrant emotions. The puzzle of evaluable experience is a puzzle for views that entail that some emotions are experiences whereas the puzzle of recalcitrant emotions applies more broadly. The challenge presented by the puzzle of evaluable emotional experience is not only to identify a rationally evaluable mental entity that is part of an emotion. In addition, one must argue that the rationally evaluable mental entity is itself an experience. Discussions of the puzzle of recalcitrant emotions have largely focused on finding a suitably evaluable attitude or commitment on the part of the subjects of recalcitrant emotions; they have given less explicit attention to the puzzle of explaining how the proposed evaluable entity could be an emotional experience.

3 Rational Evaluation and Subjective Commitment

In raising the puzzle of rationally evaluable emotional experience, I suggested that for S to be rationally evaluable in virtue of *x*, S must make a subjective commitment that involves *x*. In this section, I say more about why we should think that subjective commitment is required for rational evaluation.

Subjective commitments are personal-level entities. Daniel Dennett (1969) introduced the personal/sub-personal distinction into philosophy of mind. Dennett used the distinction to carve out space for a theory of mind that avoided substance dualism on the one hand and physicalist identity theory on the other. However, in recent years the distinction has been drawn in many different ways (Drayson 2012). As I use the distinction

theories of emotion could face the Problem of Plenty, if one developed a notion of emotional experience on which it had multiple parts as in Goldie (2012).

here, personal-level entities (including personal-level states and processes) are those that are correctly attributable to persons and more generally organisms; sub-personal level entities (including sub-personal states and processes) are correctly attributable to subsystems of persons or organisms. A subject's intentional actions, beliefs, judgments, and experiences are all personal level on this usage. For example, reaching one's arm toward a target is a personal-level action, attributable to the subject. The beating of one's heart is sub-personal on this usage: one's heart beats; one does not beat one's heart.

Emotional experiences are personal level. Necessarily, all experiences are phenomenally conscious. Being an experience is sufficient for having conscious phenomenology. So, all emotional experiences are phenomenally conscious. Necessarily, all phenomenally conscious mental entities are personal level. Something's having conscious phenomenology is sufficient for that thing to be personal level (Burge 2010). So, all emotional experiences are personal level.

The fact that *x* is personal level with respect to a subject S is not sufficient for S to be rationally evaluable in virtue of *x*. For S to be rationally evaluable in virtue of *x*, it must also make sense to ask non-causal why questions about *x*. Say that *x* is *primary* if and only if *x* is a state or process for which it does *not* make sense to ask non-causal why questions. And say that *x* is *non-primary* if and only if it *does* make sense to ask non-causal why questions about *x*. Note that the definitions do not specify that it must make sense to ask the *subject* of the experience what reason she has for the experience. There is a difference between having a reason for *x* and being able to give a reason for *x*. We're interested in which kinds of *x*s subjects have reasons for, even if they cannot give those reasons. As a result, it would be enough for S to be rationally evaluable in virtue of *x* if in principle someone could say what S's non-causal reasons are for *x*.

Emotions are non-primary: it makes sense to ask non-causal why questions about one's emotions. For example, it makes sense to ask, 'Why are you angry?' Importantly for experiential theories of emotion, emotional *experiences* are also non-primary: it makes sense to ask 'Why do you *feel* angry?' where this question does not merely ask for an account of the etiology of the anger experience. Such questions make sense in part because emotions and emotional experiences have what Deonna and Teroni (2012a: 5) call 'cognitive bases': intentional mental entities in virtue of which emotions and emotional experiences refer to particular objects. Cognitive bases include a wide range of intentional mental entities: from perceptual experiences to imaginative states to beliefs. For example, one's anger could be directed at one's boss in virtue of having a belief about one's boss as a cognitive base. Or one's fear could be about the dog nearby, because of one's perceptual experience of the dog nearby. The cognitive base provides at least part of one's reason for having the emotional experience.

The fact that it makes sense to ask non-causal why questions about *x* (*x* is non-primary) is not sufficient for S to be rationally evaluable in virtue of *x*. For S to be rationally evaluable in virtue of *x*, S's reasons for *x* must also be evaluable as good, adequate, appropriate, and the like. There must be norms governing which reasons are good, adequate, etc. The bearing of such evaluative norms will be fixed in part by how well *x* fits S's other commitments. As a result, I propose the following further necessary condition for rational evaluability: subjects are rationally evaluable in virtue of *x* only if *x* involves personal-level, subjective commitment by S. Next I illustrate the notion of subjective commitment with respect to some paradigmatic cases of it, before applying it to emotion and emotional experience. I will have more to say about how commitments get involved in the right ways in the next section.

Judgments and intentional actions are paradigm examples of mental entities that involve subjective commitments. Subjects are rationally evaluable in virtue of their judgments in part because judgments are constituted by a kind of endorsement of a propositional content. In addition, subjects are rationally evaluable in virtue of their intentional actions. Actions constitutively involve intentions to bring about a state of affairs. Such intentions are a kind of rationally evaluable commitment by the subject.

Adequacy and appropriateness conditions for rational evaluation can be understood in relation to the commitments one makes related to the thing for which one is rationally evaluated and the norms that govern such commitments. In making a judgment, a subject is rationally evaluable in virtue of the commitment she makes to the content of the judgment. The judgmental commitment can be assessed as epistemically rationally adequate or appropriate in light of the degree to which the judgment fits the subject's evidence. In performing an intentional action, a subject is rationally evaluable in virtue of the commitment she makes to bring about the intended state of affairs. The intentional commitment can be assessed as practically rationally adequate or appropriate in light of the degree to which it fits the subject's further goals or ends.[10]

[10] The subject need not be committed to the norms themselves. Plausibly, standards of rational evaluability are fixed partly by one's commitments, but not entirely by one's commitments. There may be norms of rational evaluation independent of one's commitments, and it may be partly in virtue of these norms that S is rationally evaluable.

Much has been made about the alleged judgmental (Nussbaum 2001; Solomon 1976) or quasi-judgmental nature of emotions (Brady 2013; Helm 2001). For example, although Bennett Helm holds that emotions are not ordinary judgments, he argues that they must be constituted by a kind of *assent* similar to the assent in judgment. However, not all rationally evaluable commitments involve assent, even if one excludes intentional action. Consider credence assignments. Credences are assigned to propositional contents. Credences range from 0 to 1. An assignment of 1 to *p* indicates subjective certainty that *p* is true and an assignment of 0 to *p* indicates subjective certainty that *p* is not true. Suppose S has evidence that a coin with two sides (heads, tails) is fair. S assigns credence 0.5 to the claim that the coin will land heads when tossed. S's credence of 0.5 is rationally evaluable. Given S's evidence, the assignment is epistemically rational. Note that S does not assent to the claim that the coin will land heads. Nor does she reject the claim or assent to its negation. It is also not the case that S fails to take any attitude at all to the claim that the coin will land heads, since she does assign credence 0.5 to the claim. This is an example of a mental entity (a subjective credence) in virtue of which S is epistemically rationally evaluable, but that does not involve assent.[11]

I have just been arguing that subjects are rationally evaluable in virtue of *x* only if *x* involves personal-level, subjective commitment. It is this further necessary condition that gives rise to the puzzle of rationally evaluable emotional experience. For it is plausible that in having emotional experience, things will seem to you some way, but that you need not make any subjective commitments to their being that way. If such a commitment is required for rational evaluation, experiential theories of emotion may be poorly positioned to account for it.[12]

4 Phenomenal Commitments

In Section 2, I noted that the puzzle of rationally evaluable emotional experience arises from the conjunction of two claims. According to the constitutive commitment requirement, S is rationally evaluable in virtue of

[11] One might argue that a credence of 0.5 that *p* is equivalent to a belief or assent that *p* is 0.5 probable. However, the two are not equivalent. For one thing, forming the belief that *p* is 0.5 probable clearly requires that the person have the concept PROBABLE, whereas the former does not.

[12] I should clarify that I am not claiming that personal-level attribution, non-primacy, and subjective commitment provide a jointly sufficient condition for rational evaluability. To respond to the puzzle of rationally evaluable emotional experiences, it is enough if I can show that one of the assumptions underlying the puzzle is false. Doing so does not require that I give a sufficient condition for rational evaluability.

x only if x is at least partly constituted by a rationally evaluable commitment by S. And according to the mere seeming conception of emotional experience, every emotional experience is a mere seeming, such that no emotional experiences are even partly constituted by a rationally evaluable commitment by their subject. Together these claims entail that no subject is rationally evaluable in virtue of her emotional experiences.

In responding to the puzzle, it will help to introduce some terminology concerning such commitments. The terminology will also help clarify the ways in which commitments can 'involve' emotional experiences. Say that *phenomenal commitments* are commitments involving phenomenally conscious entities, such as experiences. Such involvement can be constitutive or not. When such commitments are at least partly constitutive of a phenomenal entity, call them *constitutive* phenomenal commitments. When such commitments are not even partly constitutive of a phenomenal entity, call them *non-constitutive* phenomenal commitments.[13]

4.1 Constitutive Phenomenal Commitments

Many emotion theorists have held that the rationally evaluable commitments related to emotion must be at least partly constitutive of the emotion itself. Such an assumption has likely driven support for judgmental, quasi-judgmental, and other attitudinal theories of emotion. One way to respond to the puzzle of rationally evaluable emotional experience is to argue that there are constitutive phenomenal commitments in emotional experience.

However, arguing that emotional experiences are partly constituted by subjective commitments has its challenges. In particular, there is a worry that one will fall back into a component theory: when trying to specify the rationally evaluable aspect of emotional experience, one runs the risk of specifying a closely related but distinct entity instead.

To illustrate, we can apply the worry to Robert Roberts' (2003) concern-based construal theory of emotions. Roberts holds that emotions are concern-based construals. For Roberts, a construal is an activity of seeing-as, in which one thing is seen in terms of another. Construals come in various

[13] We could add a further wrinkle here. We could say that *c* is a constitutive phenomenal commitment with respect to a phenomenal entity *e* just in case *c* partly constitutes *e*. This terminology may be helpful when one makes a commitment to having some phenomenal experience *e*, the commitment is partly constituted by a conscious judgment *j*, and *j* is a phenomenal entity with some sort of phenomenology distinct from *e*. Such a commitment would be a constitutive phenomenal commitment on the more general definition (because *j* is a phenomenal entity), but would not count as a constitutive phenomenal commitment with respect to *e*. For simplicity, I ignore this complication in the main text.

formats: cognitive, visual, emotional, etc. As a non-emotional illustration of a construal, Roberts describes one's activity of seeing-as for ambiguous figures. Suppose you're looking at the well-known ambiguous figure of an old or young woman. Most subjects can visually construe the figure either as an old woman or as a young woman. To construe the image in these ways, one must place the image under the concept OLD WOMAN or YOUNG WOMAN. Roberts argues that the activity of construal in such a case just is one's visual experience of the figure as an old/young woman. For Roberts, phenomenally conscious visual construals just are a kind of experience of something in terms of something else. Similarly, Roberts holds that emotional experiences are concern-based conscious construals of some object in terms of emotional evaluative properties. To experience fear is to consciously emotionally construe something as dangerous in a certain way. Roberts offers his theory as what I am calling an experiential theory. He writes, 'Construals have an immediacy reminiscent of sense perception. They are impressions, ways things appear to the subject; they are experiences and not just judgments or thoughts or beliefs' (Roberts 2003: 75). In addition, since construals are intentional activities for which subjects can have or lack reasons, they are good candidates for rational evaluation. As a result, Roberts' proposal suggests a way in which some emotions could just be experiences and yet could also be rationally evaluable. Roberts could thus deny the mere seeming conception of emotional experience.

However, conscious construals are not experiences. Consider again visual construals of ambiguous figures like the old/young woman. Roberts notes that visual construal is an activity of organizing the visual scene (71). Activities are a kind of process. So construals are processes. One of the stages of a construal process involves placing the stimulus under a concept, e.g., placing the visual stimulus under the concept OLD WOMAN. But placing the stimulus under a concept occurs before one visually experiences the stimulus in terms of the concept. The activity of organizing the scene is initiated before the onset of the conscious experience of the scene thus organized. As a result, the activity of visually construing an object *o* as having a feature *F* begins before the conscious visual experience of *o* as *F*. Experimental results in vision science support this characterization of visual construal. Studies of eye movement during perception of ambiguous stimuli indicate that one sees an ambiguous figure as one does in part because of shifts in spatial attention (Long and Toppino 2004). Depending on where one fixates, one gets the image of the old or young woman. Thus the construal process involves stages of attentional shift prior to the experience. The experience may be part of the construal process, but the construal process is not identical to the experience.

As a result, Roberts' claim that conscious construals just are experiences is implausible, and Roberts' view of emotion as concerned-based construal is probably best characterized as a component theory. In a construal approach, the construal component is the best candidate for that in virtue of which emotions are rationally evaluable. Since the rationally evaluable construal component is distinct from the emotional experience, Roberts' view fails to support the claim that emotional experiences are partly constituted by rationally evaluable subjective commitments. As such the view fails to provide compelling evidence that emotional experiences are rationally evaluable or that subjects are rationally evaluable in virtue of their experiences.

There are other ways one might argue for the claim that emotional experience is partly constituted by a subjective commitment. For example, Helm (2001) argues that constitutive commitments in emotional experiences are 'focal commitments'.[14] Although they do not use the term 'phenomenal commitment', Deonna and Teroni (2012a) argue in effect that felt bodily attitudes of action readiness partly constitute phenomenal commitments in emotional experience. I am sympathetic to these lines of response to the puzzle, and I will remain neutral on them here. The mere seeming conception of emotional experience deserves scrutiny. However, in what follows I explore another route: denying the constitutive commitment requirement.

4.2 *Non-Constitutive Phenomenal Commitments*

Emotions are not rationally evaluable in isolation. Our emotional lives involve commitments concerning our emotions in various circumstances. We make some commitments concerning how our emotions will change when circumstances change and other commitments concerning how our emotions should have been, had things been different. Likewise, we make commitments as to what our emotional *experiences* will or would be in various circumstances. For example, if you feel fear that a dog will bite you, you might implicitly commit to feel relieved if the dog does not bite. In other cases, one commits to having some emotional experience in various counterfactual circumstances. For example, suppose you experience the

[14] According to Helm, an emotion has a target, formal object, and focus. The *target* of an emotion is 'the object at which the emotion is directed' (34). The *formal object* is 'the kind of import the responsiveness to which makes each emotion intelligible as the emotion is it' (62). The *focus* is 'the background object having import to the subject that makes intelligible the evaluation implicit in the emotion' (69). For example, suppose I am afraid a dog will bite me. The target is the dog, the formal object of fear is danger, and the focus is my bodily integrity. Focal commitments are commitments to the value and importance of the focus of an emotion.

positive emotion of satisfaction or joy in response to a desired circumstance. In such a case, you typically also hold the commitment that, if the desired circumstance had not obtained, you would have felt disappointment or anger. Bennett Helm calls these *transitional* and *tonal* commitments, respectively (Helm 2001: 68). They are species of what I have called phenomenal commitments.

Helm holds that transitional and tonal commitments are constitutive phenomenal commitments. On his view, one's commitment to feeling relief if the dog does not bite is partly constitutive of one's feeling of fear that the dog will bite, and one's commitment to having felt disappointment or anger if things had not gone satisfactorily is partly constitutive of one's feeling of satisfaction. The commitments are inherent in the feelings themselves on Helm's view. Call this the *constitutive commitment view.*

I think that one does not need to hold the constitutive commitment view in order to explain the rational evaluability of emotional experiences, nor the evaluability of subjects in virtue of those experiences. In my view, the commitments constraining the rational status of emotional experiences (and of subjects in virtue of them) in various circumstances need not be constitutive phenomenal commitments. The attitudes, orientations, or mental entities that constitute the commitments partly in virtue of which one is rationally evaluable for emotional experiences need not be even partly constitutive of emotional experiences. Having an emotional experience in the circumstances I rationally commit to have it in is a rational success, other things equal. Failing to have an emotional experience to which I rationally commit is a rational failure, other things equal. I am rationally evaluable in virtue of fulfilling or failing to fulfill emotional phenomenal commitments about which emotional experiences to have when, even if the commitments are not even partly constitutive of any emotional experience. Similarly, emotional experiences are rationally evaluable in virtue of their fulfilling or failing to fulfill the emotional phenomenal commitments of their subject, even if the commitments are not even partly constitutive of any emotional experience. Call this the *non-constitutive commitment view.*

Phenomenal commitments can be explicit or implicit. Some of our non-constitutive phenomenal commitments concerning emotional experiences are explicitly made. For example, when a patient promises her therapist to try not to feel so afraid in social situations, the patient makes an explicit phenomenal commitment concerning her emotional experiences. However, most of our emotional phenomenal commitments are implicit, reflected in our broader values, preferences, and social relationships. For example, most humans, including children, value their own bodily integrity. But many humans, especially children, have never formulated an explicit commitment to their own bodily integrity, let alone an explicit commitment to feel fear when they perceive or believe their bodily integrity to be threatened. In addition, a parent may be implicitly rationally committed to fear for the safety of her child in virtue of norms governing parent-child relationships. The non-constitutive commitment view covers both explicit and implicit phenomenal commitments.

To see why the non-constitutive commitment view is plausible, note that even on Helm's constitutive commitment view, a phenomenal commitment that is constitutive of an emotional experience does not constrain the rational status of that very experience. Rather, on Helm's view, the commitment that partly constitutes some emotional experience rationally constrains some *other* emotional experience. For example, an emotional experience of fearing a dog can put constraints on whether it is rational to have another emotional experience of relief that the dog did not bite, not on the experience of fear. Once we see that the constraints do not reflexively apply to the initial emotional experience itself, it is not clear why the constraining commitment must be partly constitutive of any emotional experience. As long as the thing that is rationally constrained is an emotional experience, the obtaining of the constraints helps explain why subjects are rationally evaluable in virtue of their emotional experiences.

It is important to note that on the non-constitutive commitment view, the rational evaluability of subjects cannot be explained solely in terms of their non-constitutive phenomenal commitments and the norms governing those commitments. Naturally, one's emotional experiences feature essentially in the explanation of the rational evaluation of those experiences. What makes one rationally evaluable for one's emotional experience is not only that one commits to have (or not have) an emotional experience, but that the experience is appropriate given one's commitments and the norms that govern them. For example, on the non-constitutive commitment view, the explanation of why a recalcitrant emotion is irrational must make reference to one's other commitments, to one's recalcitrant emotional experience, and to the norms governing their relation. As a result, the non-constitutive commitment view respects the desideratum that subjects are rationally evaluable at least partly in virtue of their emotions, even if those emotions just are emotional experiences.

It is also important to note that the view concerns the rational evaluability of emotional experiences and of subjects in virtue of such experiences. The non-constitutive commitment view does not entail anything about what it takes to have an emotional experience in the first place. For example, it does not require that one make some phenomenal commitment in order to have an emotional experience. If that were the view, only organisms with the ability to (at least implicitly) make phenomenal commitments about their emotional experiences could have emotional experiences at all. Such a view entails implausibly demanding requirements for having an emotional experience. The non-constitutive commitment view is about how non-constitutive commitments constrain which emotional experiences are rationally good, appropriate, etc. It entails nothing about whether such commitments are necessary to have the emotional experience in the first place.

The non-constitutive commitment view has a number of attractive features. As just noted, the non-constitutive commitment view separates the preconditions for having emotional experiences from the preconditions for such experiences to be rationally evaluable (and for subjects to be rationally evaluable in virtue of such experiences) in a way that the constitutive commitment view does not. This separation provides a potential advantage for the non-constitutive commitment view over the constitutive commitment view. When theorists adopt a constitutive commitment view, they must locate the relevant commitment in the emotional experience itself. Such theorists run the risk of offering overly restrictive necessary conditions for having emotional experiences at all. If constitutive commitment views entail that making such a commitment is part of the nature of emotional experience, such views entail that the necessary conditions for having the experience include making the relevant kind of commitment. Since the non-constitutive commitment view does not entail that the relevant commitments are even partly constitutive of emotional experiences themselves, it faces no such worry.

The non-constitutive commitment view allows that there are possible organisms that have emotional experiences but do not make the relevant further commitments, not even implicitly. If there were such beings, they might have emotional experiences but not be rationally evaluable in virtue of them, according to the view. I think that this is a nice feature of the non-constitutive commitment view. Such beings are plausibly not conceptually impossible. That one is able to have emotional experiences is insufficient for one to be rationally evaluable in virtue of those experiences. The rational evaluability of emotional experience is generated from a wider range of commitments and norms in which emotional experiences are embedded.

In addition, the non-constitutive commitment view allows for the conceptual possibility of beings that make value commitments, lack emotional experiences, yet are not irrational in virtue of this combination of features. Suppose that a highly sophisticated nonhuman being holds a set of values and preferences but is incapable of having emotional experiences. Such a being makes various value commitments without being committed (even implicitly) to having various emotional experiences. For example, such a being might value its own bodily integrity, but have no phenomenal commitment (even implicitly) to feel fear in response to threats to their bodily integrity. The non-constitutive commitment view nicely explains the conceptual possibility of such a being. On the non-constitutive commitment view, the being's failure to experience fear in such cases need not be a rational failure, since they lack the relevant phenomenal commitments.

In closing this section, I consider and respond to a worry one might have about the non-constitutive commitment view. One might wonder whether the view entails that if a subject S makes a non-constitutive phenomenal commitment to have an experience, *e*, in circumstances *c*, the commitment is sufficient to generate rational obligations for S to have *e* in *c*. If so, the view would arguably make it too easy to generate rational obligations.[15]

In response to the worry, I want to explain why phenomenal commitments alone are not sufficient to generate a rational obligation on the non-constitutive commitment view. There are at least two reasons.

First, in order for a phenomenal commitment concerning one's emotional experience to help generate rational obligations (or rational evaluability more generally), there must be rational norms governing such commitments and how those commitments constrain rationally appropriate experiences. That these norms obtain is not guaranteed by the existence of the phenomenal commitment on its own. To see why not, it is helpful to consider a different

[15] Michael Brady raises a similar worry for Bennett Helm's (2001) view of emotional rationality. Brady writes, 'Suppose that I am committed to the value of bodily integrity. This commitment plausibly grounds certain others, namely the commitment to feel fear when bodily integrity is *in fact* threatened, or to feel relief when a *genuine* threat has passed, etc. But it is implausible to suppose that this commitment rationally grounds a commitment to feel fear with respect to an object that one *knows* is not dangerous, even if this object *appears* in some sense dangerous. A commitment to a certain focal value only plausibly grounds commitments to certain appropriate emotional responses if these emotional responses are themselves *warranted*, at least from the subject's own perspective. By the same token, it seems false to claim that a *recalcitrant* forward-looking emotion rationally commits me to having the appropriate backward-looking emotion: if I am clearly aware that a certain dog is harmless but I am nevertheless scared that it will bite me, it seems false to claim that I am nevertheless rationally required to feel relieved when the dog doesn't bite me' (Brady 2009: 420). Unlike Helm, a defender of the non-constitutive commitment view need not hold that emotional rationality involves assent. And unlike Helm's view, the non-constitutive commitment view does not entail that emotional commitments are partly constitutive of emotional experiences. Nevertheless, Brady's objection may seem to apply to the non-constitutive commitment view, since the view explains the rationality of emotion partly in terms of phenomenal commitments.

kind of experience: visual experience. Many theorists hold that visual experiences are not subject to rational norms, even though it is possible to make non-constitutive phenomenal commitments regarding one's visual experiences. Suppose one phenomenally commits to seeing squares when squares are present and when images of the squares are encoded on one's retinas. On its own, this commitment is insufficient to generate a rational obligation to see squares in such circumstances. If there are no rational norms to constrain such commitments or appropriate visual experiences in response to such commitments, then visual experiences may not be rationally evaluable, nor subjects rationally evaluable in virtue of them, even when subjects make such commitments.[16] Similarly, if there were no norms governing how phenomenal commitments constrain emotional experiences, subjects would not be rationally evaluable in virtue of their emotional experiences. However, as I argued earlier, it is clear that emotional experiences are governed by such norms.

There is a second reason that making a non-constitutive phenomenal commitment to have an experience *e* in circumstances *c* is not sufficient to rationally constrain one with respect to having *e* in *c*. Suppose that you make a non-constitutive, phenomenal commitment to feel fear in response to offensive situations. Given plausible assumptions about the norms that govern emotional responses, your non-constitutive commitment is irrational. But plausibly, an irrational commitment cannot rationally constrain one's experiences. An analogous point applies to the rational constraints that hold among beliefs. Suppose that you form the beliefs that all kangaroos are immortal and that Kant is a kangaroo. Suppose that these beliefs are irrationally formed because you lack adequate evidence for them. Your commitment to the contents of these beliefs does not generate a rational requirement (or even a rational entitlement) for you to form the belief that Kant is immortal. Because your kangaroo beliefs are irrational, they fail to constrain which further beliefs are rational for you in the way they would if your kangaroo beliefs were rational. Likewise, if your non-constitutive phenomenal commitments concerning an emotional experience *e* in *c* are irrational, they do not generate rational constraints on your experiencing *e* in *c*.

The non-constitutive commitment view is consistent with all these points. There is a difference between the claim that (i) emotional experiences are

[16] Not everyone denies that vision is subject to rational norms. For the suggestion that visual experiences or visual processes are subject to rational norms, see Prinz (2004), Siegel (2017), and Vance (2014, 2015).

rationally evaluable partly in virtue of phenomenal commitments to feel further emotions and the claim that (ii) the fact that one makes relevant phenomenal commitments in conjunction with relevant norms is sufficient to give one's emotional experiences positive rational status.[17] The aforementioned worry targets a view that entails (ii). However, the non-constitutive commitment view entails (i) but not (ii). The view entails that emotional experiences are rationally evaluable partly in virtue of one's non-constitutive phenomenal commitments. But the view does not entail that fulfilling these commitments is sufficient for emotional experiences to have positive rational status if the commitments themselves are irrational.

5 Conclusion

In this chapter, I raised a puzzle for experiential theories of emotion and defended experiential theories in response. In response to the puzzle, I have argued for a non-constitutive commitment view, according to which the subjective commitments in virtue of which emotional experiences are rationally evaluable (and subjects are evaluable in virtue of them) are not even partly constitutive of emotional experiences themselves.

I have not tried to offer anything like a detailed explanation for why there are rational norms that govern emotional experience or what those norms are. Rather I have assumed that there are rational norms that govern emotions and argued that such norms can generate rational constraints on emotional experiences in conjunction with non-constitutive phenomenal commitments. This leaves important work undone concerning the details of the norms that help generate constraints on emotional experience. However, if the contours of my response to the puzzle of rationally evaluable emotional experience are correct, proponents of experiential theories of emotion do not need to find a way to fit subjective commitment into emotional experience itself in order to account for such norms.[18]

[17] Here I put the points in terms of the rational status of emotional experiences, for ease of presentation. I endorse parallel points in terms of the rationality of subjects in virtue of their emotional experiences.

[18] For helpful discussions of the rational evaluability of experience, I would like to thank Brian Ballard, Zoe Jenkin, Jesse Prinz, Jake Quilty-Dunn, Nico Silins, and Susanna Siegel. I would also like to thank Fabrice Teroni and Hichem Naar, the editors of this volume, for their very helpful comments on previous drafts.

CHAPTER 6

An Enactivist Theory of Emotional Content

Daniel Shargel and Jesse Prinz

Most of the prominent theories of emotion identify them with some kind of representational state: judgments, perceptions, desires, sui generis mental attitudes, or compounds of these states. These models emphasize the idea that emotions have meaning or content; they present the world as being a certain way. Embodied theories of emotion complicate this model. Facial expressions and accelerated heart rates do not, at least on first inspection, resemble judgments or perceptions. We believe embodied theories are right, though we won't review the evidence here (see Prinz 2004). Instead, we want to consider how embodied theories should cope with the question of content. We will review some of the dominant strategies that defenders of embodiment have taken, and we will argue that each faces problems. We will then consider two more recent approaches: one that emphasizes affordances, and another that defines emotions as "enactive." Building on the former approach, we will develop a version of the latter: an enactivist theory of emotional content. Our theory makes a strong claim about the ontology of emotions: that emotions do not represent pre-given features of the world, but rather bring new properties into existence. Thus, emotions do not represent objective features of the world, nor do they represent response-dependent features. Indeed, we don't think it is accurate to say emotions represent at all. Rather, they bring a special class of properties into existence.

1 Embodiment and Emotional Content

Embodied theories of emotion claim that bodily changes, or perceptions thereof, are essential components of emotional states. They have a long history, dating back to the earliest days of theorizing about emotions, since it has long been observed that the body undergoes changes when we experience emotions. Aristotle (1987) related anger to warm blood around the heart, and he defends a view according to which emotions involve physical states playing characteristic functional roles. Descartes (1989: 39–40) advanced the view that emotions are judgments that follow upon movements in the animal spirits. Francis Hutcheson (2003) defines emotions as confused sensations accompanied by bodily motions. Two centuries later, Charles Darwin wrote a systematic study of emotional expressions, suggesting that bodily states can be used to differentiate emotions. Such accounts reveal that the body has long figured into theories of the emotions. But embodiment got a major boost in the late nineteenth century, when William James and Carl Lange simultaneously advanced more thoroughgoing embodied theories. For James (1884), emotions are perceptions of bodily changes, and Lange (1885) rails against the view that bodily conditions are mere contingent effects of emotions.

The James-Lange approach continued to find supporters in the twentieth century and among contemporary authors (see Damasio 1994; Prinz 2004; Shargel 2014). Research has shown that emotions correlate with patterned bodily changes, that induced bodily changes can induce emotional experiences, and that disruptions in bodily perception of change can have an impact on emotional intensity. The embodied approach has not earned universal support, however. One key reason for this is that it is not immediately clear how changes in the body, or perceptions thereof, can have meaning or content. As Aristotle (1987) and Descartes (1989) argued, emotions present the world as being a certain way. In the twentieth century, this conjecture took precedence and a range of "cognitive appraisal" theories emerged, which identify emotions with judgments or other cognitive states (Kenny 1963: 14). On appraisal theories, each emotion corresponds to some kind of mental representation, corresponding to a "core relational theme" – a relationship between organism and environment that bears on well-being (Lazarus 1991a). Thus, sadness represents loss, anger represents offense, and fear represents danger. When we experience these emotions, we are representing such relations. This helps to explain the distinct role of each emotion, as well as the criteria for assessing their appropriateness, or rationality, on any given occasion. To fear a benign snake, for example, might be considered irrational because it would be mistaken to represent a benign animal as dangerous.

Under pressure from cognitive appraisal theories, defenders of embodied approaches have faced a challenge. How can one insist that emotions are embodied, while also accommodating the intuition that they have meaning? If fear is constituted by bodily changes such as blood flow to the extremities and a racing heart, how can it signify danger? Such abstract content is thought to exclusively belong to mental representations, not bodily transformations.

To face this challenge, proponents of embodied theories have adopted several strategies. We want to review these now, and also indicate why each of the leading strategies might be regarded as problematic. One strategy is to bite the bullet and simply deny that emotions have content. As we read them, both James and Lange essentially ignore the issue of content, so they might have been partial to this approach. One of us has also defended a version of the bullet-biting view, claiming that emotions may lack precise intentional content (Shargel 2015). There are benefits of bullet biting, since emotions differ in important ways from typical representational states. When we are angry, for example, the anger influences behavior directed at many things in our surroundings, not just an individual object. We will revisit this point at the end. But bullet biting also has a considerable cost. Content helps explain why emotions play different roles. It explains why anger is related to aggression by supposing that anger represents offense. It would be good to have some account that explains this.

A second strategy is to endorse a hybrid model, on which emotions have both a cognitive component and a bodily component. The challenge here is justifying the unification of these components, as well as the identification of that state with the emotion. What makes the two elements part of a single state? They are demonstrably dissociable (we can represent the presence of danger without entering into a physiological state of fear, and conversely). Moreover, such approaches implicitly concede that bodily states cannot have meaning. This forecloses the interesting possibility that embodied states make substantive contributions to content.

A third strategy, once favored by one of us (Prinz 2004), is to argue that physiological states form part of an embodied representational system. Physiological states carry information about significant situations, so by perceiving these states we indirectly perceive those situations. On this model, emotions use interoceptive modalities to achieve a form of exteroceptive perception. Prinz tries to pull this off by adopting a popular naturalistic approach to representation: informational semantics (Dretske 1981). According to informational semantics, a mental state gets its meaning in virtue of the information it carries. Information, in turn, is characterized in terms of some kind of covariation relation. If state M reliably occurs in the presence of stimulus S, then M indicates the presence of S. To a first approximation, then, a racing heart and blood flow to the extremities can represent danger because such states tend to arise when and only when we are in danger. This is called the embodied appraisal theory, since bodily states, or perceptions thereof, come to have the kind of content that is traditionally associated with appraisal judgments.

This approach faces some serious hurdles. Apart from worries about informational semantics in general,[1] standard versions of informational semantics are difficult to adapt to the case of emotions, since they presuppose that the representational content of a mental state can exist independently of that state. Representation is said to involve a reliable co-occurrence between mental states and items in the external world. But some experiences seem to represent things that lack this kind of external existence. For example, if one experiences gustatory pleasure after eating a bite of peanut butter, there is nothing in the peanut butter that corresponds to its pleasantness; others find it unpleasant. Some emotions seem to fit this model as well. Prinz (2004) tries to argue that emotions do not represent secondary qualities (things like deliciousness, which depend on us), but this is a very controversial position with respect to emotional content. Finally, the approach faces another objection, which threatens hybrid theories as well. Informational semantics claims that content is determined by covariation between mental states and the world. But, on that approach, there is nothing about a given mental state that determines what it refers to – mental states are no more than arbitrary symbols (Fodor 1990). Therefore, it is irrelevant that emotional components are realized by bodily states and bodily perceptions (Shargel 2014). One could easily represent the same content without the bodily change, since the theory appeals to their information-processing characteristics and not their bodily character. Moreover, situations such as danger can result in different bodily reactions, ranging from flight to steadfast confrontation. If content were determined by covariation, the theory might render such differences semantically irrelevant; this is an embarrassing outcome for a theory that emphasizes embodiment, since such differences seem to correspond to distinct embodied construals of the precipitating events. The embodied appraisal theory tries to make bodily states the bearers of content, but, in the same gesture, it makes them irrelevant to content determination.

2 Emotional Content and Affordances

We want to turn now to another account of emotional content, which departs from these earlier proposals. Hybrid theories and the embodied appraisal theory both follow cognitive appraisal theories when it comes to

[1] For example, informational approaches have been criticized on the grounds that a given mental state (or bodily state) can have arbitrarily many causes, so information alone cannot settle which of these fix the meaning of the state, and which are false positives (Fodor 1990).

the content of emotions. While hybrid theories simply build in cognitive appraisals, the embodied appraisal theory assigns standard appraisal contents to embodied states. Both approaches give the impression that the bodily changes that take place are irrelevant when it comes to determining content. A recent alternative promises to get around this problem. Paul Griffiths and Andrea Scarantino (2009) have advanced the interesting proposal that emotions represent affordances. We will briefly describe the account and some of its advantages and disadvantages.

The notion of an affordance owes to psychologist of perception J. J. Gibson. Gibson (1986) argues that visual states represent more than shapes and locations of objects. Vision also informs us about possibilities for action. Thus, if we see a hammer, we not only see the length and orientation of its handle; we also see that it is graspable. Graspability is an interesting feature because it is relational. It is not intrinsic to the hammer. Rather it depends on aspects of the observer's body: hand aperture, the ability to close one's fingers, the presence of a prehensile thumb, and so on. It is a feature that depends on how the observer is embodied. To see an object as graspable may also recruit motor responses. One might spontaneously prepare to grasp a hammer because its shape is associated through learning with grasping (Grèzes 2003).

Griffiths and Scarantino notice that certain aspects of affordances lend themselves to a theory of emotional content. Emotions have long been recognized to have associated actions. When the body changes during an emotion, these changes are not arbitrary, but rather underlie what Nico Frijda (1986) calls an "action tendency." However, Frijda and the many others who make this observation have not suggested that the action tendency is part of what an emotion represents. This is where Griffiths and Scarantino come in. Griffiths (2004), for example, proposes that anger represents the fact that aggression is afforded, and shame represents that the acceptance of another person's dominance is afforded. Griffiths and Scarantino (2009) elaborate on this view. Instead of aggression, they propose that anger represents a retribution affordance, and they note that retribution can take many different forms – sulking, insulting, storming out, etc. – depending on the context.[2]

The affordance theory has clear advantages over some of the proposals surveyed previously. For one thing, affordances are a kind of object that

[2] The affordance theory is part of a broader theoretical model in which the authors emphasize the communicative impact of emotions. Sometimes we show anger, for example, in order to achieve an end. We will touch on this aspect of their account in the final section. Here we want to focus on the claim that emotions represent affordances.

depends on having a particular embodiment, and the perception of affordances characteristically involves bodily changes. Aggressing, sulking, and storming out are all physical activities. The bodily changes that take place when a person is angry are not arbitrarily related to these, but rather prepare the body to act. If emotions represent affordances, emotional embodiment bears a direct relationship to emotional content.

The affordance theory also provides theorists with the opportunity to develop an account of emotional content that avoids informational semantics. Affordances depend on physical abilities, and this invites an embodied approach to content determination. Affordances also bypass the need to posit a cognitive accompaniment, as in the case of hybrid theories, since they are recognized through embodied perception. We may perceive affordances by perceiving the physical abilities that determine them.

We think the affordance theory is going in the right direction, but it still faces some problems. For one thing, Gibson (1979) regards affordances as relational, but in some sense objective; they are invariant features of the environment out there to be perceived. Just like shape and location, affordances exist even when they go unnoticed. A hammer affords grasping even when it hasn't been seen. Embodied responses to a hammer play a role in our "picking up" on the affordance, but the affordance was already there. Changes in the body can alter affordances, on a Gibsonian account, but only when these are long-lasting changes that lead to new invariant relations. For example, after doing a lot of weight training, certain heavy objects might become liftable. But, in general, liftability is a function of one's physical traits, not one's occurrent states. For Gibson, a heavy object can have the property of liftability for a weightlifter even when she is occupied by some other task. A hammer is heftable even when we have no incentive to lift it. These are standing features of the world. Scarantino (2004) notices this aspect of affordances, but he also insists, perhaps departing from Gibson, that affordances can change with context. A tree, he notes, does not afford climbing for a squirrel if there is a barrier in the way. This kind of context sensitivity is fairly minimal, however. The example implies that any accessible tree within the squirrel's immediate environment affords climbing, even if the squirrel is currently foraging on the ground. Climbability can be instantiated independent of the animal's current activities.

With emotions things seem different. It would be absurd to say, for example, that there is an affordance to aggress every time one passes another person on the street. We might just as well say that there is an affordance to compliment every stranger about the shape of their ear lobes.

We posit emotional affordances to explain emotional motivation and behavior, so we must avoid adopting a conception of affordances that saddles us with these trivial entities. In fact, it doesn't even seem plausible to suppose that there is an aggression affordance when one is insulted. In the right mood, one might be totally unbothered by biting words. In such cases, one's body might remain docile in ways that are neither conducive to aggressing nor motivated to aggress. The emotional affordance – the entity with real explanatory value – seems to arise only when an actual transformation in the body takes place. The transformation enables the body to act, and it brings with it a motivation pull. In contrast, Gibsonian affordances are dispositional properties that need not have any command over us. Griffiths and Scarantino implicitly recognize this. In their fully developed theory, they note that emotional affordances can change dynamically in the course of a social interaction. But this feature of their account marks a contrast with Gibson's idea that affordances are environmental (or relational) invariants. Without further explanation, it is unclear whether affordances can play the role required by their theory.

There is also a further worry, which concerns an assumption that Griffiths and Scarantino share with most other approaches to emotional content. They think emotions are representational; emotions represent affordances. As we have noted, embodied emotional features facilitate actualizing these affordances, so there is a non-arbitrary connection between emotion and embodied responses. However, on their theory, that connection is still contingent. It is possible to represent the relevant affordances without any bodily change, and they do not explain why alterations in bodily features should change our representations of those affordances. In these ways, their affordance theory resembles other members of the appraisal theory family.

In summary, the affordance theory strikes us as a promising approach to the content of emotions, because it makes features of the body relevant to content determination. But the theory also faces objections about the way that it characterizes affordances, and about the contingent connection between representations and embodied features.

3 From Affordances to Enaction

We have raised concerns about some of the prevailing approaches to the content of emotions. Here is a brief summary. No-content views capture the intuitions that embodied responses are unlike conventional representations (in ways we will elaborate on), but they fail to fully explain the role that emotions play in modulating motivation and behavior. Hybrid views have difficulty justifying the union of cerebral and embodied elements, and do not make much use of the later. The embodied appraisal theory puts meaning into the embodied response, but it doesn't adequately explain the bodily aspects of meaning and relies on controversial semantic theories. Affordances address these last worries nicely, but they ultimately feature some disadvantages of the hybrid view. Since they still consider emotions to be representational states, they do not fully capture the nonrepresentational contributions of emotional embodiment. It would be good to find another approach.

One idea that has been emerging in the recent literature may fit the bill. It is the enactive approach to cognition (Colombetti 2014; Colombetti and Thompson 2008; Di Paolo and Jaegher 2010). Here we want to sketch a version of the view, along with some of its implications. The details of our approach will differ a bit from the existing enactive views. For example, we will not be endorsing extended cognition, emergence, or phenomenological methodology. In these respects, our account is a limited form of enactivism. In addition, we reject the thesis that enactivism is the best approach to cognition more generally; we think it is especially suitable for the emotions.

The enactive approach that we want to recommend takes inspiration from Francisco Varela and his colleagues, since we think he provides an attractive way to move beyond the affordance theory. Our focus will be on Varela's account of how minds make meaning (Varela 1991; Varela, Thompson, and Rosch 1991). Here the term "enaction" gives a good indication of the view. Two things need to be italicized. First, to "enact" is, for Varela, "to bring forth." Enaction brings things into existence. In this sense, enaction is ontological; it creates new things. Second, enaction involves action. We bring things into existence by doing something with our bodies. It is an embodied theory of cognition because mental activity is grounded in physical activity.

The notion of "bringing forth" is meant to contrast with standard accounts of representation. A key feature of standard representational approaches is that they assume that the world is pre-given, that there are mind-independent entities, category boundaries, properties, and relations waiting to be re-presented by symbols or models inside the mind. Enaction, in contrast, implies a kind of constructive process wherein an organism adds to its environment things that weren't there before mental processes kicked in. Theories of embodiment help us develop an account of how this construction takes place. How can we alter what exists in our world? According to Varela, we can do so through embodied activity.

We think these ideas lend themselves to explaining the emotions. First of all, we think emotions are embodied, in that they essentially involve bodily states, as well as inner processes that regulate these states. We also think the bodily states in question are related to action. Each emotional episode involves a pattern of bodily change that is conducive to specific kinds of action: fleeing, aggressing, withdrawing, and so on (Prinz 2004). We also think that emotional content is difficult to characterize in terms of a pre-given world. Against the idea that minds bring forth reality, critics argue that some features of the world exist independently of particular cognizers, and, against embodiment, critics offer examples of mental processes that can be carried out without specific changes in the body. Neither line of criticism is especially compelling in the case of emotions, however, which is our focus here. We think evidence supports the view that emotions are embodied (though, for reasons of space, we cannot discuss the evidence here), and we have raised doubts about the idea that emotions represent pre-given features of the world.

Putting these two features of enaction together – embodiment and bringing forth – we can now say, in broad strokes, why we think an enactive theory of emotion may outperform rivaling embodied theories. Like no-content views, the enactive approach rejects traditional theories of representation, but, unlike them, it asserts that embodied activities are, in some sense yet to be specified, meaning-giving. Unlike hybrid views, enaction does not posit cool cognitive states to explain emotional meaning, but rather locates meaning in embodied activity. For reasons that will become clearer shortly, the enactive view does so by making reference to actual bodily changes, and is thus more cohesive than the embodied appraisal view, which calls on covariation with things in the environment.

The enactive view most resembles an affordance view. As the term is often used, affordances are things that we perceive in virtue of aspects of our bodies. We see the graspability of a hammer because its handle has proportions that could be easily grasped by hands like ours. On most affordance theories, the perception of an affordance is occasioned by an actual motor plan: when a hammer is presented, we prepare to grasp. This looks like a case where meaning is created by physical activity. As we suggested, however, affordances are also often characterized as standing features of objects, which they have even when the affordances have not been noticed. Hammers are graspable even when unseen. For this reason, it is misleading to say affordances are created by our emotions, at least if we use the visual examples as an analogy. The affordance theory does much to improve on its rivals, by relating meaning more intimately to embodiment, but it faces this technical hurdle.

The enactive view promises to overcome that hurdle. Enactive content is said to be brought forth by activity. So it is not the kind of content that is in place prior to the emotion. But what might that content be, if it is not representational? This is a question that is difficult to answer without discussing some specific examples. We will do that in the next section. But, to get started, we want to offer a schematic suggestion of how emotions might bring forth meaning. Affordances are possibilities for action, but they are possibilities that are already in place. Emotions create new possibilities for action. The embodiment of an emotion makes new actions possible because it places the body into a configuration where it can perform certain actions more easily than it could have before. One might think this is just a quantitative difference: emotions make action easier. We think it is more than that. Prior to an emotion, there is a sense in which any action compatible with our physical constitution is possible. So that claim that a given action could take place is, to that degree, trivial. When an action is potentiated by an actual bodily change, certain courses of action go from being mere possibilities to being something akin to dynamic attractors. Epistemically, a potentiated action becomes a salient option, and, motivationally, a potentiated action has a kind of command over it. When the body prepares to act, we are *eo ipso* pulled toward certain lines of behavior. Motivation is immanent: it is not merely an injunction to act, through its motivational role, but a nascent kind of acting, as a constitutively embodied state – our bodies push and pull us.

All this suggests an important contrast between emotional content and Gibsonian affordances. In perception, affordances are properties that stand in place regardless of whether they are noticed. Affordances are, thus, dispositional, and, consequently, they are not motivating. Emotional content differs on both of these dimensions. This is the difference between possibility and potentiation: Gibsonian affordances merely require possible action, while emotional content requires nascent action. Emotional content can still be expressed using the language of affordances provided this difference with the perceptual case is made explicit: the affordances associated with emotions are state-dependent (they typically arise only once the emotion has been initiated) and imperatival (they motivate action). In contrast, the affordances in Gibson's scheme are state-independent and inert. Thus, we embrace Griffiths and Scarantino's appeal to affordances, but find it useful to develop the view by making these differences explicit. The enactive approach gives us the tools for doing precisely this.

State-dependent, imperatival affordances have the attractive feature of being bound up with embodiment. These affordances arise only when the body undergoes perturbations, and they motivate because the perturbations push and pull us. This offers a more intimate link between content and bodily change than can be found in traditional embodied theories. It also implies that emotional meaning is not given in the world, but rather constructed, which is a satisfying result.

With this schematic characterization in place, we will now consider a range of different emotions, both social and nonsocial, to illustrate how the enactive view works in greater detail. We will then consider some implications.

4 Putting the Enactive Approach to Work

Emotions are often put into two classes, social and nonsocial. Here we want to give illustrations of both. Griffiths (1997) has argued that social and nonsocial emotions do not form a natural kind, and the affordance theory presented by Griffiths and Scarantino takes social emotions as their primary focus. We think that both social and nonsocial emotions are amenable to a unified analysis on the enactive view, at least with respect to content. We will not attempt to show that all emotions can be explained on our account, but by giving examples in both categories, we hope to illustrate its breadth.

We will begin with an example that illustrates the state-dependent nature of emotion enaction in a nonsocial context. A swimmer far from shore begins to struggle with a strong undertow, and realizes that it will take every bit of strength she has to make it back. In virtue of entering a state of fear, her body mobilizes more forcefully to support strenuous action, helping her return safely. This bodily change has important effects. Prior to the fear, the ocean seemed like a place to enjoy a swim, not a site of escape. The bodily response makes escape salient by actually compelling a flight response. Moreover, the physical changes actually enable the swimmer to traverse waters that would have been prohibitively strenuous before her fear set in. So both what is possible for her and what she is motivated to do have changed. In that respect it seems like her fear altered affordances for her. However, the ordinary concept of affordance does not permit this sort of state-dependent change. Gibsonian affordances are stable possibilities of action. Only through long-term training could she make an enduring change in what waters can be traversed, and, even if our swimmer has undergone such training, the ocean would afford recreational swimming to her, not escape. Fear increases her powers and changes the action type that presents itself to her. It is a temporary solution to a temporary problem, which changes her relationship to the environment.

In our second example, a dancer is thrilled when the DJ plays one of his favorite songs. Like fear, joy mobilizes bodily resources, so he can dance harder and longer. Other types of action are available to him: he could get a drink, take a break, or even go home and get some sleep. Instead, his joyful bodily activation has an imperative force that makes him dance to that song. It gives him extra stamina, compels him to carry on, and thereby makes dancing a compelling choice. Without joy, dancing would not seem feasible any longer.

Fear mobilizes resources to make dangers more escapable, and joy mobilizes resources to make opportunities more achievable. Sometimes, however, there is not much to be done, either because nothing is wanting in the case of relaxed pleasure, or, in the case of sadness, because one has suffered a loss that cannot be repaired. The adaptive response in the latter case is to avoid spending bodily resources in a futile attempt to achieve what is (temporarily at least) out of reach. When sad we reserve bodily resources in a way that changes affordances. Our bodies shift into a mode that makes any action more effortful, and that functions as an imperative to disengage, withdraw, or remain lethargic.

The enactive view can also be applied to social emotions. Here we take inspiration from Griffiths and Scarantino (2009), though we also want to emphasize the imperatival, state-dependent nature of emotional affordances in these cases. We can start with the example of joy in athletes. Joy often arises in nonsocial contexts, but, as Griffiths and Scarantino point out, there is also a social form of joy – a joy that is dependent on doing something that is valued in the eyes of others. We think it useful to mark this distinction by using the word "pride" for the social case. Griffiths and Scarantino also point to research showing that victorious athletes smile only when observed (see Fernandez-Dols and Ruiz-Belda 1997). An athlete's smile makes clear to her audience that she is happy with her accomplishments. By signaling this, she is mobilizing resources that can accomplish significant social benefits. Her smile transforms neutral observers into potential allies, since smiles are contagious, and we all want to collaborate with people who are on a path to success. Social emotions are not mere representations of social relations; they bring forth new social affordances, both for the one having the emotion and those with whom she interacts. The athlete's emotion creates a new relation with her audience that allows bond-building. Forging social connections becomes an imperative, and the bodily changes, including the expressive component, contribute to that possibility.

Displays of anger follow a similar pattern. They signal preparation to aggressively further interests or values, which rallies support from those whose interests or values align, and discourages opposition from others. Social displays create new social realities, and they do so by credibly publicizing the features that are familiar from the nonsocial cases: the creation of state-dependent, imperative affordances through bodily mobilization. Anger mobilizes the body for aggressive action. This can transform affordances regarding the ones who provoked a state of anger. It would be absurd to suppose that all people at all times afford being aggressed against. Though physically possible, we rarely feel motivated to attack others. It doesn't even make sense to say that people afford aggression when they act offensively; some react to offenses with aggression, but others with avoidance, submission, dependency, concern, disarming affection, bemused indifference, and so on. Anger does not pick up on the action that was demanded by the offense, but rather creates the demand; it temporarily transforms those who provoked anger, and potentially innocent others whom one happens to encounter while angry, into potential targets of aggression. Expression signals this, and action potentiation motivates it, thus creating new social relations that were not in place before the emotion.

These examples are just rough sketches to illustrate how the idea of state-dependent imperatival affordances can apply to nonsocial and social emotions. Our goal with these cases is not to provide precise analyses, but rather to give an idea of how enactive content works. Instead of representing core relational themes such as danger, loss, and offensiveness, emotions bring in new possibilities of action and introduce a kind of to-be-doneness that temporarily alters affordance space.

5 Implications of Emotional Enactivism

Having presented some examples, we now want to consider some implications of the enactive approach. We will begin by indicating how coming to this view relates to our own earlier commitments in emotion theory. In so doing, we hope to illustrate what's at stake for those who are already attracted to embodied approaches to emotions. Then we will consider some implications that bear on widely shared commitments in the literature. We think an enactive approach to emotional content may require the reconsideration of some deeply held views. Finally, we take up the issue of emotions and ontology. This is a central feature of our account, which we want to bring out more explicitly.

In previous work, both of us have been committed to embodied approaches to emotions. As noted, one of us has defended an embodied appraisal view, which treats emotions as perceptions of bodily states that carry information about core relational themes (Prinz 2004). This account shares features with enactive approaches (see Colombetti and Thompson 2008), but also faces objections (see earlier in this chapter and Colombetti 2014). If our enactivist approach is on the right track, the embodied appraisal theory must be revised. First, it is wrong about the content of emotions: rather than representing core relational themes, such as danger and loss, emotions represent state-dependent, imperatival affordances. In principle, one could define core relational themes broadly enough to accommodate this revision. A core relational theme is an organism–environment relation that bears of well-being. State-dependent, imperatival affordances satisfy this definition. Still, loss and danger seem to be response-independent properties; one can be in danger, for example, without realizing it. One of us (Prinz 2004) did embrace this point, and denied that emotional content is response-dependent. We now think this is a mistake, since emotional content depends on our responses. In fact, we think this dependency goes even deeper than the dependency found in standard secondary qualities, such as colors. If Locke (1690/1979) is right, colors are powers to cause sensations; and such powers exist in things even when they are not having their effects. Emotional content is not dependent on our responses in this dispositional sense; it depends on an organism actually being in an emotional state (state-dependence is stronger than response-dependence). Moreover, the content is imperatival. It has a kind of to-be-doneness, which standard secondary qualities lack. One can define terms such as danger and loss to reflect these two features. One can stipulate, for example, that something counts as a loss only when it is perceived affectively in a way that motivates certain kind of coping strategies. So the revised account can still be characterized as an embodied appraisal view, but these differences in content are significant.

Another departure from Prinz (2004) concerns the correlates of emotional states. In that earlier work, emotions were said to supervene on brain states in somatic input systems. The peripheral nervous system and body were excluded. Enactivists like to argue for a stronger form of embodiment, according to which "mental states" can include actual changes in the body. We are inclined to agree with this. Drawing a principled distinction between brain and body is difficult and tends to promote a kind of dualistic thinking. Also, we explained the motivational aspect of emotions by saying that the body is engaged in activities when we are in emotional states.

Emotions are a kind of doing. This idea is easiest to capture if we treat the body as part of the emotion. That also allows us to say, in social cases, that others can directly perceive the emotions we are in, which is one way in which emotions literally change extant relations in the world. One could stipulate that emotions are internal, but we think that would be both contrived and unhelpful. A theory of how emotions work, and how they come to have their content, is easiest to state if emotions include both internal and external bodily changes.

This brings us to the prior work of Shargel. Shargel (2014) picks up on the ideas in William James's contemporary, Carl Lange. James and Lange are said to have innovated the embodied approach to emotions independently around the same time (James 1884; Lange 1885), hence the popular label, the James-Lange theory. But Shargel observes a subtle difference; James says emotions are perceptions of bodily changes and Lange seems to suggest that emotions encompass actual changes in the body. The enactive approach defended here fits nicely with that Langean thesis, which Shargel also endorses. In following Lange, Shargel (2015) also raises doubts about the idea that emotions are representational states. In what follows, we will describe a way in which our enactive account may qualify as nonrepresentational. At the same time, the enactive account does commit to the view that emotions have content. This, and the specific content proposed, require extending the views expressed in Lange and endorsed by Shargel.

Before we address the difference between content and representation, we want to draw attention to a few features of enactive content that might require revision in many emotion theories, whether embodied or otherwise. First, the enactive view allows a more parsimonious view of what Griffiths (2004) calls Machiavellian emotions. Theorists in the transactional tradition have emphasized cases where emotions serve as strategic moves in an ongoing negotiation. Fernández-Dols and Ruiz-Belda's (1997) athlete example is relevant here, or Hinde's (1985) example of birds that display anger but quickly flee. Griffiths and Scarantino (2009) argue that we cannot understand these cases without locating each emotional response in the context of the ongoing, open-ended transaction. However, these cases complicate representational accounts of emotional content, even for their own affordance view. The agent enters the emotion that is the best next move for advancing that agent's interests, not the emotion that best represents some features of reality. As Griffiths (2004) acknowledges, this makes the emotion seem insincere. After all, if the emotion is sincere, but still misrepresents reality, then the agent's strategic move to enter that emotional state requires self-delusion. Transactional emotions, for the representationalist, are therefore either Machiavellian or Orwellian.

The enactive view allows us to avoid this dilemma. In the enactive view, the content of an emotion is simply a function of the affordances it enacts. Emotions produce the same affordances as usual in the transactional cases, plus additional social affordances that are determined by the specific circumstances of the transaction. Hinde's angry bird really is mobilized to fight – there is nothing false about the mobilization. The goal behind the mobilization is to intimidate the rival, affording greater access to valuable resources. However, there is a big difference between mobilizing to fight in order to alter social affordances and actually initiating a fight with a stronger rival. If the attempt to intimidate fails, it is only sensible to enter a state of fear, redeploying resources to afford more effective flight. On our view, it is sensible to alter emotional states as a negotiation develops, because different stages of the negotiation require different affordances. We can explain this progression without implying insincerity or self-delusion.

With our revised view of emotional content, it is necessary to reconsider associated properties such as intensity. Within a representational framework, there are two natural ways to conceive of the strength of an emotion: as the degree of credence in the representation, or as the magnitude of the features perceived. The former seems more appropriate because it corresponds more closely to the strength of other states, such as belief, with a mind-to-world direction of fit. A strong belief is a belief we hold with greater credence. However, strong credence in a minor danger does not explain the occurrence of a strong fear. The enactive theory of emotions has a very simple explanation of intensity. Emotions modify state-dependent, imperatival affordances, so a strong emotion modifies affordances more strongly. Strong fear mobilizes the body more thoroughly to enhance escape, which leads to a greater imperative to escape.

It is commonplace to say that emotions have two kinds of objects: formal and particular (de Sousa 1987; Kenny 1963). The formal object is, roughly, the type of self–world relationship that any token of a given emotion type would represent (for example, anger might concern offensiveness), and the particular object is the specific thing toward which a given emotion is directed (for example, anger about a new government policy toward immigrants). On the enactive view, this distinction may break down to some degree. Once the body is engaged, it is liable to create new relations to a wide range of things that an organism happens to encounter. For example, when something makes a person angry, the anger tends to leak, and the person may lash out at those who did not cause the anger in the first place. Plus, in expressing anger, a person creates a palpable impression of hostility that can be picked up by others, temporarily altering social relations.

Such diffusion could be described as a kind of mistake, and in some cases it does harm – a person might regret an aggressive response to someone who did not cause the initial state of anger. But it is also a pervasive aspect of how emotions work, and the broad relational changes that take place are perfectly real and demand explanation. Shargel (2015) uses this observation to challenge the claim that emotions have intentional content. The enactive approach suggests another way to put the point: emotions usually can't be confined to having precisely circumscribed particular objects. They have a kind of content that spreads, because the affordances themselves spread. The content doesn't impact everything (anger will not be extended to things that are too distant in space and time), but it impacts more than the objects that elicit the emotion. In fact, there are good reasons for this content to spread. When anger alters our bodily mobilization, the effects on the efficacy of our actions aren't limited to any particular object. Imperatival content should have the same broad scope.

Just as we vary emotional states in sync with changes in social dynamics, as in our discussion of transactional cases, we manage the scope of our emotional responses in accordance with social norms. Although our enactive theory does not feature emotions with particular intentional objects, our social norms sometimes do. In order to comply with these norms, we often attribute an intentional object to our emotions. When our anger threatens to violate social norms by impacting someone who was not responsible for making us angry, we respond by selectively suppressing the imperatival character of the emotion so that it does not impact that person. This attribution does not reflect representational content, but it has instrumental value in such cases. We think that emotion theory may need to abandon or revise the notion of particular objects to reflect these facts about how emotions operate (cf. Shargel 2015).

This brings us to another issue, which is the rationality of emotions. On many theories, emotions have a conventional kind of content, which can be assessed for something like truth or fit. Emotions aim to represent relations with the world, and they may do so accurately or inaccurately. Emotions can be criticized as unwarranted or irrational, when they arise in situations that they fail to fit. The enactive account is consistent with the possibility that emotions may go wrong, but there is a way in which it also invites rethinking about these issues. Consider fear. Fear, we have said, brings an imperatival affordance into being – something that might be glossed in terms of escapability together with an impulse to flight. Along with standard theories, we grant that such a state might arise under conditions that, objectively speaking, do not warrant flight. The enactive account can borrow from other approaches when trying to articulate grounds for saying that certain emotional episodes are inapt. At the same time, there is a way in which enactive content is self-fulfilling. The property of escapability is brought forth by the emotion. It is really there. If one has a fear response to something benign, such as a harmless snake, the emotion will still cause escapability to be instantiated in the situation. In this sense, the emotion is not misrepresenting anything. It can't misrepresent anything. It is bringing an action-related property into existence. One can be criticized for false beliefs about the dangerousness of the snake, or for acting in ways that are unnecessary, but the emotion itself does not misrepresent. This differs from standard theories, which suppose that fear represents something like danger. In addition, the enactive theory may introduce the possibility of another kind of irrationality, which relates more directly to action. In some cases, emotions potentiate behaviors that we cannot carry out. Fear when constrained would be an example. In such a case, standard theories would say the fear is perfectly rational (chances are a person is in danger if constrained). But constraints prevent fleeability, so an emotion that potentiates flight cannot fully succeed in bringing that property into being. This, for us, would be a kind of misfire – a failure to enact a property. We think such misfires deserve consideration in discussions of how emotions can go wrong. We will not develop the point here, but flag it as a direction for future work.

Now we come to the issue of representation. The originators of the enactive approach to cognition make the provocative claim that mental states are not representational (Varela et al. 1991). Most cognitive scientists embrace a representational theory of the mind, according to which behavior is underwritten by mental representations – inner states that aim to represent things, features, events, or states of affairs in the world. The wholesale rejection of mental representation is a radical view, and it is not one that we will endorse. But the view does have plausibility when applied to emotions. If the enactive account of emotional content is right, then emotions are not in the business of informing organisms about external features of the world. They do not tell us about something that is already there, prior to the emotion itself. Rather, they bring something into being. This bringing forth can be regarded as a kind of content: that which is brought forth is a kind of embodied interpretation. When a body prepares for flight in response to a predator, it presents the predator as something that demands escape, and had it prepared, instead, for aggression, it would represent the predator as demanding confrontation. Like other kinds of mental content, enactive content also drives action and decision-making, and can, thus, play a role in explaining behavior. The term "content" here means something like significance for the organism. The term "representation," in contrast, often carries the further assumption that there is something out there in the world that can be represented by the organism. On this use, the reference relation is like pointing or labeling; it implies a fixed and independent object. Enactive content is not like this. It is more like making or doing. It creates something that wasn't there to begin with. This can be expressed by saying that emotions are not representations (or, more conservatively, they differ from how mental representations are standardly understood).

Much more can be said about the topic of representation. For instance, it raises questions about whether emotions have truth conditions and questions about the content of judgments (e.g., moral judgments or aesthetic judgments) that may have emotions as component parts. We will not take up these issues here, but we do want to end by drawing attention to a related issue. The contrast between representing and making underscores the point that emotions bring properties into being. This has been a repeated refrain in our discussion, but our emphasis so far has been on the semantic implications. The notion of enacting or bringing forth also bears on questions of ontology. There are two ontological implications that we would like to emphasize. First, whereas representational mental states are said to register properties that already exist, enactive content is brought into being. Emotions are, thus, adding to the furniture of the world. Without emotions, the properties that they enact would not exist. This is an interesting case where minds construct reality. Second, the kinds of properties that emotions bring into being are quite unusual. As noted, they are neither primary qualities nor secondary qualities, as these terms are usually understood. Nor are they mere affordances, as that term has been used in accounts of perceptual content. Their imperatival character means that they are properties that have a built-in to-be-doneness. This can be thought of as a kind of normativity. It may be that other mental states also enact such properties (pains, desire, and evaluative attitudes, for example). It may also be these other states enact such properties only because they constitutively involve emotions. We need not settle that here. The crucial point is that enaction allows us to articulate the existence of a kind of property with interesting characteristics. These properties play an important role for many organisms, and they warrant philosophical reflection. The enactive theory, unlike other accounts of emotional content, draws attention to this aspect of ontology, and that may be its greatest source of interest. On the enactive theory emotions furnish the world with normative properties. This ontological implication is easily missed on other theories of emotional content.

We leave the elaboration of these implications to future occasions. Our goal here has been to motivate and articulate an enactive approach to emotion content. We think this approach has advantages over rival theories, and some surprising implications – psychological, semantic, and ontological. Our enactive theory leaves out aspects of enactivism that some other authors have emphasized, and we stop short of the view that all cognition is enactive. But our theory builds on this tradition, which is sometimes dismissed as excessively radical. We have tried to show that aspects of enactivism lend themselves to emotions. Taking enactivism seriously may deepen our understanding of what emotions are and why they matter.

Acknowledgments

We would like to thank Fabrice Teroni and Hichem Naar for extremely detailed and helpful comments.

CHAPTER 7

The Perceptibility of Emotion

Joel Smith

Perceptibility is the claim that suitably placed and endowed observers can perceive others' emotions. In §1 I distinguish *Perceptibility* from some other claims with which it is liable to be confused. In §2 I set out a first constraint on *Perceptibility*: that the perception of emotion is only possible via the perception of some distinct entity, paradigmatically an expression of the emotion in question. This rules out views according to which we perceive others' emotions 'directly'. In §3 I set out a second constraint: that *Perceptibility* must respect the fact that an explanatory relation exists between emotion and emotional expression. This rules out views according to which we can perceive emotions via their expressions because the former are grounded in the latter. In §4, by far the longest section, I set out a third constraint: that the claim that we perceive entities of a certain sort must cohere with the most plausible account of the ontological category that such entities fall into. I go on to argue that since there is reason to accept the claim that emotions are states and expressions are processes, we must reject the view that we can perceive emotions via their expressions because the latter are parts of the former. In §5 I propose a version of *Perceptibility* that meets these constraints. This is the view that we can perceive emotions via their expressions because the latter are manifestations of the former.

1 Perceptual Accounts of Emotion Recognition

Perceptibility is a claim that may form a part of a perceptual account of emotion recognition.[1] Consider a situation in which *A* perceives *B*, who is screaming in terror, and, on this basis, judges *B* to be afraid. Perceptual accounts of emotion recognition are united in the claim that, in suitable

[1] For perceptual accounts of emotion recognition (or mindreading more generally), see Cassam 2007: ch. 5; Dretske 1973; Green 2007, 2010; McDowell 1982; McNeill 2012; Stout 2010.

circumstances, this belief can be grounded non-inferentially, by the perceptual experience itself. But this can be fleshed out in a number of non-equivalent ways, among which we can distinguish between the following:

> ***Perceptibility***: *A* perceives *B*'s fear
> ***Perceptibility-that***: *A* perceives that *B* is afraid
> ***Perceptibility-as***: *A* perceives *B* as afraid
> ***Appears***: *B* appears afraid to *A*

The relations between these are controversial (Dretske 1969; Maund 2003). In particular, some will deny that *Perceptibility-as* and *Appears* really represent distinct claims. Whatever one supposes about that question, though, it seems reasonable to suppose that *Perceptibility* is not equivalent to any one of the others. To see this, consider what I will take to be the uncontroversial claim that *A* can perceive *B*'s screaming. That *A* perceives *B*'s screaming does not entail that *B* appears to *A* to be screaming, for she might appear to be singing. Nor, for the same reason, does it entail that *A* perceives *B* as screaming. Further, on the supposition both that *A* takes her perceptual experience at face value and that *B* appears to be singing, it would not be true that *A* perceives that *B* is screaming. Nor is there an entailment in the other direction. From the fact that *A* perceives that *B* is screaming, it does not follow that she perceives *B*'s screaming, since she may perceive that *B* is screaming by way of perceiving her shadow. From the fact that *A* perceives *B* as screaming, or that *B* appears to *A* to be screaming, it does not follow that *A* perceives *B*'s screaming, for *A*'s perceptual experience may be illusory in this respect. It seems, then, that *Perceptibility* is not equivalent to any one of the other claims and that if *Perceptibility* is to play a role in a perceptual account of emotion recognition, it will be a role distinctive to it.[2]

That we can perceive others' emotions is a claim that has recently been advanced by a number of philosophers. Here are three examples:

> Not only can we know of one another's emotions; in some cases we can also literally perceive them. (Green 2007: 89)

> We somehow directly see another's mental life, including their thoughts, emotions, intentions, etc. (Krueger 2012: 150)

> What displays or manifestations of the anger do is to *reveal* his state of mind without *being* his state of mind; one perceives his anger by perceiving displays of it. (Cassam 2007: 165)

[2] I defend a version of *Perceptibility-as* in (Smith 2010), a version of *Appears* in (Smith 2015), and a version of *Perceptibility-that* in (Smith 2016).

In each case is articulated a perceptual account of emotion recognition (or mindreading more generally) that endorses something like *Perceptibility*. It is with these claims that I shall be concerned.

A number of factors might motivate defenders of a perceptual account of mindreading to adopt *Perceptibility*. First, we should not downplay the fact that we do actually speak this way. There is nothing more natural than to say that we see the fear in someone's eyes or the joy in their smile, that we hear the disgust in someone's voice, and so on. If we are interested in preserving surface appearances, then it may seem that a defence of *Perceptibility* is the right way to go.

Second, since 'perceives' is factive, if *A* perceives *B*'s fear, it follows that *B* is afraid. Since many defenders of perceptual accounts of mindreading are interested, ultimately, in our *knowledge* of others' psychological states, and knowledge requires truth, this fact can make *Perceptibility* seem attractive. More attractive, perhaps, than claims couched in terms of the non-factive 'perceives-as' or 'appears'.

Third, it is plausible to suppose that perceiving is non-inferential and at least relatively immune from top-down effects (cf. the papers in Zeimbekis and Raftopoulos, 2015). An answer to the question of whether *A* perceives *o* need not refer to *A*'s beliefs or conceptual capacities. It is at least debatable whether the same can be said regarding the question of whether *A* perceives that *o* is *F*, the question of whether *A* perceives *o* as *F*, and the question of whether *o* appears *F* to *A*. Non-inferentiality is typically deemed crucial to perceptual knowledge and, thereby, perceptual accounts of mindreading. In this vein, McNeill (2012) argues that a successful defence of *Perceptibility-that* actually depends on *Perceptibility*.

Combining these features, as it does, *Perceptibility* might seem to be the strongest claim that a proponent of a perceptual account of mindreading might seek to defend. In what follows I will not further consider the motivations for or significance of *Perceptibility*.[3] At the very least, though, we have reason to determine whether it is a plausible view.

2 Emotion Perception Is Indirect

The quotation from Cassam highlights a puzzle for *Perceptibility*, one that points towards a constraint on an acceptable account. It is, let us suppose,

[3] I outline what I take to be some limitations of the claim in Smith (2015).

unproblematic that one can perceive emotional expressions.[4] Indeed, the perception of emotional expressions is the paradigm case to which defenders of *Perceptibility* appeal. We say, after all, that we see the fear *in* the expression. Such emotional expressions, however, are evidently not identical to emotions. Rather, they express those emotions. But if an emotional expression is not identical to an emotion, as Cassam explicitly claims, we need to know how it can be that the perception of the expression amounts to the perception of the emotion. How can *A*'s perceiving *B*'s screaming amount to her perceiving *B*'s fear?[5]

Defenders of *Perceptibility* must claim, then, as Cassam does, that it is possible to perceive one thing by, or in virtue of, perceiving another. In particular, they must claim that one can perceive an emotion in virtue of perceiving its expression, despite the fact that these are not identical. This is to say that there is a sense in which the perception of others' emotions must be indirect. One sees someone's fear in virtue of seeing their facial or other bodily expression. The converse is not true: one sees someone's joy *because* one sees their smile, but one does not see their smile *because* one sees their joy.

The claim that emotion perception is indirect due to its resting on expression perception must be distinguished from the claim that emotion perception is indirect due to its resting on the perception of representations or other psychological entities. There is no suggestion in the foregoing considerations of the 'indirect realist' theory of perception (although there are parallels to be drawn with Jackson's (1977: ch. 1) view). Rather, the claim is that one perceives one aspect of a person (her emotions) in virtue of perceiving others (the bodily behaviour that expresses them).

Some defenders of *Perceptibility* claim that one can 'directly perceive' the emotions of others (e.g. Gallagher 2008). If by this they mean to deny the preceding point, then their positions are, in that respect at least, implausible. That some philosophers have thought that *Perceptibility* is false (e.g. Jacob 2011) is testament to the fact that we see others' emotions, at most, indirectly. Were the emotions of others seen directly, in just the same way as are expressions of emotion, say, then there would be no more temptation to deny *Perceptibility* than there is to deny that one can see the smile of

4 I argue later that emotional expressions are dynamic entities that occur over time. As such, the claim that they can be perceived, whilst taken by many as a phenomenological datum, is not without difficulties. For discussion of the sorts of issue that arise with respect to the perception of dynamic entities, see Phillips (2010).

5 Cf. Jacob's dilemma, 'either another's overt bodily expressions do constitute her emotional or affective experiences or they do not. If they do not, then clearly by perceiving another's expressive behavior, one does not thereby perceive the other's emotional or affective experience. But if they do, then it is quite unclear how the . . . model can distance itself from behaviorism' (Jacob 2011: 531).

another. That is, there would be no temptation at all. If we are seeking to defend the manifest image of our awareness of the emotional life of others, then we must recognise that we perceive others' emotions in virtue of perceiving their bodily behaviour and, paradigmatically, their expressive behaviour. The question is not *whether* the perception of emotion is indirect, but *how* it is. That is, what we want to know is what relation holds between emotion and expression such that it can be true that one perceives the former by perceiving the latter.

3 Emotions Explain Emotional Expressions

If asked to explain why someone is smiling, we might respond that they are smiling because they are happy; if asked why a person is scowling, we might cite their anger; and so on. In short, emotions explain expressions. This can be expanded in two ways. On the first, emotions explain their expressions at least in part because they cause them: Joy explains smiling as cause explains effect. On the second, the explanation is of the non-causal variety typically referred to as 'grounding' (Fine 2012). We often use the term 'because' in non-causal contexts, for example I am in pain because my c-fibres are firing. On this second view, joy explains smiling as ground explains grounded. Both of these relations – causation and grounding – are asymmetric. Thus, whichever way one fleshes out the view, the point is that emotions explain expressions, but not vice versa.

I propose this as a part of our ordinary folk conception of the relation between emotion and emotional expression. It can, of course, be challenged. For example, some subscribe to an account of emotions as feelings of bodily reactions to stimuli (James 1884). According to this view, the standard picture of emotions as explaining, causally or otherwise, emotional expressions gets things exactly backwards. Despite our ordinary talk seemingly presupposing the opposite, it is in fact the smile that explains the joy, the frown that explains the anger, and so on. This is not the place to argue against the Jamesian view of the relation between emotion and emotional expression. The view has been criticised extensively elsewhere (e.g. Deonna and Teroni 2012a). I just add that the view is inconsistent with most accounts of what it is that makes a piece of behaviour an expression of emotion (e.g. Green 2007).

I will simply assume the falsity of the Jamesian picture, and the truth of the common-sense claim that emotions explain expressions.[6] This claim

[6] See Pickard (2003) for a Jamesian account that discusses some issues closely related to those that follow.

places a constraint on *Perceptibility*. If emotions are perceptible, they are so in virtue of the perceptibility of their expressions. Our question is what relation, holding between emotion and expression, could explain this. Given that, as mentioned previously, grounding is a relation that supports explanation, one might be tempted to suppose that grounding will do the work here. That is, one might point out that one can perceive grounded entities by perceiving their grounds.[7] So, for example, one might perceive a city by perceiving a group of streets, buildings, and so on. The idea would be that the existence of the city is grounded in the existence of its streets, houses, etc. Another example, somewhat closer to our present concern, would be the claim that an appropriately situated neuroscientist could see someone's pain in virtue of seeing the firing of c-fibres.

The fact that emotions explain their expressions constrains *Perceptibility* and it does so in such a way as to rule out the possibility that one may perceive an emotion in virtue of perceiving the expressions that ground it. For this proposal gets the explanatory connection back to front. If a grounding relation exists between emotions and their expressions, it is the former that ground, and so explain, the latter. But one cannot perceive grounding entities by way of perceiving that which they ground. I do not perceive the buildings in virtue of perceiving the city, or the c-fibres in virtue of perceiving the pain. Of course, it may be that there are cases in which I perceive both the ground and the grounded, but, insofar as I perceive the former, it is not because I perceive the latter. Grounding, it seems, is not the relation that the defender of *Perceptibility* is looking for.

4 Emotions, Expressions and the Part–Whole Relation

A general and entirely plausible constraint on *Perceptibility* is that claims about the scope of perceptual experience, about what we perceive, should be sensitive to ontology. That is, a claim that we perceive entities of a certain sort must cohere with the most plausible account of the ontological category that such entities fall into. In this way, ontology may constrain what we may feasibly claim can be perceived. Thus, whatever relation accounts for the possibility of perceiving an emotion via perceiving its expression must be consistent with the best available account of the

[7] This may seem like an odd suggestion if, as many think, grounding is a relation between facts. Since my concern is not to make any positive claims about grounding, I will allow that there is a legitimate sense in which all manner of entities (objects, properties, processes) may ground and be grounded in others.

ontology of emotion and expression. This innocuous constraint, I will argue, rules out a popular view.

a The Part-Whole View

Some defenders of *Perceptibility* assert that the relation that enables one to perceive an emotion by perceiving its expression is the part–whole relation. That is, they claim that expressions are parts of emotions, and that, quite generally, one can perceive a whole by perceiving one of its parts. So,

> I defend the view that some mental states and processes – or at least some *parts* of mental states and processes – are at times visible, capable of being directly perceived by others. This is because some forms of expressive behaviour constitute proper parts of some mental phenomena. (Krueger 2012: 151)

> In some cases we perceive emotions by means of part-whole perception . . . a facial signature of anger is a characteristic component of anger. (Green 2007: 89)

This 'part-whole view' combines two claims and derives a third: we can perceive emotional expressions; emotional expressions are parts of emotions; so we can perceive emotions. Thus is *Perceptibility* vindicated.[8]

Let us assume that we can see objects in virtue of seeing their parts. Some might hold that in every case in which we see an object, we do so by way of seeing one of its parts, namely its facing surface (cf. Jackson 1977: ch. 1). One need not endorse that claim, however, to suppose that one can on occasion see an object by seeing only a part of it, for example in cases in which it is partly occluded.[9] For the sake of argument, we can also assume that this claim is true for any other sensory modalities for which *Perceptibility* might want to be asserted.

The success of the part-whole view rests on the plausibility of the claim that emotional expressions, for example screaming, are parts of emotions, for example fear. Such a way of speaking is encouraged by certain approaches to emotion taken within the cognitive sciences where, as

[8] For an earlier formulation of the view, see Tormey (1971: ch. 2).

[9] Green's formulation employs the phrase 'characteristic component'. On his view, it is not possible to perceive an object by perceiving just any old part; only certain parts will do. On his definition, a characteristic component is a part the perception of which justifies one in inferring the existence of the whole (2007: 86). This isn't really elaborated much further, although he is clear that what counts as a characteristic component is relative to context. I won't be concerned with this issue but will simply assume that if expressions are parts of emotions, then they meet whatever conditions there are on being the *right sort* of part.

Scherer says, 'there is now increasing consensus on a componential approach to emotion' (2009: 1307). For example, in their introduction to the psychology of emotion, Parkinson and Coleman speak for many:

> Emotion is conceived as a syndrome of more or less integrated components usually including the following four factors: cognitive appraisals, bodily reactions, action tendencies, and expressive movements. (Parkinson and Colman 1995: xii)[10]

Such componential accounts might be thought to lend support to the part-whole view. Indeed, this element of Green's perceptual account of mindreading relies on the view, which he takes to be supported by cognitive scientific work, in particular that of Ekman, that 'the basic emotions are complex, coordinated, and automated' (2007: 88), including expression as a part. It can seem, then, that the part-whole view is on solid ground.

b Dynamic Entities, Static Entities and the Parts

The following line of argument can be mounted against the part-whole view: if something is part of a static entity, it is itself static. Emotions are static. Expressions, however, are not static, but dynamic. It follows that componentialism is false; expressions are not parts of emotions. From this it follows that the part-whole view fails; perceiving an expression does not, via part-whole perception, enable us to perceive an emotion.

Each element of this argument requires some elaboration, and I begin with the distinction between static and dynamic entities. The most familiar way in which this distinction is made, and one that I rely on, is that these two sorts of entity differ with respect to the way in which each occupies time. This can be summarised by saying that dynamic, but not static, entities occur or happen. As things that occur, dynamic entities are extended in time, either taking or going on for a certain period of time. Static entities, on the other hand, are not extended in time; rather they persist through time. My travelling from Manchester to London takes time, my being on the train does not take time; rather it persists or obtains for an amount of time. The former is a dynamic entity, unfolding over time through the happening of successive phases; the latter is a static entity that I instantiate for the duration of that process. This is a difference in what Steward (1997) calls an entity's 'temporal shape'.

[10] Also see Scherer (1987, 2001).

The category of dynamic entities includes events and processes.[11] The category of static entities includes properties or states, and property instances or tropes. For the most part in what follows, the differences between entities that fall within the broad categories of the static and dynamic will not much matter, my concern being with what unites the categories, i.e. the difference between occurring over time (or at a time), on the one hand, and persisting through time, on the other.

How are we to determine whether any given type of entity is static or dynamic? This is a specific instance of the more general question of how we are to determine the ontological category of some entity. There are, no doubt, various ways to proceed. However, here I adopt a thought of Austin's on the relation between linguistic and metaphysical distinctions. He writes that:

> Our common stock of words embodies all the distinctions men have found worth drawing, and the connexions they have found worth marking, in the lifetimes of many generations: these surely are likely to be more numerous, more sound, since they have stood up to the long test of the survival of the fittest, and more subtle, at least in all ordinary and reasonably practical matters, than any that you or I are likely to think up in our armchairs of an afternoon – the most favoured alternative method. (Austin 1956: 8)

In the first instance, following Austin's recommendation, I shall turn to the way in which ontological distinctions are marked in language. The distinction between the dynamic and the static is indeed marked in the way in which we speak. As such, linguistic indicators give us a defeasible reason to determine whether some entity is static or dynamic. Whilst I do not suppose that the linguistic considerations that follow are conclusive, they surely do some significant work in shifting the burden of proof onto those who wish to deny their deliverances.

A number of linguistic markers of the dynamic/static distinction have been proposed. Dynamic, but not static, verbs typically accept the progressive aspect, can serve as infinitival complements of perception verbs, and allow for anaphoric reference via 'to happen'.[12]

Dynamic verbs typically take the progressive aspect, a device used to indicate that something is now occurring:[13]

[11] On these distinctions, and further sub-distinctions, see Vendler (1957), Kenny (1963: ch. 8), and Mourelatos (1978).

[12] Here I draw on the work of Maienborn. See her (2005) for a full discussion in which she also claims that static verbs can combine with neither locative and temporal modifiers, nor with manner adverbials, instrumentals, or comitatives.

[13] Vendler (1957: 146–8) claims that achievement verbs (such as 'reach the top') do not take the progressive whilst nevertheless picking out entities that are (in my terms) dynamic. It is for this

A is running
A is thinking
A is smiling
A is screaming

Static verbs, however, never do:

! *A* is believing
! *A* is knowing
! *A* is being happy
! *A* is being afraid

This is *prima facie* evidence that the referents of static verbs are not things that can be happening now.[14] Related to this is the seeming fact that only dynamic verbs allow for anaphoric reference via 'to happen' (Maienborn 2005). So,

A ran for the bus. This happened while . . .
A thought about kittens. This happened while . . .
! *A* believed that *P*. This happened while . . .
! *A* knew French. This happened while . . .

Again, the thought is that only dynamic verbs refer to entities that happen. Finally, dynamic verbs can serve as infinitival complements to perception verbs; indeed various forms are available[15]:

A saw *B* run(ing)
A saw *B*'s running
A heard *B* think(ing)
A heard *B*'s thinking
A saw *B* smile(ing)
A saw *B*'s smiling
A heard *B* scream(ing)
A heard *B*'s screaming

Static verbs, however, cannot; only the nominalised adjectival is acceptable:

! *A* saw *B* believe(ing) that *P*
! *A* heard *B* know(ing) French
! *A* saw *B* be(ing) happy
! *A* heard *B* be(ing) afraid

reason that I say that dynamic verbs *typically* take the progressive. Since I assume that nobody will wish to claim that emotions are achievements, I do not think that this matters too much for present purposes. As it happens, I agree with Parsons (1989: fn. 25) that Vendler's claim is 'far from obvious'.

14 Additionally, the unavailability of past-tense variants ('I was knowing') supports the more general thought that they cannot happen.

15 It is worth emphasising that the point here concerns grammaticality, not the possibility of truth.

A saw *B*'s happiness
A heard *B*'s knowledge of French
A saw *B*'s belief that *P*
A heard *B*'s fear

The fact that this behaviour pairs with that concerning the progressive and anaphor via 'to happen' gives us a further way of testing for whether a given verb is static or dynamic.[16]

I will assume that, in the absence of compelling reason to suppose otherwise, a dynamic verb picks out a dynamic entity while a static verb picks out something static. Thus, running is dynamic; its occurrence is extended in time. Believing, on the other hand, is not; a person may hold a belief for a certain amount of time, but that belief is not itself something that unfolds over time. As Vendler puts it:

> This difference [static/dynamic] suggests that running, writing and the like are processes going on in time, i.e., roughly, that they consist of successive phases following one another in time . . . But although it can be true of a subject that he knows something at a given moment or for a certain period, knowing and its kin are not processes going on in time. It may be the case that I know geography now, but this does not mean that a process of knowing geography is going on at present consisting of phases succeeding one another in time. (Vendler 1957: 145)

The fact that static and dynamic entities occupy time differently suggests a constraint on what can count as a part of a state. If a part *p* of a whole *w* occurs, then it follows that *w* occurs, for it must take, or go on for, at least as much time as does *p*. Since static entities do not occur, it follows that no part of any static entity occurs. Thus, all the parts of a static entity are themselves static or, at least, non-occurring entities. If, then, some *w* has a dynamic part, what Vendler calls a phase, it follows that *w* is itself dynamic. Another way to make this point would be to borrow the 'wholly present' terminology familiar from discussions of universals. So, static entities are wholly present at each time at which they exist whereas dynamic entities, since they have temporal parts, are not. Since a static entity is wholly present, there is no point during its existence at which some (part) of it has not yet happened. It follows that

[16] The fact that only the nominalised adjectival form is acceptable suggests that insofar as some static entities are perceptible, these are property instances, or tropes, which are plausibly the referents of nominalised adjectivals.

states cannot have dynamic entities as parts.[17] This is important in what follows.

c (Most) Emotions Are Static, Expressions Are Dynamic

As is suggested by these examples, emotion verbs, or at least the large majority of them, are static and so, if static verbs pick out static entities, emotions are static. '*A* is being happy' is ill-formed, as are, '*A* is being afraid,' '*A* is being angry', and '*A* is being sad'.[18] Of course, there are readings of some of these according to which they are not illicit. For example, '*A* is being sad' can mean '*A* is being a loser,' but then 'sad' does not denote an emotion.[19] Similarly, in the case of emotion verbs we cannot use anaphor via 'to happen', so '*A* was happy. This happened while . . .' is illicit. Finally, while '*A* saw *B*'s happiness' is acceptable, 'A saw *B* be(ing) happy' is not. According to these tests, then, emotion verbs are static.

That emotions are states that people are in, rather than events or processes that people undergo, is I assume the default position.[20] Of course, as with the journey from Manchester to London, static and

17 It does not follow that every part of a dynamic entity is itself dynamic. I will remain neutral on whether dynamic entities can have non-dynamic parts. I do not, therefore, assume that Steward (1997: 73) is right to suppose that all of an entity's parts must possess the same temporal shape as it does.

18 In passing, Arpaly and Schroeder (2014: 26–7) provide a lovely discussion of the grammaticality of 'I'm loving'. The fact that 'I'm loving' is frequently used in popular culture (e.g. MacDonalds', 'I'm loving it') may be evidence that there is 'a linguistic change in process' (27). Perhaps this is so. Compare the way that 'begs the question' is often used to mean 'raises the question'. This reminds us in the present context of the provisional nature of the conclusions reached via the Austinian method of metaphysics.

19 One emotion verb admitting of the progressive picks out grief, as in '*A* is grieving'. This lends at least some support to Goldie's (2011) contention that grief is a process. Perhaps there are others. Richard Dub has tried to convince me that examples such as 'I am admiring the painting' qualify. I am less than sure since I suspect that these are typically used to pick out expressive actions (the act of looking closely, etc.). Nevertheless, I set such cases aside, focusing on less cognitively sophisticated emotions such as fear, sadness, and joy.

20 This point speaks to a distinction commonly made between episodic and dispositional emotions (see for example Deonna and Teroni 2012a: ch. 1). It might be thought that my claim that emotions are states is inconsistent with the way that this distinction is typically understood. There are some subtle issues here that I can only gesture at. First, there is no reason to suppose that the claim that emotions are states is inconsistent with the distinction between, say, being afraid of *this snake now* and being afraid of snakes. Second, it is sometimes suggested that the distinction between episodic and dispositional emotions is at the same time a distinction between emotions that do, and emotions that do not, reside within the stream of consciousness. O'Shaughnessy (2000), for example, would take the claim that emotions are states to entail that they are not experiences, since only processes can be experiential. Wollheim (1999), who, although employing a different terminology, argues that emotions are states, would probably agree. Soteriou (2013), on the other hand, allows for experiential states. I will remain neutral on this question. Also, see later in this chapter for a related point regarding emotional feelings.

dynamic entities are often related. So, while being afraid is static, persisting without occurring, becoming afraid and getting over one's fear are both dynamic. One's fear itself, however, persists without occurring.[21] Further, one may go through a number of sorts of fear, from mild concern to abject terror. There is something here that may justly be called an emotional process, but it is a process consisting in the transition between different emotional states (cf. O'Shaughnessy 2000: ch. 1). It is not itself an emotion. Finally, there are a number of dynamic entities that are very closely associated with emotion. For example, when angry I may experience a number of bodily and non-bodily 'emotional feelings' that we might collectively refer to as 'feeling hot under the collar'. The acceptability of sentences such as '*A* is feeling hot under the collar,' '*B* saw *A* feel(ing) hot under the collar,' and '*A* felt hot under the collar. This happened while . . .' suggests that such feelings are dynamic and so not identical to emotions themselves (cf. Scherer 2009: 1318 ff.).[22]

Again, as the earlier examples suggest, expression verbs are dynamic and so, on the assumption that dynamic verbs pick out dynamic entities, emotional expressions are dynamic. '*A* is smiling,' '*A* is screaming,' '*A* is scowling,' and '*A* is weeping' are all perfectly well formed, each indicating that the smiling, screaming, etc. is happening now. Emotional expressions occur. In fact, in many cases, they are things that we do.[23] A smile, for example, consists in a series of successive phases – voluntary or involuntary movements of the facial muscles – the accomplishment of which takes a period of time. Similarly, in the case of expression verbs we may use anaphor via 'to happen', so '*A* smiled. This happened while . . .' is fine. Finally, both '*A* saw *B*'s scream' and '*A* saw *B* scream(ing)' are acceptable. According to these tests, then, expression verbs are dynamic.

So, quite plausibly, emotions are static and emotional expressions are dynamic. If, as I claimed previously, static entities cannot have dynamic

[21] I therefore disagree with Scherer when he says that 'the term "emotional state" is misleading' (2009: 1320). I do not, however, take my claim that emotions are states to be inconsistent with the central insights of his account, since his view can be construed in a number of ways, including as the view that (modal) emotions are *grounded* in what he calls 'component processes', i.e. appraisal, feeling, etc. For the notion of a process-grounded state, see §4d.

[22] Some may wish to defend the view that some such processes can be perceived in virtue of the perceptibility of their expressive parts. I will not discuss that view here other than to point out that it is unlikely to aid a defence of *Perceptibility* or perceptual accounts of emotion recognition more generally. For the reasons already presented, feeling hot under the collar (an occurring entity) is not a part of being angry (a state).

[23] According to Kenny's (1963) performance/activity distinction, most expression verbs will be activity verbs, although some expressive actions will be associated with performance verbs (for e.g., jumping for joy).

entities as parts, it follows that emotional expressions are not parts of emotions. This is not a contingent matter, but follows from a consideration of the ontological category that each occupies. If so, then the part-whole view should be rejected. It is not the case that perceiving an expression is perceiving a part of an emotion, so we as yet have no adequate answer to the question of how perceiving an expression amounts to perceiving an emotion. This is not to say that such an answer cannot be given. Rather, it is to say that the part-whole view cannot provide one.

d Homogeneity and Process-Grounded States

The claim that expressions are dynamic entities might be challenged on the grounds that they are homogeneous down to their instants, a feature that some take to be a defining feature of the static. On this view, despite passing the aforementioned linguistic tests for being dynamic, expression verbs would nonetheless pick out static entities.[24]

Suppose that some object *o* is *F* for the period t_1-t_n. If *F* picks out a homogeneous entity, it follows that *o* is *F* for every sub-interval, down to instants, of t_1-t_n. If *F* picks out a non-homogeneous entity, this does not follow. So, for example, if *A* knows French for the period t_1-t_n, it follows that *A* knows French for any sub-interval of that period. Freeze time at any point during t_1-t_n and it will be true, at that time, that *A* knows French. However, if *A* is running for the period t_1-t_n, it does not follow that *A* is running for every sub-interval of that period, since there are intervals too small for it to be the case that *A* is running during that interval.

It might be maintained that at least some emotional expressions are homogeneous in this sense.[25] So, if *A* is smiling for the period t_1-t_n, it follows that *A* is smiling for any sub-interval of that period. Freeze time at any point during t_1-t_n and it will be true, at that time, that *A* is smiling. If so, and if we think that a sufficient condition of something's being static is that it is homogeneous, then perhaps at least some emotional expressions, e.g. smiles, are static after all. This result might be bolstered by

[24] Maienborn (2005) argues for the existence of what she calls 'Davidsonian-state verbs' which, whilst accepting the progressive and happily serving as infinitival complements to perception verbs, do not allow for anaphoric reference via 'to happen', and pick out homogeneous, so static, entities. In this category, Maienborn includes the verbs *sit, stand,* and *sleep*. Expression verbs, such as *smile*, do not fit neatly into this category so defined, since, as I pointed out earlier, they do allow anaphoric reference via 'to happen'.

[25] Only some since I take it that there is little to recommend the thought that screaming, for example, is homogeneous down to its instants.

consideration of pictorial representations of smiles: a smiley face is smiling, yet there is no event or process involved.

But this has moved too fast. First, the obvious point is that just as a picture of a pipe is not a pipe, the 'smile' of a smiley face is not a smile but a representation of a smile, and it certainly isn't an expression of emotion, at least not in the sense with which I am concerned. What, then, makes a real smile a smile? That is a difficult question to answer, but one highly plausible thought is that whether or not some facial muscular configuration is a smile depends in part on the movements that brought it about (and perhaps also whether and how it will continue to develop). It is not incoherent to suppose that if we froze a smiling face it may be indiscriminable from a similarly frozen grimacing face. The one face, however, would be smiling whilst the other grimacing. The point here is that *if* smiling is homogeneous down to its instants, then it is plausible to hold that, at those instants, a face is smiling in part because of the facial movements occurring before (and perhaps after) that instant.

Compare Steward's (1997: 72) example of temperature. As she points out, the temperature of a gas depends on the movements of its constituent molecules. If a gas is a certain temperature for t_1-t_n, then it follows that it is that temperature for any sub-interval of that period. So temperature is homogeneous. But, certainly when it comes to instants, it will only be so in virtue of certain movements occurring at times other than that instant. Temperature is 'process-grounded' (cf. Soteriou 2013).

On this picture, however, even if smiling is homogeneous, it will not be *strictly* homogeneous. Let us say that an entity F is strictly homogeneous if and only if when an object o is F for the period t_1-t_n, then for any instant t falling within t_1-t_n, o is F at t and its being so is grounded in entities existing at t. I take it that smiling is not strictly homogeneous.

The question now is which, if either, of homogeneity and strict homogeneity is sufficient for being static. The answer to this question, I suggest, is strict homogeneity. I said previously that if A is running for the period t_1-t_n, it does not follow that A is running for any sub-interval of that period, since there may be intervals too small for it to be the case that A is running during that interval. But one might deny this. That is, one might deny that the fact that an instant during t_1-t_n does not contain the grounds for the fact that A is running entails that A is not running at that instant. This would be to claim that running is, despite what was suggested earlier, homogeneous. For all that, though, it will not be strictly homogeneous. But since running is evidently a process, passing the test for homogeneity cannot be sufficient for being static. So, since smiling, even if homogenous, is not strictly homogenous, it is not static.[26] Considerations of homogeneity, then, give us no reason to doubt the earlier conclusion that expressions of emotion are dynamic.

5 The Manifestations of Emotion

I have set out three constraints on *Perceptibility*. The first is that the perception of the emotions of others must be indirect, proceeding via the perception of emotional expressions. The second is that it must be consistent with the fact that emotions explain expressions, not vice versa. The third is that it must be consistent with the correct account of the ontology of emotion and expression, in particular it must respect the fact that emotions are static while expressions are dynamic. With these constraints in mind, it is possible to elaborate *Perceptibility* in a way that looks back to the previously noted fact that some explanation is causal. The idea, in short, is that we can perceive an emotion via perceiving its expression because the former causes the latter. More than this, the latter is a manifestation of the former.

I have argued in this chapter that (most) emotions are states. But more can be said. I suggest that emotions are *functional* states, individuated by their pattern of stimulus conditions (inputs) and manifestations (outputs). That is, an entity is an instance of emotion, *e*, if it instantiates the particular pattern of inputs and outputs definitive of *e*. In short, an entity is an instance of *e* if it realises the relevant causal profile. Exactly what the relevant inputs and outputs are for any given emotion is an open question. However, quite plausibly, the list of inputs will include evaluative appraisals and the list of outputs will include emotional expressions (Scherer 2001, 2009). For example, the inputs definitive of joy are likely to include positive evaluation of some object or event, the outputs are likely to include the exhibition of a genuine, or

[26] The persistent might still deny that 'smiling' always names a process. For it may be claimed that there is some static entity grounded in the processes of smiling. Call this process-grounded state 'smiling$_s$'; an initial grip on which we can gain by consideration of pictorial representations of smiles. As mentioned previously, a smiley face is smiling in some sense. It further might be argued that smiling$_s$, being a state, could happily be a part of happiness.

This move would not help the defender of *Perceptibility*, however, for the reason that smiling$_s$ cannot both be grounded in smiling and a part of happiness. In §3 I claimed that since emotions explain expressions, not vice versa, it cannot be that emotions are grounded in expressions. It is furthermore plausible that if *A* grounds *B*, and *B* is a proper part of *C*, then *A* (partly) grounds *C*. Thus, if smiling grounds smiling$_s$, and smiling$_s$ is a proper part of joy, then smiling (partly) grounds joy. But this is, once more, to get the explanatory relation the wrong way around. Happiness is not grounded, even partly, in smiling. The present suggestion reverses this order of explanation in the manner of the Jamesian picture of emotions as feelings of bodily responses to stimuli. To this extent, the view is deeply at odds with common sense.

Duchenne, smile. This is not to say that every instance of joy causes smiling. Rather, it is to say that joy is partly defined by its tendency to cause smiling.[27]

Assuming this, I propose the following as a sufficient condition of the perception of others' emotions:

> Where *F*ness is a functional/dispositional state, *S* indirectly perceives *o*'s *F*ness if *S* perceives (a sufficient number of) the manifestations of *o*'s *F*ness (the *G*ness of o, the *H*ness of o, etc.).[28]

By 'the manifestations of *o*'s *F*ness', I mean those features, including property instances, that *o*, and perhaps other objects, instantiate in virtue of *o*'s possessing *F* and being in the appropriate stimulus conditions.[29] This condition is perfectly general, offering an account of how it is that one may perceive functional properties. Consider, for example, poisonousness. Suppose that one sees a person ingesting a poisonous substance that has an immediate visible effect. Since this effect is a manifestation of the functional state of poisonousness, our condition allows (but, given the 'sufficient number' condition, does not mandate) that in such a scenario, one sees (but need not see-that, see-as, etc.) the poisonousness of the substance. There will, of course, be objections to this picture, but this is not the place for a full defence.[30] Rather, in what follows, I will sketch how the account meets the three constraints on *Perceptibility* elaborated earlier.

The first constraint is that the perception of the emotions of others must be indirect, proceeding via the perception of emotional expressions. This constraint is evidently met by the manifestation view. On this view, one perceives an emotion (but need not see-that, see-as, etc.) in virtue of perceiving a sufficient number of its manifestations. Thus, when one

[27] Of course, this is just a thumbnail sketch; for more details of the general approach to functional states, see Whittle (2008). For functionalism as applied to emotion, see Nussbaum (2003). For the application of the approach in an account of *Perception-as*, see Smith (2010).

[28] Note that this does not require that *S* perceive *o*. One might suppose that one can perceive *o*'s *F*ness without perceiving *o*. Consider seeing the strength of a hidden magnet by seeing iron objects flying towards it. The same point may, arguably, hold for direct property perception. Consider seeing *o*'s redness by glimpsing some small part of *o*, too small for it to be true that one sees *o*.

[29] The 'sufficient number' condition is intended to allow for the possibility that attributions of indirect property perception are context-sensitive.

[30] For one objection, since properties interact in an indefinite number of ways, the account would probably have to rely on some distinction between a property's 'core' and 'peripheral' manifestations. For another, if we think of the colours as functional/dispositional properties, won't even redness be perceived only indirectly? Well, such a view wouldn't immediately follow from the account, for it depends on what the manifestations of redness are, and whether they are perceived. On the view that the relevant manifestations of redness are colour experiences, one might reasonably deny that they are perceived. I leave a consideration of these issues to another occasion. For an alternative, more detailed, account of the visual perception of functional/dispositional properties, see Cohen (2010).

perceives the emotion, one does so indirectly, on the back of the direct perception of, for example, its expressions.

The second constraint is that the account must respect the fact that emotions explain expressions, not vice versa. This is built into the account. The functionalist view of emotional states sees emotional expressions as on the output side of the causal profile definitive of the emotions in question. Put in terms of explanation, the idea is that one sees the emotional state in virtue of seeing a sufficient number of the things that it explains, including expressions.

The third constraint is that the account must be consistent with the fact that emotions are static while expressions are dynamic. The functionalist view sketched earlier is an account of what it is that individuates states of a certain kind, the key claim being that functional states are those that are individuated by their causal profile. As an account of functional states, it evidently respects the fact that emotions are static. Beyond this, the account leaves as an open question the ontological category into which the relevant stimuli and manifestations fall. In all likelihood, there will be no single answer to such a question. For example, it is plausible to suppose that the manifestations of joy will include both smiles (processes) and other emotional and cognitive states (gratitude, the desire for more of the same, and so on). The account, then, is neutral with respect to the ontology of emotional expression, and the constraint is met.

The manifestation account meets the three constraints on *Perceptibility* that I set out earlier. The account is, of course, merely a sketch and I have done nothing to defend the functionalism on which it depends. Nevertheless, the fact that the constraints are met, and in an intuitive way, puts the account ahead of the rivals that I discussed in §§2–4. Tentatively, then, I suggest that suitably placed and endowed observers can see others' emotions by way of seeing a sufficient number of their manifestations.

Conclusion

Whether *Perceptibility* plays an important role in a complete account of emotion recognition, and if so what, is a question that I have not addressed here. There is, nevertheless, some reason to think that it might be true. The plausible constraints on a defence of *Perceptibility* that I have outlined can be met, but not by all existing views. In particular, I suggest that the popular suggestion that we perceive emotions in virtue of perceiving their (expressive) parts is mistaken, paying insufficient attention to more general issues concerning the ontology of emotion. Nor are emotions directly perceived, or perceived via the perception of their grounds. They are perceived via the perception of their manifestations. I hope that I have made this position seem plausible and if not, at the very least, to have displayed the importance of approaching the question of the perceptibility of emotion – one typically addressed from a purely epistemic or phenomenological standpoint – with a clear view of the ontology of emotion.[31]

[31] I have discussed this material in Geneva, Milan, and Manchester and have benefitted enormously. Thanks, in particular, to Tim Bayne, Julien Deonna, Richard Dub, Santiago Echeverri, Jonathan Farrell, Anil Gomes, Pierre Jacob, Federico Lauria, David Liggins, Michele Davide Ombrato, Alain Pe-Curto, Corrado Sinigaglia, Tom Smith, Fabrice Teroni, Emma Tieffenbach, Ann Whittle, and Silvano Zipoli Caiani. Thanks especially to Hichem Naar and Fabrice Teroni for detailed comments on an earlier version.

CHAPTER 8

Sentiments

Hichem Naar

1 Introduction

Consider the following sentences:

(1) John has been in love with Jane for the past ten years.
(2) Miriam spent her entire life with a deep hatred for injustice.
(3) Matt cares deeply about his mother.
(4) Akio has been deeply jealous about Tim since he was a teenager.

In these sentences, the speaker seems to be predicating a certain kind of affective state of a subject. This affective state, moreover, is predicated for a significant period of time. John's love for Jane is a matter of years rather than seconds or minutes. The same is true of Miriam's hatred and Akio's jealousy.

The predications involved in (1)–(4) seem to contrast with the predication of what philosophers and psychologists typically call 'emotions'. Here are some examples of attributions of emotion:

(5) When he finally meets Jane, John feels very joyful.
(6) Miriam is angry that Tom hasn't called her.
(7) Upon seeing his sick mother, Matt is overwhelmed by sadness.
(8) Akio is feeling a pang of jealousy toward Tim.

If we take (5)–(8) at face value, emotions are a matter of seconds or minutes rather than months or years. A cursory look at the literature, indeed, indicates that a common assumption is that the nature of an emotion is such that its typical temporal extension is rather limited. Emotions have been thought to be judgments (Solomon 1988; Nussbaum 2001), perceptual experiences (De Sousa 1987; Tappolet 2000, 2016; Döring 2003) and processes involving relatively short-lived mental states/events (such as physiological arousal, appraisal) (Robinson 2005, Chapter 3, this volume). If any of these views is right, then it is unsurprising that emotions are generally predicated for short periods of time. Assuming the major ontological treatments of the emotions are on the right track, emotions lasting ten years should be as puzzling and exceptional as perceptual experiences or judgments lasting ten years.

Let's call 'emotions' the kind of seemingly short-lived mental state predicated in (5)–(8) and 'sentiments' the kind of seemingly long-lasting mental state predicated in (1)–(4). Facing the linguistic contrast between attributions of emotions and attributions of sentiments – that emotions and sentiments are typically predicated for different periods of time – we can ask how sentiments fit into a general ontology of the affective, and in particular how they are related to emotions. Are sentiments *sui generis* affective states, or do they reduce to some other affective phenomenon such as emotions?

Adopting the first option by maintaining that sentiments are *sui generis* affective states – call this the distinctness view – is a way of maintaining that the linguistic appearances should be taken at face value. Sentiments are predicated for significant periods of time because they are the sorts of things that can last a long time, whereas emotions are predicated for much shorter periods of time because they are the sorts of things that exist only for a short time. Observe that an implication of this view is that when the same term – 'jealous', 'angry', etc. – is used for both short-term and long-term predication, it is ambiguous (Goldie 2010: 63). When I utter the sentence 'I have been angry with him for the past ten years,' therefore, I do not refer to the same kind of mental state as when I utter the sentence 'His remark made me angry'; in the first sentence, I refer to a sentiment, while in the second I refer to an emotion.

The distinctness view should be resisted, however, if a view reducing sentiments to emotions can be made to work. For such a view would provide at once a more parsimonious ontology of the affective and a unifying account of our attributions of sentiments and emotions, avoiding thereby the consequence that terms such as 'jealous' and 'angry' are ambiguous. In doing so, a reductive view would to a large extent avoid the task of providing an account of the relationship between sentiments and emotions, unlike the distinctness view.

In Section 2, I introduce and motivate a natural way to pursue this reductive project. I argue that the resulting view either fails to be extensionally adequate – it does not deliver the intuitively right verdicts on various cases – or else it is subject to problems that motivate its rejection. In Section 3, I argue that, absent some alternative reductive view, the distinctness view should be accepted as the best – or at least default – account of the distinction between sentiments and emotions. In Section 4, I fill out the details of the distinctness view in order to answer an objection to it. I conclude in Section 5.

2 Reducing Sentiments: The Pattern View

Consider our attribution of a state of jealousy to Akio. On what basis are we justified in attributing it to him? One simple answer is that we have noticed that Akio's behavior changes when he is around Tim or when he is talking about Tim; he looks at him, talks to him and talks about him in certain ways, and so on. Presumably, we take Akio's behavior to indicate something about the way he feels about Tim. And, after further investigation into Akio's behavior, we conclude that he is jealous about Tim.

At this stage, we might wonder whether, in attributing a state of jealousy to Akio, we are really attributing to him a *psychological* state. One way the story could indeed be filled out is by saying that our attributions of sentiments (love, jealousy, etc.) are made true by certain patterns of behavior. Perhaps Akio's jealousy toward Tim just *is* his looking at Tim in a certain way, talking to him in a certain way and so on and forth.

It should be clear that the resulting view, thinking of sentiments as constructed out of behavioral patterns as it does, has not much going for it. Surely, Akio could behave exactly the way he does without being jealous about Tim; he might for some reason or other decide to pretend being jealous of Tim. And he could be jealous about Tim without behaving as he does; he might constantly succeed in hiding his true feelings. Furthermore, by reducing sentiments to behavioral patterns, the view does not accommodate the conceptual link between sentiments and *emotions*. Clearly, Akio's jealousy about Tim has something to do with the discrete episodes of jealousy he might experience at various times.

The sensible move here for the advocate of a reductive account is to reduce sentiments, not to behavioral patterns, but to patterns of *emotions*.[1] By constructing sentiments out of collections of emotions, the view provides a parsimonious account of affective states that accommodates the seemingly necessary link between sentiments and emotions.

The view of sentiments at issue – call it the pattern view – appears to be a bit of a default view in the literature on emotions, in both philosophy and psychology (see Ekman 1994; Helm 2001; Shoemaker 2003; see also

[1] I am here setting aside the view that sentiments are instances of emotions experienced for a very long time, for I am assuming here that the major theories of emotions are on the right track in identifying emotions with mental states that typically exist for a relatively short time (perceptions, judgments, etc.).

Deonna and Teroni 2009). According to Paul Ekman, (what I call) a sentiment is nothing more than a summation of emotions; he says: 'I believe those who claim emotions endure for much longer time periods are summating what is actually a series of briefer emotion episodes' (1994: 16, quoted in Goldie 2000: 104). David Shoemaker argues that an appeal to sentiments makes intelligible distinct emotions by placing them in a broader context. Speaking about caring, he writes:

> Caring is a kind of conceptual-linguistic structural framework we overlay upon emotional reactions to render them intelligible . . . Talk of caring is simply a way of referring to the range of emotional reactions one is expected to have with respect to the fortunes of the cared-for object. (2003: 94)

Bennett Helm (2001) has put forward a similar proposal.[2] According to him, patterns of emotions are distinctive in that they have members that entertain rational connections. When one feels a given emotion, Helm claims, one incurs two sorts of commitments. First, we have 'transitional commitments', whereby undergoing an emotion of a given type at a time commits oneself to undergoing an emotion of a different type at a later time. For instance, my hoping that it will not rain tomorrow commits me to *being relieved* if it finally doesn't rain. Second, we have 'tonal commitments', whereby the having of a positive emotion in a certain situation commits one to feeling the corresponding negative emotion in relevant counterfactual situations. For instance, if one feels joy because it doesn't rain, one is thereby committed to feeling sadness or disappointment in a counterfactual situation where it does. As a result, an appeal to sentiments makes distinct emotions intelligible by revealing their being connected in some way.

Although there are differences between these accounts in how sentiments are supposed to be related to emotions, all seem to agree that emotions are ontologically basic and that sentiments are somehow derivative of emotions. The reductive strategy here, indeed, is to have first in hand an account of emotions, and then understand sentiments in terms of that account. One's account of emotions[3] will therefore determine one's account of sentiments. For instance, if one follows Helm in thinking that emotions may entertain certain relations, one is free to adopt a view on which sentiments are complexes of emotions entertaining such relations. If one, by contrast, has a simpler account of emotions – construing, for

[2] Followed by Jaworska (2007).

[3] Plus some further assumptions about sentiments, such as their typical temporal lifespan.

instance, emotions as primitive reactions to external events – one can hold a 'summary' view of sentiments according to which a sentiment is a mere collection of emotions. Despite the different ways one might pursue the reductive project, we can extract a view common to all such accounts:

> *Priority Thesis* (PT): A subject possesses a given sentiment over a particular period of time if and only if, and because, the subject experiences a certain pattern of emotions over that period of time.

According to PT, if a subject undergoes a certain pattern of emotions with respect to an object O, she thereby cares about, loves, is angry with etc. O. This is the sufficiency claim. And in order to care about, love or be angry with O, she must undergo a pattern of that sort. This is the necessity claim.

At least two questions may be raised with respect to these claims. First, what kind of pattern must one undergo in order to be in love rather than angry? In order to be able to distinguish between different kinds of sentiments, presumably, we must provide a story about the sorts of emotions one must feel over time in order to have a given sentiment; one must, in other words, tell what the components of that sentiment are. This question, of course, is not the hardest we can ask a pattern theorist. For we seem to have a good grasp of the sorts of emotions a person in love typically undergoes over time – she feels joy in the presence of the beloved, worried when she is in danger, proud when she succeeds in life, angry when someone has insulted her, missing her when she is gone, and so on. A similar, but simpler story holds for anger (in the sentiment sense): a person angry with someone else should be angry at various times. Although the details must be filled in here, I will assume that the pattern theorist has available to her a principled way to distinguish between the various sentiments.

A more difficult question concerns the intentionality of sentiments. What does undergoing a pattern of emotions *with respect to an object O* involve? Sentiments, it seems, have intentional objects just as emotions do. But if sentiments just are patterns of emotions, does this mean that, in order for a sentiment to be *about O*, then all the emotions composing it must be *about O*? If this is the case, then this is problematic. For sentiments clearly need not have the same object as all the associated emotions. I may be angry with John for hurting someone I care about. In this case, the object of my anger is John, not the person I care about. But it is clear that my anger is the sort of emotion a caring person would experience in this case; we might say it would be in this case an *expression* of care. A pattern theorist, therefore, should claim that the anger is part of the pattern constituting my care, even though it is not directed at the same person. Sensitive to considerations of this kind, Helm distinguishes between the *intentional object* of an emotion and its *focus*. While the intentional object of an emotion is the object toward which it is directed, its focus is the object an appeal to which renders the emotion intelligible. For instance, it is because an individual has insulted my mother that I am angry with him. Here, although the individual is the object of my anger, reference to my attitude toward my mother is needed to explain why I feel the way I do – why I am angry rather than joyful or indifferent. The question now is how a given emotional episode gets to have the focus it has. A natural thought is that my anger has my mother as focus in virtue of the fact that I *love* her. In other words, the focus of my anger is the intentional object of my love. Had I not loved her, I may not have felt angry at all. Given that sentiments seem necessary to ground facts about the intentional structure of emotions, it seems, the pattern theorist should tell us how they can do so if they are at bottom nothing over and above patterns of emotions.[4]

We will see in Section 3 that the distinctness view has a straightforward answer to this question. But for now, let's assume that the pattern theorist has available to her a story of the relevant sort. There are problems with the pattern view, however, that will motivate the alternative account of sentiments I called the distinctness view. In particular, there seem to be counterexamples to both the sufficiency and the necessity claims involved in PT. The pattern view, it seems, fails to deliver the intuitively right results in a variety of cases. And even if these counterexamples only constitute *defeasible* evidence against the pattern view, they each point to significant worries about its viability. It turns out that the pattern theorist faces the burden of showing us that her view can adequately address these worries. The pattern view, therefore, is a view for which one needs to argue and cannot simply be taken as the default account of the distinction between sentiments and emotions. I'll present apparent counterexamples to the

[4] A possibility open to the pattern theorist is to appeal to 'non-emotional' elements that may be part of the pattern and that would explain my reaction. Perhaps it is because I have a long-term desire that my mother be respected that I get angry when someone insults her. An appeal to this desire clearly makes my anger intelligible. Two points may be raised in response, however. First, it seems that we can still ask why I desire that my mother be respected, and an appeal to my love for her would be an adequate, but non-obvious answer to this question (it is one possibility among others). Second, even though the appeal to the desire reaches rock bottom when it comes to the psychological explanation of my anger, we still need an account of how whole patterns get to be intentionally directed at one thing as opposed to another. Appealing to an element of the pattern that is directed at it does not tell us how and in what sense the whole pattern is directed at it. Thanks to Fabrice Teroni for pressing me on this issue.

sufficiency and the necessity claims, and explain what I take each of them to reveal about the pattern view.

Consider a scenario presented by David Pugmire:

> Suppose there are two people of contrary character. There is Nick, who is ill at ease with others and over-anxious to please. He can't abide silence and has to maintain a barrage of constant, random banter. Rick, on the other hand, is ruminative, laconic and doesn't suffer fools gladly. When their professional circumstances force them together Nick finds Rick perversely unforthcoming and even hostile – thankless company and, frankly, intimidating. For his part, Rick finds Nick an irritating twit. Not surprisingly, they bring out the worst in each other: insistent nervous chatter confronts bristling silence. Their working relationship suffers. However, their Company has a resourceful Personnel Department. Without their knowledge the Department medicates both men with a new psychotropic drug called Amity. Their perceptions of one another remain, but their mutual responses are wonderfully transformed. Thus, despite Nick's admittedly pathetic foibles, Rick warms to him. Irritation and disdain yield to bemused indulgence. On the other hand, Rick's ominous silences no longer prevent Nick from dubbing him somehow likable. As if by grace, an unaccountable fondness arises on both sides, and the working relationship prospers. (Pugmire 1994: 106)

The question we should ask ourselves is, do Nick and Rick really *care* for each other? In the scenario, we have, it seems, a pattern of emotions that, if it wasn't for the pill, would give us a strong reason to attribute a state of mutual care to the characters. Yet, given that we know about the pill's presence, we may be reluctant to say that they genuinely care.

The pattern theorist may object that, given that it is unclear what work the pill is doing here, we should not trust our judgment. The pill, after all, must be able to track certain relevant facts in order to be activated at all. In order to avoid this sort of mystery, let's imagine that, instead of the pill, a high-tech device is implanted into the characters' heads that triggers the relevant emotions whenever the relevant cognitive states are present. For instance, whenever it detects a belief that the other is in the vicinity and that he is in a state of distress, it triggers friendly compassion for him. We can assume that the device is so sophisticated that it triggers not only the right sort of emotions, but does so in a way that feels natural to the protagonists. I think that there is at the very least ground for saying that it is an *open* question whether Nick and Rick genuinely care for each other, suggesting in turn that the instantiation of a pattern of emotions is not sufficient for caring.

We have here an apparent counterexample to the claim that a pattern of emotions is sufficient for having a certain sentiment. The case is about caring, but I take it that we can construct cases involving a pattern associated with any kind of sentiment. It seems as though any pattern of emotions can in principle be induced in the way described in the case. And for each of these cases, it is not clear that we are in the presence of the relevant sentiment. If this is right, patterns of emotions are not sufficient for the presence of sentiments.

Although cases of emotional inducement constitute clear evidence against simple forms of the pattern view, they may not be as devastating against more sophisticated ones. Recall what PT says. It says that a *certain* pattern is sufficient for the presence of a sentiment, not that *any* pattern is sufficient. The pattern theorist is free to supply details about the kind of pattern sufficient for the presence of a sentiment. Note, though, that this is not an easy task. In order for the pattern view to be acceptable, it should provide an adequate story about the relationship between the various emotions that are part of a given pattern that is needed for this pattern to count as a sentiment at all. In particular, she must tell us what prevents the pattern instantiated by Nick and Rick from being a genuine instance of caring.

Cases like this put pressure on the pattern theorist to lay down certain restrictions on the sort of pattern that constitute a given sentiment, restrictions that are not satisfied in the Nick and Rick case. One possibility is that the emotions composing the pattern should be rationally connected in the way described by Helm, or at the very least the pattern should be internally coherent in a fairly broad sense. But it is far from clear that the emotions induced in the case fail to be rational or coherent in the way Helm has in mind. Of course, there is something fishy about a pattern of such emotions – and the challenge is to say exactly what that is – but it doesn't appear that being internally incoherent is what explains this fishiness. What explains why there is something fishy about the pattern arguably has more to do with the *source* of the emotions than any other relation they might entertain to one another. After all, the case involves people whose emotions are *directly produced by a drug*.[5] The challenge for the pattern theorist, then, is to say why the source of a certain pattern of emotions matters when it comes to the composition of a given sentiment

[5] Notice that it is not the fact that the emotions in question are induced *artificially* that is of concern here, only the fact that the drug *directly* produces the emotions. Indeed, it is open to an advocate of the distinctness view defended in the next section to admit the possibility of cases where a *sentiment* is induced artificially, sentiments being here conceived of as distinct from the relevant patterns. In these cases, the sentiment, rather than the drug, would still be the direct cause of the emotions.

if – as the pattern view claims – a sentiment is nothing over and above that pattern. Why can't Nick and Rick be said to genuinely care for each other, if they manage to experience all the emotions characteristic of an attitude of caring? Call this the *wrong kind of origin problem.*[6]

Although patterns of emotions might not be sufficient for sentiments, they might still be necessary. Perhaps, indeed, sentiments are patterns of emotions that have a source of a certain kind.[7] However, there are reasons to deny even this claim. I'll provide a counterexample involving love, but I believe similar counterexamples can be given for other kinds of sentiments. The counterexample involves a subject who, although loving deeply a particular thing, fails on certain occasions to feel the relevant emotions such that no pattern of emotions can be attributed to her. Of course, the pattern theorist can allow occasional gaps in patterns (Helm 2001); the subject can be said to love as long as gaps are only occasional, that is, as long as they do not falsify the claim that there is a pattern. But it should be kept in mind that the pattern theorist is committed to the impossibility of love (or any other sentiment) without patterns.

Consider the following case. John loves his dog, Mindy, very much. She is his best friend. He experiences all the emotions someone loving their dog would feel – joy when she is around, sadness when she is sick, anger when someone attempts to kick her and so on. Knowing this about John, his worst enemy, who happens to be a gifted hypnotist, Tim, somehow manages to make John emotionally indifferent to Mindy. Thus, every time he sees or thinks about her, John experiences no emotion whatsoever. If it wasn't for the hypnosis, John would feel again all the emotions he used

[6] One might suggest that the problem is not that the emotions have the wrong origin, but that they are not appropriately related to the subject's reflective perspective. Indeed, it may be the case that, in order for a pattern to be an instance of caring (say), the subject must endorse, or identity with, such a pattern. The problem with such a view, however, is that it implies that creatures incapable of reflective endorsement are incapable of caring. See Jaworska (2007).

[7] One possibility would be to claim that the emotions constituting a pattern are subject, not simply to norms of internal coherence, but to more substantial norms, such as epistemic norms. How should we understand such a claim? Suppose emotions are subject to world-involving norms. We might then understand the claim as saying that, in order for a pattern to constitute an instance of caring, there must be a pattern of emotions subject to these norms. The problem is that, just as the beliefs that are induced artificially are still subject to epistemic norms, emotions induced artificially are still subject to whatever norm they are subject to. Alternatively, we might understand the claim as saying that the relevant emotions must *comply* to these norms, such that a pattern of emotions constituting love (say) comprise emotions that are appropriate responses to certain features of the object. Making love depend on such appropriate emotions is implausible, however, for the simple reason that the fact that all our emotions toward a person do not adequately respond to features he or she actually has might make our love inappropriate or 'blind', but certainly not disingenuous. Just as inappropriate fear is still fear, inappropriate love is still love.

to feel toward Mindy. In fact, with one word, Tim has the power to make the hypnosis go away. Unfortunately for John, Tim doesn't want to make it go away.

Suppose that the hypnosis is sufficiently strong that John fails to instantiate a pattern characteristic of love over a significant period of time. Does this mean that John does not love Mindy anymore? The pattern theorist is committed to answering this question positively, for on her account a pattern of emotions is necessary for the presence of a sentiment and John fails to instantiate any such pattern. Notice, however, that it doesn't *follow* from John's failure to experience emotions toward Mindy that he stopped loving her. If the pattern view provided an adequate account of at least the concept of love, then we shouldn't think it an open question whether John still loves Mindy while under hypnosis for such a long time. We should think instead that the absence of a pattern is sufficient to falsify the claim that John loves Mindy.

This point can be made stronger if we reflect on the *role* the hypnosis is supposed to play in the case. In what way does the hypnosis manage to make John indifferent? One hypothesis – the one, it seems, the pattern theorist is committed to – is that the hypnosis does so by *destroying* the love John used to have for Mindy. Given that, by hypothesis, the pattern of emotions he used to instantiate does not exist anymore, his love doesn't exist anymore either. But there is an alternative hypothesis we would be able to give if we rejected the pattern view. Rather than destroying John's love for Mindy, the hypnosis makes John emotionally indifferent to Mindy by *blocking* his love for her. Just as a state of sleep may prevent one from manifesting certain long-lasting psychological states, a state of hypnosis of the sort involved in the case may prevent John from manifesting his love.

I think that the hypothesis involving prevention should appear more plausible than the one involving destruction once we look at how the hypnosis is supposed to work in the case. As stated in the scenario, the uttering of a simple word is sufficient for the state of hypnosis to be over and for everything to be back to normal. For this to be the case, it seems, hypnosis should not have too big of an impact on the subject's psychology. It should not damage his brain, for instance. Had Tim hit John hard on the head instead, damaging various areas associated with emotions, it would have been very hard to maintain that he still loves his dog. The hypothesis involving destruction would thereby have appeared very plausible. We are less tempted by this hypothesis, however, when it comes to the original case. There does seem to be an intuitive difference between the impact the hypnosis has on John's love and the impact the head banging may have on it.

While it seems to us that the hypnosis – even when persistent – may have no impact on his love even though it has an impact on the pattern of emotions he undergoes, the head banging may clearly have an impact on it. This difference in impact, it seems, cannot be accounted for by the pattern view.

Furthermore, the prevention hypothesis should appear better than the destruction hypothesis if we consider a variation of the case where, rather than being in state of hypnosis all the time, John is somehow hooked up to a device that triggers the activation word every time it senses that John is about to experience an emotion for his dog. Facing this case, the pattern theorist is forced to say that, because John fails to feel any emotion toward his dog, he doesn't love her in the first place. This claim is dubious, however, since if John didn't love his dog, there would be no point in hooking him up to the device. The device's *point* is precisely to prevent John's love from manifesting itself. If that's right, then the pattern view fails to allow a kind of explanation we might naturally give of cases like this one.

Suppose now that, in the original case, Tim decides to use the magic word on some occasion, but then decides a moment later to use another word restoring the state of hypnosis. During the time John is no longer under Tim's influence, he feels joy upon seeing Mindy. What explains the appearance of this lonely state of joy? As there is no pattern, the pattern theorist is unable to say that the joy is an expression of John's love, for on her account John no longer loves Mindy. One thing she can do in order to explain the joy is to appeal to some underlying neurophysiological facts about John that obtained upon the removal of the hypnosis. Since there is no pattern of emotions of which the joy would be a part, there seems to be no other way than furnishing a sub-personal explanation of this sort in order to make its appearance less chancy. (I take it that even the pattern theorist would not find John's reaction very surprising.) She has to admit that, as a matter of psychology, the appearance of John's emotion is a brute fact about him.[8]

[8] One might wonder whether, in addition to providing a mere sub-personal explanation that would render the lonely emotion intelligible, we could provide some sort of rationalizing explanation whereby we describe the *reason* why John feels the way he does. If he reacts a certain way, indeed, this is presumably because he is responsive to some feature of the situation that might make his response appropriate. Citing this feature, furthermore, may allow the pattern theorist to appeal to something other than sub-personal states of the subject in order to make sense of the lonely emotion. If that's right, then the pattern theorist could help herself with a species of personal explanation after all. One worry with this response, however, is that, since the pattern theorist cannot appeal to the presence of love, she cannot appeal to features of the situation whose status as reasons would only make sense if love was indeed present. For instance, she cannot appeal to facts such as *My best friend is here* or *Mindy – my beloved dog – is in front of me*. At best, she could only appeal to facts that connect to other cares and concerns of the subject, such as the subject's liking of dogs. In this case, she would still be

We might think, though, that it is because John *loves* Mindy that he is happy – even for just a moment – to see her. This is, I think, a natural and perfectly acceptable psychological explanation of his reaction. Of course, the pattern theorist may be right in claiming that the appearance of the lonely state is explained by some facts about John's brain. Yet, this kind of explanation is typically not what we are looking for when we attempt to make sense of other people's seemingly idiosyncratic reactions. What we are looking for, in these cases, are details about the subject's psychology that would make the reactions look less idiosyncratic. I think that a case like John's is of this kind, and that the way we would make sense of it (assuming the hypnosis works the way I pictured it and we know how John used to react in front of Mindy) is by appealing to some underlying state of attachment toward Mindy that was there all along.

If a sentiment is appealed to in order to explain isolated emotions, then there is no reason to think that it cannot be appealed to in order to explain *entire* patterns of emotions. Indeed, it seems perfectly adequate to explain a certain sequence of emotions by saying that the subject is in love, an explanation that would not be open to us if the sequence were identical with the love. In fact, it isn't even clear that the 'intelligibility' story the pattern theorist gives of individual emotions – placing them in a broader context – preserves the thought that sentiments can be explanatory. The strategy is to subsume an emotion under a series of emotions the subject has felt or is likely to feel, and that might be related in certain ways (by satisfying Helm's rational requirements, for instance). It might thereby look explanatory 'only in the limited sense that it takes away the oddity that the single happening might otherwise have' (Wollheim 1999: 5). This falls short of the kind of explanation we might wish to give of the occurrence of our emotions. By appealing to sentiments in order to explain individual emotions, it seems, we do more than claim that such episodes are things we can expect, or that they entertain certain relations (such as rational relations). Rather, it is tempting to say, we *explain* them.[9]

able to give a rationalizing – and even a full-blown *psychological* – explanation, but, it seems, not the one we would intuitively give, namely one that preserves the appearance that the lonely joy at play in the case is an expression of love rather than some other sentiment and that, as a result, it is responsive to features of the situation whose status as reasons can only be made sense of by appealing to this love. Thanks to Mauro Rossi for pressing me on this point.

[9] If the sort of explanation we find missing in the pattern view is *causal* explanation, then it may seem that the pattern theorist can allow the possibility that the emotions forming a pattern are causally – and not just rationally – connected to each other, for it is clear that emotions can cause other emotions. We might worry, though, that this sort of explanation can explain the occurrence of every emotion that is part of a given pattern, for the temporal gap between two successive emotions may be

The pattern view plausibly fails to do justice to some aspects of our explanatory practices with respect to our affective lives. Call this the *explanatory problem.* First, the view rules out explanations of massive disruption in patterns of emotions couched in terms of blocking or masking, admitting only explanations couched in terms of destruction. Second, it rules out explanations of lonely emotions couched in psychological terms, admitting only explanations couched in sub-personal terms.[10] Third, it rules out explanations of entire patterns of emotions couched in terms of sentiments, admitting only quasi-explanatory stories about their members.

3 The Distinctness View

It seems that the pattern view is not as plausible as we might have initially thought. Perhaps there are ways it can be pursued that avoid the problems raised against it. More generally, there might be alternative reductive views that could deliver everything we want from an account of the distinction between sentiments and emotions.[11] That said, it is important to realize how neatly a *non*-reductive view – which I called the distinctness view – avoids the problems facing the pattern view. Absent some plausible reductive view, indeed, I think we should accept the distinctness view as the best – or at least, the default – account of the distinction between sentiments and emotions.

too significant for the first emotion to be said to cause the second. It would be odd to claim, indeed, that the joy one feels toward one's beloved before work at 9 AM causes the joy one feels toward him or her after work at 6 PM, assuming no emotion of the relevant sort has occurred in between.

[10] Or, as seen in Note 8, couched in terms of sentiments other than the one we would intuitively appeal to.

[11] One possibility is a view on which, in order for a sentiment to exist, a pattern must exist at least *counterfactually.* So even though John's actual emotions do not form a pattern, they *would* if the hypnosis were not in place, and so John could still be said to love Mindy even under the influence of the hypnosis. Putting forward this sort of view would therefore allow the pattern theorist to avoid the John and Mindy counterexample. It might not so easily avoid the Nick and Rick counterexample, however, and the two problems raised earlier. In particular, although explanations by prevention (rather than destruction) are possible on this view, the kind of prevention explanation it would give of the relevant cases is a bit odd. In the John and Mindy case, the pattern theorist would account for the role of the hypnosis by saying that it prevents counterfactual states of affairs from being actual. Facing this story, we might naturally wonder *by what means* the hypnosis manages to do this. In other words, the story it gives might not be all we can give of the role of the hypnosis in the case. In this and the next sections, we will see that the distinctness view gives us what we want by way of explanation of this kind. Overall, it is unclear what could be the motivation (except the purported intuitive link between sentiments and emotions, a claim I show in Section 4 to be consistent with the distinctness view) of the modified pattern view over the more straightforward distinctness view.

The distinctness view clearly avoids the counterexamples raised against the pattern view. Given that on this view sentiments and emotions are distinct existences, it is not surprising that dissociations are possible. Just as a chair can exist without a table, and vice versa, a sentiment can exist without a pattern of emotions, and vice versa. Of course, we might wonder whether sentiments and emotions are as independent from each other as tables and chairs are (see next section), but we can note for now that this account of the distinction has a clear advantage over the pattern view in not being subject to the counterexamples introduced earlier.

We have seen that each of these counterexamples reveals a difficulty that the pattern theorist must avoid in order for her view to be successful. The Nick and Rick case seems to show that the origin of one's emotions matters as to whether they are genuinely indicative of a given sentiment. For instance, the fact that a pattern characteristic of love is directly produced by a drug appears to make a difference to the pattern's identity. The John and Mindy case, by contrast, seems to show that the pattern view neglects some aspects of our explanatory practices. In particular, it seems to rule out certain kinds of explanations we might naturally give with respect to our affective lives: (i) explanations involving prevention rather than destruction of a given affective state, (ii) psychological explanations of seemingly idiosyncratic reactions rather than mere sub-personal ones, and (iii) explanations of whole patterns of emotions rather than 'intelligibility' stories about individual members of these patterns.

It should be clear that the distinctness view avoids the wrong kind of origin problem. By positing an extra species of affective state – sentiments – the distinctness theorist is free to claim that what is wrong with Nick and Rick's reactions is that – produced by the drug as they are – they do not really come from an attitude of *care*.[12] A sentiment being conceived of here as something distinct from the relevant patterns of emotions, it is something that can fail to exist while a pattern characteristic of it is at play. One straightforward thing this allows us to say is that, for a pattern to constitute a manifestation of a given sentiment, *it must be produced by that sentiment*. Problem avoided.

The explanatory problem is avoided by the distinctness view as well. First, given that sentiments are distinct from patterns of emotions, the absence of a pattern doesn't imply the absence of the associated sentiment. As a result, in cases where a pattern is removed, it still may be the case that the sentiment is not destroyed as well, but merely masked. Second, given

[12] Again, nothing I say here commits me to the claim that caring (and other sentiments) could not be induced artificially. In fact, I don't see why it could not.

that sentiments are both distinct from emotions and properly psychological, we can appeal to them in order to provide psychological explanations of isolated emotions. Last, again given that they are distinct from emotions, sentiments can explain both individual emotions and patterns of emotions.

Before moving on, recall a potential difficulty for the pattern view introduced earlier. After distinguishing between the intentional object of an emotion and the object the appeal to which makes the emotion intelligible – its 'focus' – we wondered how the emotion gets to have the focus it has. A natural answer was that the intentional object of the sentiment associated with it is the emotion's focus. An appeal to sentiments, we concluded, seems necessary to ground certain facts about the intentional structure of emotions. It was not clear, however, whether a pattern theorist is really free to help herself with this account, given the role sentiments seem to play here over and above the relevant pattern of emotions. Although the pattern view may have the resources to avoid this difficulty (after all, the distinction between object and focus was initially introduced by Bennett Helm, an advocate of this view), notice how easily the distinctness view gets around it. On this view, indeed, love, anger and other sentiments are distinct from any sort of pattern of emotions with which they might be associated. Love, anger and these other sentiments, furthermore, are intentional states: we always love, are angry with etc. some thing or other. The distinctness view thus claims there are states called 'sentiments' that are distinct from both emotions and intentional. Although the sort of story we have given of the intentional structure of emotions is not *part* of the distinctness view, it is certainly open to its advocate to accept it, for nothing on her account prevents her from claiming that sentiments not only explain the occurrence of various emotions, but also account for some aspect of their intentionality.

4 Explaining the Necessary Link: Sentiments as Powers

We have seen that a major motivation for the pattern view is the intuitive link between sentiments and emotions. There seems to be some sort of conceptual or necessary connection between the two kinds of mental states that makes it plausible to think that they are not completely independent from each other. The pattern view does justice to this plausible thought by reducing sentiments to patterns of emotions. We have seen that the distinctness view claims that sentiments and emotions are distinct, and that this claim is what enables it to avoid the problems raised previously against the pattern view. If we accept the existence of a necessary link between sentiments and emotions, this feature of the account – its claiming that sentiments and emotions are distinct – may nonetheless constitute the very reason we should reject it. For doesn't it plainly imply that sentiments and emotions are related only contingently? If the distinctness view fails to accommodate the necessary connection between sentiments and emotions, then it seems that the pattern view – even though somewhat revisionary of common sense – may have some traction after all.

I do not think that the claim that sentiments and emotions are contingently related follows from the distinctness view. Let me offer two responses to the charge that the distinctness view has this implication. The first response starts by noticing that we haven't been very precise in our description of the link between sentiments and emotions. The necessity relations at play in this connection may be of various forms, some of which might be so weak that it is uncontroversial that they can obtain between distinct entities. For instance, it might be a platitude surrounding our concept of love that a person in love is likely – at least in normal circumstances – to experience a range of emotions in various situations over time. The fact that this conceptual relation obtains between sentiments and emotions, it seems, does not give us any reason one way or the other to accept a particular account of the distinction.

Another way sentiments and emotions might be related that might explain their seemingly intuitive link has to do with Shoemaker's claim that the function of attributions of sentiments such as caring is to refer 'to the range of emotional reactions one is expected to have with respect to the fortunes of the cared-for object' (2003: 94). Although, as we have seen, talk of sentiments cannot be reduced to talk of emotions, it might still be the case that one function of this discourse – a reason why we tend to *use* it in the first place – is to express our predictions concerning the way we or other people will feel in the future. If talk of sentiments has this function, then this might explain our initial suspicion that sentiments and emotions are more than contingently related; in this case, the relevant necessary connection would be conceptual. But notice that this fact about the discourse is perfectly compatible with the distinctness view, just as the view that we attribute mental states to others in part in order to predict their behavior is compatible with the view that mental states and behavior are distinct.

The first response, then, was to show that there are ways of spelling out the intuitive link between sentiments and emotions that are easily shown to be consistent with the distinctness view. The second response is now to show that the distinctness view is compatible with more robust forms of necessity relations that might obtain between sentiments and emotions.

Suppose that there exists a not merely conceptual/analytic connection between sentiments and emotions. Say the relation that obtains between them is of a robust metaphysical sort, having to do with the nature of these entities. Surely, one might say, *that* claim is inconsistent with the distinctness view. On a natural reading of it, indeed, it might simply be impossible for sentiments to exist without patterns. Indeed, how could two entities X and Y be necessarily connected in the relevant way if it is possible for one to exist without the other?

There is a way to show that the distinctness view is compatible with relations of this sort obtaining between sentiments and emotions, however. By contrast with the first response, this response consists in filling out some details of the view in a way that removes this apparent tension. The strategy is to show that the relationship between sentiments and emotions is of a kind that allows us to posit robust necessary connections between them. In particular, sentiments' *ontological category* is such that they might be necessarily, or essentially, related to other things. Although the proposal I will make is controversial, it is rooted in a metaphysical framework that has gained some traction in recent years.

The basic idea of the view I favor is that sentiments are *dispositions* to experience various emotions. The relation that obtains between a sentiment and its associated emotions is therefore the relation that obtains between a disposition and its so-called manifestations: emotions are – at least in many cases – the manifestations of sentiments. Given that it is plausible that the relation between dispositions and their manifestations is necessary, it is thereby plausible that the relation between sentiments and emotions is necessary too.

At this point, one might reasonably doubt that I have really offered an account of the distinction between sentiments and emotions that is a version of the distinctness view. For dispositions and manifestations might be necessarily connected because they are not distinct in the first place. A view like this one is found in David Hume, who claims that the distinction between dispositions or powers and their manifestation or exercise is without foundation. He writes: 'the distinction, which we sometimes make betwixt a *power* and the *exercise* of it, is entirely frivolous, and . . . neither man nor any other being ought ever to be thought possest of any ability, unless it be exerted and put in action' (1739–40/1896: 311). Hume's view on dispositions is in part premised on the suspicion that there cannot be necessary connections between distinct entities. If dispositions and their manifestations are essentially related, then they cannot be distinct, and if they are distinct, then they are – to use

Hume's phrase – completely 'loose and separate' (Hume 1748/1975: 74), hence only contingently related.

It is not the place for a complete refutation of Hume's ontology. It will suffice for my purposes that a plausible alternative to it be available for the advocate of the distinctness view. On a distinctively anti-Humean ontology (e.g., Shoemaker 1980; Mumford 1998; Heil 2003, Chapter 2, this volume; Molnar 2003), some aspects of the world are essentially related to other aspects that are nonetheless distinct. This is the case of dispositions or – as they are called by 'realists' – powers. On a realist account, dispositions are irreducible entities whose identity is fixed by what they do. A disposition is the very disposition it is in virtue what it is a disposition *for* (see Heil, Chapter 2, this volume), that is, in virtue of the range of events or occurrences it might produce in a range of circumstances. For instance, a glass is fragile in virtue of possessing a property that is essentially connected to a range of events or occurrences such as breaking, cracking, and so on; fragility is a property that has a certain causal role necessarily rather than contingently, even though there are things possessing it that never get the chance to manifest it.

One might be suspicious of the view just introduced, and rightly so. No argument was provided to the effect that dispositions thus construed exist. And many subtle details of the relevant literature and important issues have been passed over for reasons of space.[13] I will then content myself with the following conditional statement: *if* one thinks that sentiments and emotions are necessarily connected to each other in a fairly robust way, and *if* one is attracted to the anti-Humean ontology alluded to (though not defended) previously, then there is a view that both counts as a distinctness view and preserves the supposed necessary connection between sentiments and emotions.[14]

[13] One such issue is how it is possible for a disposition to bear a necessary relation with something – its manifestation – that may not exist (for discussion, see Mumford 2009: section 3.2). Another issue concerns the legitimacy of appealing to powers in the context of a discussion about nonfundamental aspects of the world, such as psychology (Bird 2016).

[14] Even though my view of sentiments is resolutely at odds with Hume's metaphysical commitments, it might be seen as aiming at providing an account of a distinction that he himself makes in Book II of the *Treatise* between *calm* and *violent* passions (1739–40/1896: 276). However 'vulgar and specious' (276) this distinction might have appeared to Hume, an adequate account of it may render it acceptable for further inquiry into our affective lives. On one understanding of the distinction, violent passions possess, while calm passions lack or possess to a significantly lesser degree, some phenomenological content (Smith 1987: 51). The epistemology of calm passions, Hume seems to hold, is thus more indirect than the epistemology of violent passions; the calm passions, indeed, 'are more known by their effects than by their immediate sensation' (1739–40/1896: 417, quoted in Smith 1987: 52) This description appears to be true of sentiments as well, suggesting that sentiments are

5 Concluding Remarks

To sum up: there seems to be a distinction in ordinary language between affective states predicated for a relatively short time and affective states predicated for a relatively long time. Somewhat stipulatively, and not worrying too much about what precisely falls under these two categories, I called the former 'emotions' and the latter 'sentiments'. The question was how we should understand this distinction. One way is to understand it as a mere conceptual distinction that does not really map onto a genuine ontological distinction. A natural version of this strategy, the pattern view, suggests that we understand sentiments as collections of emotions (which might be related in some way). Despite its initial plausibility, we have seen that the pattern view faces a number of counterexamples and difficulties that motivate its rejection and the acceptance of an alternative view, the distinctness view. The distinctness view takes the appearances at face value: the conceptual/linguistic distinction between sentiments and emotions corresponds to a genuine ontological distinction; sentiments and emotions are equally basic psychological states. The fact that sentiments and emotions are distinct allowed us to avoid both the counterexamples and the problems raised against the pattern view. And in order to answer a worry one might have to the effect that sentiments and emotions are only contingently related on the distinctness view, I showed that there are various – more or less controversial – ways to accommodate the idea that there is a necessary connection between them. I conclude that the distinctness view should be accepted as the best – or at least, the default (until an adequate reductive alternative is put on the table) – account of the distinction between sentiments and emotions.

Of course, this account leaves many questions unanswered. For one, which mental states fall under the category of sentiments? Although I have helped myself with an intuitive way of placing various affective states on one side or the other of the distinction between sentiments and emotions, a principled way of individuating them should still be found. A principled way to distinguish between various sentiments – perhaps in part by means of their manifestations – should be found as well. Other questions we might ask concern the nature and epistemology of sentiments. If sentiments can be said to have strength, but their strength cannot be accounted

calm passions in Hume's sense: if sentiments are dispositions to experience various emotions, then they are plausibly known by means of their manifestations, namely the emotions we experience.

for by an appeal to phenomenology,[15] what is the nature of this feature and how do we know about the strength of our sentiments? To take a concrete example, what is it for one's love to be strong, and how does one know how strong it is? Furthermore, we have seen that sentiments might be necessarily connected to emotions in virtue of the fact that the latter are manifestations of the former. We might wonder, though, what events and occurrences other than emotions could count as the manifestation of a given sentiment. It is plausible, for instance, that certain desires, intentions and actions could count as the manifestation of a sentiment. An adequate account of these other manifestations, and the way they might relate to each other and to emotions, is yet to be found. Finally, given that sentiments are distinct from emotions, though closely related to them, we can ask ourselves about the potential connections they might bear to normativity and value. Are sentiments things that can be supported by reasons? And what relationship could there be between sentiments and value? Are sentiments responses to value? And if so, is this responsiveness what makes them valuable? The distinctness view, then, not only is a very plausible account of the distinction between sentiments and emotions, but also, if suitably fleshed out, promises to answer deep questions about the nature, epistemology and value of our affective lives.[16]

[15] For an attribution of this claim to Hume's conception of calm passions, see Àrdal (1989: 98).

[16] In writing previous versions of this chapter (whose ideas were first developed in a doctoral thesis at the University of Manchester), I have benefited from very helpful comments from or discussion with Helen Beebee, Michael Brady, Florian Cova, Julien Deonna, Peter Goldie, Moritz Mueller, Michele Palmira, Mauro Rossi, Michael Scott, Joel Smith, Matthew Soteriou, Christine Tappolet, Fabrice Teroni and audiences in Cambridge, Geneva and Manchester.

CHAPTER 9

The Metaphysics of Moods

Christine Tappolet

It snows outside, and you feel lazy, in the mood for doing little else than watching the first snow of the year slowly cover the city. But as you sip your coffee and think about all the work that needs to be done, you start feeling discouraged and depressed. Shifting from one mood to another, we seem to be in a mood or another most if not all of the time. What is more, far from being only watercolours on the surface of consciousness, moods have broad-ranging effects on what we think and what we do. Yet, their nature is elusive. Everyone would agree that moods are psychological phenomena. But what kind of psychological phenomenon are they? Are moods *sui generis* or can they be reduced to beliefs, desires or emotions? More generally, what kind of ontological entity are they? Are they mental dispositions, states of subjects, events in our mental life, or else mental processes, to name but a few prominent possibilities?

Because of the striking similarities between moods and emotions, a common way to proceed is to ask how moods compare to emotions. Indeed, most accounts of moods can be cast as variations on theories of emotions. Moods have been claimed to be nothing but prolonged emotions (Owens and Maxmen 1979; Oatley and Johnson-Laird 1990), or else, low-intensity emotions (DeLancey 2006). They have also been claimed to consist in objectless emotions (Armon-Jones 1991; Clore, Schwartz, and Conway 1994; Frijda 1994b). Alternatively, an influential account holds that moods are emotions that have more general objects – all the things in your environment or even the whole word – compared to the particular

Thanks to Adam Morton, Hichem Naar, Carolyn Price, Mauro Rossi, and Fabrice Teroni for their comments on previous versions, as well as to Murat Aydede, Renée Bilodeau, Paul Boswell, Marc-Antoine Dilhac, Jens Gillessen, Valéry Giroux, Bruno Guindon, Jasper Heaton, Kousaku Hui, Sandra Lapointe, Eric Margolis, Dom McIver Lopes, Iain Macdonald, Shaun Nichols, Michele Palmira, Jean-Philippe Royer, Paul Russell, and the audience at the philosophy departments at UBC, Concordia University, and Université Laval for questions and discussions. I gratefully acknowledge the support of the FRQ-SC and the SSHRC.

objects towards which ordinary emotions are directed (Solomon 1993; Goldie 2000; Prinz 2004).[1] On all these accounts, moods are taken to be kinds of episodic emotions. According to a different approach, by contrast, moods differ from episodic emotions but are considered to involve dispositions to feel emotions. According to a prominent way to spell out this approach, moods are thought to consist in dispositional or functional mental states that affect the formation of other mental states, among which emotions, but also beliefs and desires (Lormand 1985; Griffiths 1997; Siemer 2009).[2]

I shall argue that even though these accounts capture some important aspects of moods, they fail to be satisfactory. In my view, moods are affective phenomena that share important features with, but are nonetheless distinct from, emotions. What I shall propose is that in the same way as emotions are perceptual experiences of evaluative properties that are taken to be actually instantiated, moods are perceptual experiences of evaluative possibilities. More precisely, the claim is that moods are perceptual experiences of the evaluative possibilities that are taken to be likely.[3]

My plan is as follows. After having presented three largely pre-theoretical characteristics of moods, I shall first consider the accounts of moods I want to leave behind, that is, dispositional accounts and accounts according to which moods are kinds of emotions. I shall argue that the former fail to make room for one important pre-theoretical characteristic, and that the latter, while superior to dispositional accounts, are also flawed. The last section presents the "modal" account of moods I favour and offer replies to three objections.

1 Preliminary Characterization

A variety of psychological phenomena commonly counts as moods: good and bad moods, of course, but also peacefulness, tenderness, boredom, elation, excitement, irritability, sulkiness, suspicion, apprehension, anxiety, longing, melancholia, gloom, discouragement, and depression. This list might well need tidying. Maybe there is no deep difference between some of the enumerated items, such as longing and melancholia, or apprehension and anxiety. And maybe some items are too different from

[1] See also Broad 1954; Kenny 1963; Lyons 1980; Baier 1990; Lazarus 1991a; Crane 1998; Tye 2008; and Brady 2014.

[2] See also Höfler 1897; Witasek 1908; Shand 1914; Morton 1980; de Sousa 1987; Thayer 1989; Davidson 1994; Elster 1999; Sizer 2000; Fish 2005; and Wong 2015.

[3] See Price 2006 for a congenial approach in terms of appraisals that concern likelihoods.

the others to belong to the same kind. In any case, the list is most certainly incomplete, because it mentions only cases that are picked out by a single concept. Yet, we can be in the mood for a hike, in the mood for adventure, or else in the mood for love; and we can be in the mood to read a book or in the mood to have a glass of Scotch.[4]

All in all, moods make for a motley crowd, and one important question is whether a unified account of all such phenomena is available. In general, the accounts that have been proposed assume that moods form a sufficiently unified class, but some raised doubts about this claim. Eric Lormand, for instance, distinguishes between locutions of the form "S is in a . . . mood" and "S is in the mood to . . . " and claims that what he calls "moods-to" are not moods at all, but desires (1985: 385–6, 404). Similarly, Carolyn Price suggests that states such as suspicion, optimism, or laziness are distinct from states such as irritability and apprehension in that the former, in contrast to the latter, are not closely associated with emotions (2006: 50). According to her, suspicion and optimism are more like modes of thinking, while laziness is associated with a general level of motivation. The strategy I shall adopt here is to focus primarily on paradigmatic cases of moods, such as irritability, anxiety, and elation. I will argue, however, that the account I propose can be extended to less obvious cases, such as laziness and the mood for love.

In any case, most would agree that at least paradigmatic cases of moods share a number of features. The first of these features is that moods have a characteristic affective phenomenology, which is similar to the phenomenology of emotions. In all likelihood, this shared phenomenology is to be explained at least in part by the physiological and psychological changes that are involved, such as the release of adrenal hormones, a heightened heartbeat, and shifts in the focus of attention. But there also appear to be phenomenological differences between moods and emotions. As both philosophers and psychologists have highlighted, one aspect that distinguishes moods from emotions is that moods seem to involve a kind of *diffuseness* (Morris 1989: 11; Frijda 1994b: 60; Siemer 2009: 256; Kind 2013: 121). Even though there seems to be a grain of truth in this idea, it is not easy to pin the notion of diffuseness down. One way to do so is to claim that moods seem typically, even if not always, to involve less intense feelings compared to episodes of emotions – think of the mood of irritability and an explosion of anger, for instance (Morris 1989: 2; Price 2006: 56). Even so, one should not forget that the feelings involved in moods allow for important variations in intensity. What

[4] As literary works amply show, it can take more than a few words or sentences to characterize a mood.

it is like to be in a mood ranges from the subtle tones of tenderness and longing to the more intense feelings of depression (Sizer 2000: 51).

It is natural to relate the alleged diffuseness of moods to an important feature that concerns their intentionality. To put it simply, moods do not seem to be directed at specific objects.[5] Thus, when you are in a lazy or gloomy mood, you are not lazy or gloomy about something or someone, or lazy or gloomy that something is the case. By contrast, emotions typically target specific objects.[6] You are angry at your sister, you fear her wrath, and you hope that you will escape safely. All the same, it is not clear that moods have no intentional object at all. Indeed, moods seem to be about both nothing and everything (de Sousa 2014: 9; see also Goldie 2000: 17–18). Less paradoxically, it seems that moods are not about specific things, but concern the whole world, or at least our environment as a whole. When in an irritable mood, for instance, most of the things around you will tend to appear offensive. The question is how to account for this apparent lack of specific object *plus* seeming all-inclusiveness that seems to characterize moods.

A third feature of moods is their *pervasiveness*: moods involve far-reaching or global effects on our psychological lives.[7] In contrast with emotions, moods do not seem to directly motivate intentional action. At least in standard cases, an emotion like fear involves a desire that aims at preserving oneself from harm, but this is not so with the mood of anxiety, which typically does not directly result in intentional action (Goldie 2000: 147; Price 2006: 5; Morton 2013: 31). All the same, moods give rise to expressive behaviour, such as when you drum your fingers on the table when nervous (Goldie 2000: 147–8; Price 2006: 55–6). Moods also influence facial expression (Griffiths 1997: 249–50; Goldie 2000: 147–8; Price 2006: 55–6). Indeed, everyone would agree that moods are often expressed at the level of the whole body, sad moods being for instance associated with a specific posture such as sagging shoulders. Moods also come with specific gait patterns, such as reduced speed and arm swing for sad moods (Michalak et al. 2009).

[5] See Thalberg 1964; Searle 1983: 1–2; Isen 1984: 186; Lormand 1984: 389; Morris 1989: 2; de Sousa 1987: 7, 68; Armon-Jones 1991: 48; Frijda 1994b: 60; Siemer 2009: 56; Deonna and Teroni 2012a: 4; and Morton 2013: 35.

[6] It might be thought that some emotions are objectless. You can feel intense fear that seems not directed at a specific object, such as when you wake up in the grip of panic. Against the claim that your fear is objectless, it can be argued that it is directed at something, even though you don't know what it is. As Price puts it, you had "an overwhelming feeling that *something* terrible was about to happen" (Price 2006: 62, my emphasis; see also Goldie 2000: 17–18).

[7] See Isen 1984: 186; Lormand 1985: 389; Morris 1989: 2–3, 11; Sizer 2000: 746; DeLancey 2006: 259; Siemer 2009: 256.

Another important point is that moods influence judgements, notably in that there is a tendency to make mood-congruent judgements. For instance, sad people manifest a kind of "favouritism" for unpleasant concepts, attributes, and outcomes, and a happy person has the tendency to believe good weather is more likely than bad weather (Mayer et al. 1992: 119; Mayer and Hanson 1995: 237; see Siemer and Reisenzein 1998: 783–4 for a list of mood congruent effects). Moods also have an influence on attentional processes and memory tasks, as well as on categorization tasks. Thus, negative moods, such as anxiety, come with a narrower attentional focus, while positive moods, such as elation, involve an opposite effect on attention (Fredrickson and Branigan 2005). Also, when in a sad mood, for instance, we tend to remember sad events instead of happy ones (Bower 1981: 147; Mineka and Sutton 1992). As Laura Sizer puts it, moods come with "biases and modulations in the operation of processes such as attention allocation, memory retrieval, and categorization", and indeed, according to her, moods consist in such biases (Sizer 2000: 766).

The question is how to account for the alleged diffuseness, the apparent lack *plus* all-inclusiveness of their intentionality, and the pervasiveness that characterize at least paradigmatic moods.[8] Let us see how a first family of theories attempts to deal with these features.

2 Dispositional Accounts

The pervasive influence moods have on our mental lives has led a great many theorists to embrace dispositional accounts. According to such accounts, moods would be on a par with solubility and fragility. Whatever the details, everyone agrees that if a substance is soluble in water, then it is such that, *ceteris paribus*, it would dissolve were it put into water.[9] Given the close link between a mood like irritability and the emotion of anger, one could thus suggest that the mood of irritability consists in the disposition to feel anger. Unlike the disposition to feel anger at one specific thing or person, something that can be considered a sentiment (Naar, Chapter 8, this volume), the mood of irritability would

[8] This list is close to, but distinct from, that of Lormand, which includes a) apparent lack of intentional object, b) pervasiveness, and c) the causal character of explanations of moods and of explanations in terms of moods (1985: 389–90). For reasons that will become clear, I would reject c).

[9] This claim is neutral between different accounts of dispositions. Solubility could be thought to be grounded in categorical properties, such as chemical or physical structures, or it could be thought to consist in a property that explains what happens to a substance when plunged into water. (See Heil, Chapter 2, this volume and Naar, Chapter 8, this volume.)

be such that the emotion of anger gets triggered by more or less everything that comes in the way of the irritated person. This is the core of Matthias Siemer's account, according to which moods are "*temporary dispositions* to respond to a wide variety of situations with emotional reactions (experiences) that correspond to the mood" (2009: 257).[10] Call this the simple dispositional account.

The simple dispositional account nicely fits two of the three aforementioned features of moods. In particular, it does well with the thought that moods are about both nothing and everything. While the account can plausibly deny that moods have intentional objects, it can explain the intentional all-inclusiveness in terms of the different intentional objects of the emotions that constitute the manifestation of the disposition. The account also appears to be well-placed with respect to the pervasiveness of moods. On the account under consideration, moods are by definition correlated with episodic emotions, which themselves are plausibly taken to have wide-ranging effects.

However, on reflection, this explanation of the pervasive character of moods does not seem quite right. What is problematic is that moods appear to have a more direct causal role. As we saw, moods can directly result in expressive behaviour. More generally, moods are plausibly taken to directly influence cognitive processes such as the retrieval of memories and attentional shifts. In response, the obvious move is to leave behind simple dispositions and embrace the view that moods are complex or multi-track dispositions involving not only emotions, but also a number of cognitive changes as well as motivational and expressive changes (Griffiths 1997: 250). The mood of irritability, for instance, would involve the complex disposition to feel anger at most of the things that come your way, but also to act in an irritable way, to express one's irritation in a frown, to focus attention on what are deemed offenses, among other things.

The complex dispositional account clearly constitutes an improvement. Yet, it fails to be entirely satisfactory. A first objection is that moods do not appear to be mere dispositions, whether simple or complex. As Jesse Prinz notes, moods such as depression "are occurrent states" (Prinz 2004: 184; see also Frijda 1994: 65). Prinz notes that depression is notoriously miserable to endure. The thought here, I take it, is not that depression feels a certain way, something that raises another issue to which I shall turn. The objection is rather that in contrast with their manifestations, dispositions are not things that occur in time, so that

[10] See also Witasek 1908; Shand 1914.

moods cannot be dispositions. From this, one can conclude with Prinz that moods are mental states, or else that they are events or processes. Whatever the correct account, the objection to the dispositional accounts is that moods involves more than mere dispositions, the assumption being that dispositions need not ever manifest themselves.[11]

In reply, the assumption that dispositions have no temporality might be questioned. On at least some accounts of what dispositions are, they can persist through time. Indeed, as we saw, Siemer holds that moods are "temporary dispositions" (Siemer 2009: 257; see also Naar 2013: 352). Thus, insofar as dispositional accounts hold that moods consist in the temporary possession of dispositions, they make room for the idea that moods can persist over time. The question, however, is whether this way of accounting for the temporality of moods matches our intuitive grasp of how moods occupy time. It is not clear, in particular, that the dispositional accounts can make room for the event-like quality of moods. Moods have a beginning and an end, and they change in intensity. By contrast, the possession of disposition does not seem to be something that can wax and wane.

In any case, there is another, more concessive reply to the objection that underscores the occurrent character of moods. What can be held is that moods are not dispositions, but dispositional, or indeed functional, states, i.e., states that are defined in purely functional terms (Lormand 1984: 399; Griffiths 1997: 250).[12] The model here is functionalism about pain. According to a functionalist account, roughly, pain is a state that tends to be caused by bodily injury, to produce the belief that something is wrong with the body along with the desire not to be in pain, among other things (see Levin 2013: 17). In the same way, a mood could be thought of as a state that realizes a certain causal role. Irritability would be the state that tends to be caused by things like lack of sleep or too much coffee and the like, but also believing one has been slighted, and that is likely to produce fits of anger, higher attention to putative obstacles, etc. Since irritability would clearly be an occurrent state, the objection in terms of temporality would be dispelled. As with the previous suggestion, one can wonder whether the states in question share enough of the event-like qualities of moods. It would seem that functional states have a beginning and an end, but do they

[11] One reply might be to claim that moods are necessarily manifested dispositions (Tappolet 2000: 128). The problem with this suggestion, however, is that it would seem that you can be in a mood without undergoing any of the emotions or indeed any of the cognitive, motivational, or expressive states that are supposed to manifest the mood.

[12] Similarly, Sizer (2000: 766) holds that moods are biasing processes at the level of the functional architecture.

allow for changes in intensity? The analogy with pain suggests that there might well be room for such event-like qualities – headaches certainly can increase and decrease, for instance. The question is whether this is something that can be spelled out in purely functionalist terms. I shall leave this question open and turn to a second objection.

The main problem with both dispositional and functional accounts, in my view, is that they fail to do justice to the phenomenology of moods. Again, the example of depression is telling: the misery you endure is something that you feel, just as is the aching sense of ennui, the bubbling of manic elation, to use Prinz's examples (2004: 184). What dispositional accounts, whether simple or complex, have to deny is that moods are states characterized by phenomenal properties. As far as I can see, a disposition to undergo emotions is simply not something that in itself feels a certain way; and neither is a complex disposition, of course.[13] What you experience can only be the phenomena, such as, foremost, the emotions, to which you are disposed.[14] By contrast, the account in terms of functional states seems better placed. Nothing bars one from claiming that in the same way as pain is a functional state that feels a certain way, moods are functional states that feel a certain way. But as the debate about functional accounts of pain shows, this suggestion raises the familiar spectre of qualia inversion (Crane 1998: 240–1; Fish 2005; see also Mulligan 1998). A functionalist account of pain entails that the qualia of pain could be the one we associate with pleasure. Now, just as this seems difficult to believe, it is difficult to believe that the state that plays the functional role of anxiety, say, could feel like elation or laziness. As Tim Crane notes, the possibility that "emotions have their distinctive 'feel' only contingently does not really make sense" (1998: 241), and much the same is true of moods. In reply, one might suggest that what determines the phenomenal properties of a mood are the affective states that it causes.[15] On this suggestion, anxiety could not feel like elation because anxiety would be the state that realizes a causal role defined in terms of fear. The problem, however, is that even if anxiety is defined in such terms, it could well feel completely differently compared to anxiety as we know it. In principle, nothing excludes that a state that feels like elation plays that very causal role.

[13] But see Heil, Chapter 2, this volume.

[14] See Siemer 2009: 257, 260–1. In fact, he sees it as a virtue of his account that it allows for unconscious moods. While one need not realize that one is in a certain mood, the claim that one can be in a mood without there being anything it feels like to be in this mood is, at best, questionable.

[15] Thanks to Fabrice Teroni for this suggestion.

These remarks regarding the phenomenology of moods suggest that one should turn to an account that takes moods to be kinds of emotions.

3 Moods as Emotions

Moods and emotions share a number of features, the most striking of which, perhaps, is that there is a way it is like to be in a mood or to feel an emotion. Both moods and emotions appear to essentially involve affective feelings (Deonna and Teroni 2012a: 4). Given this, it is natural to suggest that moods are nothing but kinds of emotions. The most popular account along these lines is that moods are emotions that have more general objects. But before considering that account, let me say a word about the other options. According to a first view (Owens and Maxmen 1979; Oatley and Johnson-Laird 1990), moods are prolonged emotions. Even though he is not committed to the view that moods are prolonged emotions, Paul Ekman holds that "what we call moods last much longer than emotions" (1994: 56). In Ekman's view, moods last for hours, sometimes days, while emotions typically last for seconds or at most minutes. However, as seems clear from the example of laziness I started with, moods can be quite fleeting (Davidson 1994: 51; Prinz 2004: 183). Emotions, on the other hand, can surely last for longer than minutes (Lazarus 1994: 83; Prinz 2004: 183). The suggestion that moods are low-intensity emotions (DeLancey 2006: 535) does not fare better. As we saw previously, moods may be characterized by a certain diffuseness and are typically less intense than emotions, but this feature does not prevent them from being sometimes quite intense. Depressive moods or elation, for instance, can be very intense, while the corresponding emotion may lack intensity, such as when you feel a tiny bit of joy at some good news while generally in a morose frame of mind.

Similarities between moods and emotions as well as the characteristic diffuseness and puzzling intentionality of moods might suggest that they are nothing but emotions that lack intentional objects (Armon-Jones 1991: 80; Clore et al. 1994: 326; Frijda 1994b: 60). Depending on how emotions are thought of, what would be left after stripping the intentional object can be expected to be different. In fact, it is far from clear that the idea of stripping the intentional object of an emotion is coherent. To see why, consider stripping the intentional object of a belief. Beliefs are representational and as such are essentially tied to intentional objects. Given this, the thought of an objectless belief does not make sense. It is only if emotions are constituted by distinct and separable parts that the stripping strategy can be made to work. If emotions are taken to consist in a feeling associated with an evaluative belief, for instance, moods can be thought to be feelings that are stripped from the belief. However, because emotions appear to form organic wholes, it is far from clear that emotions can be conceived of in such a way.[16]

The main difficulty with the view that moods are objectless emotions is that, as Prinz notes, moods do not occur at random, but appear to have a function, something which, according to him, entails that they are intentional states (2004: 184). Indeed, moods are responses that can be assessed in terms of how they fit the world. The moods we are in appear to be at least sometimes in tune with how things are. For instance, someone's sad mood after the loss of a close friend is a response that seems to fit how things are for that person. But if moods were mere feelings, one could not assess them in terms of how they fit someone's situation. Moods would have to be considered as nothing but phenomenal noise.

In reply, it might be argued that moods, unlike emotions, fail to be assessable in terms of how they fit the world (Deonna and Teroni 2012a: 12). To make this claim convincing, one would have to explain away the impression that moods allow for assessment in terms of how things are. What could be claimed, thus, is that the assessment in question is one that concerns the emotions that caused the mood. So, being in a depressive mood after the loss of a close friend would not, as such, be assessable; if we believe so, that comes from the fact that grief, like all emotions, is assessable in terms of whether it fits how things are. At most, a depressive mood could be assessed derivatively, as the effect of an appropriate or inappropriate emotion. The problem with this reply is that moods need not be caused by emotions. As has been often noted, they can be caused by all sorts of things, such as lack of sleep, hunger, or too much caffeine (Ekman 1994: 58). Since moods often cause emotions, one might try to use the same strategy with the emotions that results from moods. But here again, the problem is that moods need not culminate in a full-blown emotional episode. We surely can feel itchy and irritable for a day or so without undergoing any episode of anger.

That moods are responses that can be assessed in terms of how they fit things militates in favour of the account that is most popular among philosophers, and according to which moods are like emotions apart from the fact that their object is more general. In the terms of Robert Solomon:

16 For objections to what he calls "add-on theories", see Goldie 2000: 40–1 and Deonna and Teroni 2012a: 56–8.

> *Moods* are generalized emotions: An emotion focuses its attention on more-or-less particular objects and situations, whereas a mood enlarges its grasp to attend to the world as a whole, without focussing on any particular object or situation ... Moods, in their indiscriminate universality, are metaphysical generalizations of the emotions. (1993: 71)

In a similar way, Prinz argues that "moods refer to things or situations quite generally" (2004: 185) the mood of anxiety, for instance, representing general peril, as opposed to a specific danger.[17]

There are several versions of the generalized emotion account of moods, depending on how we draw the contour of the intentional object of moods (Tye 2008; Kind 2013). Following Solomon's suggestion in the quote, the intentional object could be one all-encompassing object, i.e., the world. While emotions would represent specific objects as having an evaluative property such as fearsomeness or offensiveness, moods would represent the world as having such evaluative properties. An alternative suggestion, which Solomon also mentions, is that moods are targeted at "anything that comes our way, casting happy glows or somber shadows on every object and incident of our experience" (1993: 112). According to this second account, moods are directed at a plurality of objects, i.e., all or most of the things in your environment.[18] On both versions, it is plausible to hold that the distinction between moods and emotions is not a strict one. As Peter Goldie argues (2000: 17–18), moods and emotions could be located on a continuum, which ranges from the most specific to the most general objects, or from smaller to a larger sets of objects.

The main motivation of the generalized emotion account is to capture the intentional all-inclusiveness of moods, so it is no surprise that it is well-placed to explain this feature. The account also has the potential to explain the phenomenological diffuseness of moods. This diffuseness would be due to the fact that their object is not as specific as that of emotions, whether this is because they are directed at the world as a whole or at a plurality of objects, something that is likely to come with a kind of attentional openness. The pervasiveness of moods, for its part, could be explained in terms of the tendency to consider specific objects as having the same kind of evaluative property as a given general object. This would explain why we tend to feel

[17] According to Prinz, however, moods can be directed at specific objects, the difference with an emotion being that the intentional object is represented as bearing on one's general position in life. The mood of depression and the emotion of sadness can be directed at the same event, such as one's failing relationship, but whereas sadness represents this event as an isolated loss, the mood of depression represents the event as meaning that things are not going well in general (2004: 185).

[18] Of course, if the world is taken to be nothing but a plurality of objects, there would be no difference between the two ways of specifying the object of moods.

episodes of fear when feeling anxiety, for instance. The idea is that if you consider the whole world, or else the plurality of things in your environment, to be fearsome, it is to be expected that you will consider particular things to be fearsome.

A first objection to the generalized emotion account is that emotions can well take quite general objects. You may fear a pack of wolves, admire an exaltation of larks, or despise mankind. In reply, one might appeal to the idea of a continuum and claim that moods occupy the far end of the continuum between the more specific and the more general. This may be so, but then, the question that arises is whether you cannot feel emotions towards the most general objects. It seems possible to fear all (or most of) the things in your environment or even to fear the world, and on the face of it, there seems to be a difference between the mood of anxiety, on the one hand, and such all-encompassing fears. The generalized emotion account has to reject this distinction and this seems intuitively wrong.

Another objection to the generalized emotion account has been raised by Julien Deonna and Fabrice Teroni. As they emphasize, what follows from the account is that moods would almost always have to be assessed as incorrect (2012a: 13). The reason for this is that, strictly speaking, the whole world never (or very rarely) instantiates the evaluative properties in question. As such, the whole world is surely not often fearsome or offensive. And the same is true of the plural object version: strictly speaking, all of or even most of the things in your environment are never (or very rarely) such as to be characterized by an evaluative property such as fearsomeness or offensiveness. The lesson Deonna and Teroni want us to draw is that moods are not subject to fittingness standards. In reply to this objection, the generalized emotion theorist could bite the bullet and accept that moods are always or nearly always inappropriate.[19] The problem with both this reply and the claim that moods are not subject to standards of fittingness is that they simply fail to do justice to the fact that moods appear on occasion to be in tune with how things are. One of the main motivations for the account to which I wish to turn now is that it is well-placed to make sense of the assessment of moods.[20]

[19] Armon-Jones, for one, holds that moods are subjective projections onto the environment (1991: 104). Note that Prinz's account of moods in terms of the impact of things on someone's whole life can make room for appropriate assessment of moods. It can on occasion be true that things are not going well for you, or that your whole life is threatened. However, if that is the content of moods, they seem to be targeted not at the world or at the all the things in the environment, but at you and your life, something that hardly counts as a general object.

[20] An alternative possibility is to claim with Mendelovici (2014) that moods have as intentional objects unbound properties, such as scariness or rosiness, that are not attached to anything. As Kind (2013) notes, it is not quite clear what it is to represent unbound properties.

4 Perceiving Evaluative Possibilities

The account I would like to propose is like the generalized emotion account in that it locates the difference between moods and emotions at the level of the intentional object. What the proposed account holds is that the difference between the object of moods and the object of emotions is a matter of modal status and not a matter of generality vs. specificity. The "modal account", as I shall call it, claims that moods are directed at possible states of affairs, or more precisely possible states of affairs that are taken to be likely, in contrast with emotions, which are directed at actual evaluative states of affairs. In a nutshell, the suggestion is that moods represent evaluative possibilities.[21]

This general suggestion is compatible with a number of theories of emotions, but because this is the conception of emotion I find most plausible, I shall assume a perceptual account.[22] On such an account, emotions consist in perceptual experiences of evaluative facts, such as the admirableness of someone or the fearsomeness of a situation. This entails that emotions, like evaluative judgements, have representational correctness conditions. In contrast with evaluative judgements, which have conceptually articulated contents, the content of emotions need not be conceptually articulated. What has to be stressed is that the evaluative states of affairs at stake are taken to be actual ones. Put differently, emotions are perceptual experiences of evaluative properties seen as actually instantiated. When you are afraid of a dog which is savagely growling at you, you have a perceptual experience of the dog as actually fearsome. In the same way, when you admire a friend, you have a perceptual experience of the friend as actually admirable, and when you are angry with someone, you have the perceptual experience of that person as actually infuriating.

By contrast, moods are directed at possible states of affairs that are taken to be likely. For example, while the emotion of fear consists in the perceptual experience of something as actually fearsome, the mood of anxiety consists in the perceptual experience of the likely possibility of fearsomeness being

[21] Interestingly, possibilities figure prominently in Heidegger's account of moods. He holds, for instance, that basic existential possibilities are disclosed in anxiety (1927/1962: 235). See Mulhall 1996: 204.

[22] See de Sousa 1987; Tappolet 2000, 2016; Döring 2003; Prinz 2004; Tye 2008; among others. Other accounts that would work well are judgmental theories (Solomon 1993; Nussbaum 2001) and appraisal theories (Arnold 1960; Lazarus 1991a; Scherer et al. 2001). Indeed, Price's account is spelled out in terms of appraisals. She writes: "we might express the content of the state that triggers Annie's irritable mood roughly as follows: *It is more likely than usual that people will behave offensively towards me in the near future*" (2006: 60).

instantiated by something or other. When you are in such a mood, you feel the likely possibility of instantiations of fearsomeness by something or other. In the same way, when you are in an irritable mood, you feel the likely possibility of instantiations of offensiveness, and when in an elated mood, you feel the likely possibility of instantiations of delightfulness or enjoyableness. More generally, what the modal account holds, then, is that moods are perceptual experiences of evaluative possibilities that are taken to be likely, which are characterized by a certain amount of indeterminacy.

Insofar as it is spelled out in terms of perceptual experiences, the modal account is well placed with respect to the specific affective phenomenology of moods. Indeed, the plausibility of an account in terms of perceptual experiences hangs on the assumption that there is a way it is like to be in a mood. The modal account is also in a good position to explain the diffuseness that seems to be characteristic of how moods feel. That moods are readily described in terms of diffuseness is to be expected if moods concern evaluative possibilities that involve unspecified objects, which do not call for a focused attention. By the same token, the all-inclusiveness of the intentionality that characterizes moods is also well accounted for on the view under consideration. Moods would not be about anything in particular, but since an indeterminate number of things will be seen as likely bearers of evaluative properties, the apparent all-inclusiveness of moods would be readily explained. Finally, the proposed account is also well positioned with respect to the pervasiveness of moods. When in the mood of anxiety, the air will seem filled with possible dangers, and thus of possible instantiations of fearsomeness for which you will be on the lookout. Given this, moods are naturally taken to involve expectations as to how things will develop, so moods are likely to have an important biasing effect. You will tend to form the belief that things really are threatening, and it is thus likely that you will undergo episodes of fear. Let me also emphasize that insofar as moods are concerned with possibilities, the modal account predicts that there are important interactions between imagination and moods: imagining certain evaluative possibilities is likely to have an impact on your mood, while the moods you are in will itself orient what you will tend to imagine.

Another virtue of the proposed view is that it not only makes room for the assessability of moods in terms of how things are, but it explains why moods can, on occasions, fit how things are. On the proposed account, emotions are in the business of informing us about actual instantiations of evaluative properties, while moods have the function of signaling the likely possibility of evaluative properties being instantiated. Even if moods are often misleading, they would thus have am important epistemic function.[23] As Price, who argues that moods are states of vigilance that "represent how things are likely to turn out in the immediate future" (2006: 65), puts it:

> while the function of anger or fear is to enable the subject to deal effectively with an offence or threat that has actually occurred, the function of irritability or apprehension is to adapt the subject to an environment in which there is an increased probability than an offense or a threat will occur. (2006: 57)[24]

Thus, depending on how moods fulfil their function, they can be said to be in tune with how things are, or more precisely with what is likely to happen. The instances in which moods are appropriate would alert us to what good and bad things are in the offing, thus allowing us to get ready to deal with what comes our way.[25] For instance, if you are in an environment that is full of possible threats, and thus of possible instantiations of fearsomeness, your anxiety surely can be considered appropriate. Whether a feeling of anxiety will be considered appropriate or not depends not only on the environment, but also on how things stand with you. If you are weakened by a long illness and especially vulnerable, say, there will be more things that are likely to harm you, so feeling anxious will make sense and might well be instrumental in preventing harm from happening.

This seems a promising account which nicely fits the main characteristics of moods, but does it have any plausibility? The first objection likely come to mind is that it cannot make sense to talk about perception in this context. Let us set aside the question whether emotions can be considered perceptual experiences.[26] In the case of moods, the question is how one could make sense of the idea of perceptual experiences of evaluative possibilities and their proximity. The problem is that such metaphysically rarefied items have no causal traction, so that they hardly can be thought to be the object of perceptual experiences. Perceptual experiences are naturally taken to be answerable to a causal constraint, in the sense that their

[23] See Mulhall 1996: 194, for a version of this claim that draws on Heidegger.

[24] In a different passage, Price notes that the appraisal that corresponds to fear represents the *presence* of a threat, not past threat. Note also that Price's general argument relies on a teleosemantic theory of intentional content, according to which the function of state determines its intentional content (Price 2006: 53; see also Millikan 1984). For my part, I prefer to remain neutral with respect to the theory of representation.

[25] As Price suggests, the mechanisms underlying moods might be designed for sensitivity rather than accuracy, so that even if moods are sometimes accurate, they may often be wide off the mark (2006: 66).

[26] For doubts about the idea that emotions could be perceptual experiences of evaluative facts, see Deonna and Teroni 2012a: chap. 6, and Brady 2013: chap. 3; for a defence of the perceptual account, see Tappolet 2016: chap. 1.

object needs to be causally responsible for the experience. So, there is no way one could have perceptual experiences of likely possibilities.

As far as I can see, there are two ways to go for the advocate of the perceptual account of moods. The first is to retreat to a safer theoretical position, which avoids talk of perception and instead appeals to the notion of appraisals. Following Price, moods could be claimed to involve, or indeed to consist in, appraisals that concern evaluative possibilities. A good question, however, is how these appraisals would differ from perceptual experiences. Insofar as it is plausible that they are not conceptually articulated and have a rich affective phenomenology, it might well be argued that they are perceptual experience of a kind, or at least that they are quasi-perceptual experiences. This question leads to the other reply, which is to question the assumption that the objects of perceptual experiences need to be causally responsible for the experiences. Surely there is a causal story to be told, but it is likely that it is more complex than the one we find in sensory perception. Moods are formed in response to how things are presently taken to be, but they are comparable to guesses about what is likely to happen next. So the causal chain goes from how the world is now and how it is taken to be now to expectations about how things will unfold in terms of evaluative possibilities. On the basis of what you take the world to be, something that can involve sensory perception, imagination, or indeed emotional experiences alerting you to the presence of evaluative properties, you form a sense of what is likely to happen in the future. The suggestion, then, is that the sense you form of what good and bad things are in the offing can well count as a perceptual experience even if it is not caused in any sense by these possibilities. On a liberal account of what counts as perceptual experiences, one might well accept this claim. For the less liberally minded, what could be accepted instead is that moods are quasi-perceptual experiences.[27]

The second objection that is likely to be raised concerns the generality of the story. Maybe the proposed account has a chance of being true of irritability and anxiety, but what about laziness, peacefulness, or tenderness? What about the mood to read a book, or the mood for love? A first reply to these questions is to limit the theory to the class of states that have clear emotional correlates and that clearly concern the same type of evaluative property.[28] A more ambitious reply is to propose to extend the story to the less obvious cases. The recipe to follow is to start by specifying

[27] The deep question here is what should count as a perceptual experience (see Tappolet 2016: chap. 1).

[28] This is what Price proposes (2006: 50). Note, however, that she leaves open the door for extending her account to what she calls "more complex cases".

types of evaluative possibilities is at stake, where these possibilities might be more narrowly characterized than the ones that correspond to moods such as anxiety or irritability. The mood in question can then be characterized as consisting in the perceptual experience of the evaluative possibilities in question. Described in this general way, this seems a feasible strategy. There is no space here to examine this strategy in any depth, but here are a few example of how to implement it. When in the mood of laziness, what you feel is the likelihood that opportunities for laziness arise, opportunities that you see in positive terms. When in the mood to read a book, what you feel are positively envisaged opportunities of reading books. When in the mood for love, what you feel are that opportunities for love and romance. What these cases share is that they concern the positively evaluated possibilities, i.e., opportunities that are welcome.[29] Whether this strategy can be made to work for all plausible candidates to the status of mood remains an open question, but on the face of it, it seems promising.[30]

A third objection one might make is that the proposed account fails to sufficiently distinguish between moods and emotions, given that emotions can well have possible states of affairs as objects.[31] Surely you can be afraid about the possibility of freezing rain overnight. Similarly, you can hope that it will snow, the possibility of snow being the object of your emotion. The problem is that on the proposed account, there would be nothing that sets such emotions and moods apart. A first reply one might want to make is that the possibilities in question differ in terms of generality. Emotions would concern specific possibilities, such as the possibility that it freezes overnight, while moods would concern more general possibilities, such as the possibility that all kinds of bad weather occur. The problem, as we saw earlier, with this reply is that fear can concern general possibilities. You surely can fear that all your friends will forget your birthday, or you can hope that friendship will remain possible in the future. Fortunately, there is a better reply. As I have tried to make clear, the modal account holds that difference between moods and emotions lies in the contrast between the actual and the possible. Given this, what can be claimed is that moods are

[29] Thanks to Carolyn Price and to Mauro Rossi for discussing this point. By contrast, when we say that we are not in the mood for something, it seems that we sense negatively evaluated possibilities.

[30] Intriguingly, some moods, such as melancholia or boredom, seem to be concerned more with the absence of positively evaluated possibilities. What could be suggested is that melancholia is a sense of the likelihood of loss, while boredom is a sense of the likelihood of the absence of fun.

[31] Thanks to Hichem Naar for raising this issue.

about the possibility of the instantiation of evaluative properties, while the emotions that concern possibilities are about possible states of affairs that have actual evaluative properties. So, what an appropriate emotion of fear represents is that it is actually fearsome that it might freeze overnight. By contrast, the mood of anxiety concerns the likely possibility that fearsomeness be instantiated by something or other.

Conclusion

I have argued that moods, like emotions, are perceptual (or quasi-perceptual) experiences of a certain kind: they are perceptual experiences of evaluative possibilities that involve a certain amount of indeterminacy. On this account, moods have a distinct epistemic function, which is crucial to decision-making. What militates in favour of this modal account of moods is that it fits well with the commonly acknowledged characteristics of moods, that is, their phenomenological diffuseness, all-inclusive intentionality, and pervasiveness. In addition, it makes room for the plausible idea that moods, even if often entirely misleading, can sometimes be fitting responses.

I started the discussion by asking what kind of things moods are. I mentioned two questions. What kind of psychological phenomenon are moods? What kind of ontological entity are moods? On the proposed account, moods are akin to emotions in that both are perceptual (or quasi-perceptual) experiences. However, because on this account moods and emotions have distinct contents, it can be argued that moods form a *sui generis* class of affective phenomenon, which is categorically different from emotions. In particular, what would be excluded is a view according to which moods and emotions stand on a continuum, the difference between the two being only a question of degree. Insofar as moods and emotions would both be perceptual (or quasi-perceptual) experiences, however, they would nonetheless fall into the same ontological category. I argued that the view according to which moods are dispositions or functional states lacks plausibility. So, if the argument is correct, dispositional and functional accounts of emotions would also be ruled out. I suggested that moods have an event-like quality, but this is compatible with a number of possibilities. Whether the experiences in which moods, or for that matter emotions, consist are better thought of as states, events, processes, or something entirely different remains an open question.

CHAPTER 10

Night Fight

Clare Mac Cumhaill

When the Romanian existentialist writer E. M. Cioran died in 1995, it was reputed that he had not slept for more than half a century. A 'career insomniac', Cioran claimed to have stopped sleeping at the age of seventeen, after which time, by his own account, everything he wrote – all his 'divagations' – issued from his insomnia. Regier remarks that the poet wore his pyjamas 'like a hairshirt' (2004: 994), insomnia a kind of blissful martyrdom which, despite the 'heights of despair' that his sleeplessness induced, brought its own 'blessings':

> Just as ecstasy purifies you of the particular and the contingent, leaving nothing except light and darkness, so insomnia kills off the multiplicity and diversity of the world, leaving you prey to your private obsessions. What strangely enchanted tunes gush forth during those sleepless nights! Their flowing tones are bewitching, but there is a note of regret in this melodic surge which keeps it short of ecstasy. What kind of regret? It is hard to say, because insomnia is so complex that one cannot tell what the loss is. (Cioran 1992: 83)

In this chapter[1] I explore to what extent, and along what dimensions, a link between regret, wakefulness, and insomnia can be excavated – and, as I will show, Cioran's lyric phenomenology speaks somewhat obliquely to this connection. But in doing so, I also aim to echo something of Cioran's difficulty in finding it 'hard to say' just what the peculiar loss of regret is, or, cast differently, what its proper object is. It is striking that the philosophical literature on regret should be likewise undecided, variously

[1] Some of the ideas in this chapter arose out of discussion with Edoardo Zamuner and owe much to him. I am grateful too to the *thumos* research group, Geneva, from whose activities and support I have greatly benefitted. Work for this chapter was started while a post-doc on the Swiss National Science Foundation project 'The Intentionality the Mark of the Mental'. I also thank participants of the 'Dream, Sleep, Emotion' workshop which I organised in September 2013 in Geneva, and Ralph Schmidt, whose work on the affective dimensions of insomnia prompted this exploration. I thank Hichem Naar and Fabrice Teroni for their thoughtful comments on a first draft.

offering, among other things, states of affairs (Williams 1976), blunders (Jacobson 2013), valuable unchosen alternatives supported by reasons (Bagnoli 2000), and objects of attachment, including one's own life (Wallace 2014). My dialectical strategy will be to try to show that such multiplicity can be read as speaking not just, or even primarily, to the potential variety of the objects of regret, but also to aspects of its ontology. In particular, my exploration will attempt to uncover regret's relationship to time through consideration of the nature of the wakeful state. Considering the extent to which the mental activities of thinking and imagining which intuitively accompany regret are partly constitutive of it, I will argue that such activities may sometimes be helpfully understood as *mental* expressive actions – a category of expressive action so far neglected in the literature.

A leading thread of my argument is to suggest that regret is an affective state of the wakeful. The puzzle that frames my 'divagation' is why the state of regret is not merely *incompatible* with sleep but precludes *falling* asleep – that is why regret may occasionally be, to coin a word, insomniacal. My conclusion is that those episodes of regretting that are insomniacal have a peculiarly self-reflexive character that reflection on the ontological character of occurrent regret helps make articulate: they bear a certain relation to the subject who is in that occurrent state.[2] To this extent, disputes over the proper object of regret, insofar as I engage with them, act only as a prism through which my primary concern can be brought into view – the link between regret, wakefulness, and, ultimately, insomnia. That regret may be variously theorised as having very different proper objects is, I explain, symptomatic of the fact that the state of wakeful consciousness is itself complex, a complexity that reflection on the nature of regret reveals and, I suggest, replicates.

The analysis I offer hinges fairly uncritically on the insight of Brian O'Shaughnessy, and in particular his 'Anatomy of Consciousness' in *Consciousness and the World*, which I detail in §§1–2.[3] For the most part, it cleaves closely to O'Shaughnessy's analysis, applying it to the case of regret. In this sense, this chapter is synthetic and expository, though along the way some novel claims are drawn, specifically regarding the link between regret and mental activity. We can get an early glimpse at this connection by noting what Janet Landman in her expansive *Regret* calls the 'occasions of regret'.

[2] For discussion of the ontological category of occurrent state, see Soteriou (2013).

[3] Some aspects of O'Shaughnessy's proposal require further defence or are questionable. For the purposes of this chapter, the idea is only to set out the general explanatory framework. See also Matthew Soteriou's chapter in this volume (Chapter 4). In various respects, I am also indebted to a reading of Soteriou (2013).

Landman notes a link between the availability of time for thoughtful reflection and regret. Reflectiveness, she says, is typically enhanced when alone and unencumbered by daily tasks and hence 'by far the single most frequently reported time for regret [is] evening or night-time' (1993: 204).[4] Likewise, Schmidt and Van der Linden observe that 'bedtime may often be the first quiet period in the course of the day available to review one's own behaviour' (2013: 873) and that 'this time window might be particularly suitable for the emergence of feelings of regret, shame and guilt' (873). But if regret typically emerges at the 'first quiet period' of the day, the link between bedtime and regretting is no surprise – it is a mere correlation. That regret may preclude sleep – as Schmidt and his collaborator also seek to establish – is more mysterious.[5] Why should regret induce insomnia?

Like other writers, Schmidt and Van der Linden take it that regret is a counterfactual emotion. Zeelenberg and Pieters gloss this as follows:

> Feeling regret requires the ability to imagine other possibilities than the current state of the world. One has to reflect on one's choices and the outcomes generated by these choices, but one also has to reflect on what other outcomes might have been obtained by making a different choice. Put differently, regret is a counterfactual emotion. (2007: 5)

Regret, then, involves mental activity. But in what sense is this mental activity *affective*? The authors do not say. They do, however, make a suggestive remark in passing: regret 'both stems from, and produces, higher order cognitive processes' (5). Part of my exploration will be to consider just how the higher-order processes of actively thinking and imagining may be involved in regretting in this dual sense. As I explain, however, while certain patterns of thought and imagining may well *produce* feelings of regret, and while regret may in turn *precipitate* further thoughts and imaginings, there is also reason to think that at least some thoughts and imaginings may be constitutively regretful in the sense that they may be understood not as productive of, nor as produced by regret, but rather as expressions of regret.

The chapter unfolds as follows: in §1, I sketch Brian O'Shaughnessy analysis of wakeful consciousness (readers familiar with O'Shaughnessy's

[4] Jacobson implicitly notes a connection between regret and nocturnal wakefulness. In discussing an individual for whom feelings of regret would *not* be appropriate, he notes: 'If any unwanted feeling keeps her up at night, it is more likely anxiety' (2013: 101).

[5] Schmidt and Van der Linden (2011) provide empirical evidence showing a correlation between self-reported regret and insomnia.

work can skip this section). I explain that although on certain accounts of regret the proper object of the emotion lies in the past, the kind of temporal orientation that wakefulness enables cannot yet explain the link between regret, wakefulness, and, specifically, insomnia (§2). I then focus on the question framed earlier: assuming that regret involves mental activity, in what sense is that mental activity *affective*? In this part of my discussion, I draw on the illuminating work of Carla Bagnoli, and more narrowly on her divergence from Bernard Williams concerning the proper object of regret. I pick up her disagreement with Williams to motivate the claim that sometimes the mental activity that occurs in regret can be understood as *expressive*, in turn bringing work by Peter Goldie to bear on a number of suggestive comments that Williams makes when elucidating his celebrated conception of agent-regret in 'Moral Luck' (§§3–4). In particular, I bring two features of Williams' characterisation of so-called agent-regret (in a sense to be made plain) into synchrony: the idea that agent-regret involves a particular *mode of expression*. And the thought that regret involves a wish. Drawing these together, I will suggest that the mental activity that attends and as I claim partly constitutes regret is in fact *expressive of a wish*: namely the wish that things were otherwise was satisfied *now*.

In closing, I return to the puzzle that Cioran's despair makes striking: the puzzle as to why occurrent regret is not merely *incompatible* with sleep, but may preclude *falling* asleep. I offer a tentative response in closing, focusing on the self-conscious character of occurrent regret (§5).

1 O'Shaughnessy on the State of Wakeful Consciousness

For O'Shaughnessy, consciousness is 'that vastly familiar light that appears in the head when a person surfaces from sleep or anaesthesia or dream. In other words with the state we call "waking"' (2000: 68). The 'problem of consciousness', as he understands it, is not, then, what theorists have elsewhere called the 'hard problem' of consciousness – after all, the hard problem arises as much for sensory experience in dream as it does for wakeful experience. Rather the problem O'Shaughnessy addresses is what the correct analysis of wakeful consciousness is, where here he takes it that wakeful consciousness is only one among a variety of states of consciousness of which the wakeful state of consciousness is the 'parent sub-variety'.[6] I spell out this peculiar taxonomic terminology.

[6] Somewhat confusingly, O'Shaughnessy refers to wakeful consciousness as *consciousness*. For clarity, I systematically refer to wakeful consciousness.

As O'Shaughnessy explains, every living animal is in some state of consciousness. But consciousness does not relate to unconsciousness as life relates to death –

> [w]hereas the paths to death lead to the monolithic state of death, the paths leading away from consciousness conduct one in different directions towards diverse states. (70)

– specifically, they lead one to the states of sleep or unconsciousness. And sometimes wakeful consciousness itself can be 'disordered', in a sense to be made plain.

In sorting among these states of consciousness and in insisting that wakeful consciousness is the 'parent sub-variety', O'Shaughnessy makes plain his methodology. We are not, he says, dealing with real essences or natural kinds. Rather, diverse states of consciousness can be individuated a priori:

> Conceptually we begin with [properly formed wakeful] consciousness and privatively derive the others by denuding it of powers. The state of waking marshals our central mental powers – to experience, sense-perceive, think, and reason cogently and actively manipulate the environment with a view to fulfilling our needs – and all other states are noteworthy for the absence of some or even all of the above. (70)

His methodology, then, is to descriptively analyse diverse states of consciousness by considering what such 'denuded' states of consciousness fail to enable in their owner. For example, deepest unconsciousness involves the 'total suspension' (73) of psychological events – the subject is divested of the powers to imagine, sense-perceive, and reason – while light sleep permits dreaming. Likewise, drunkenness may inhibit or, occasionally, enhance certain powers (see Crowther forthcoming (a), 2016 for discussion – curiously, O'Shaughnessy thinks that the drunk are not properly awake).

An important power that O'Shaughnessy discusses involves the ability to apply the indexical 'now'. A dreamless sleeper cannot entertain beliefs about the present instant picked out as 'now': '[i]f he fell asleep at 6.00 a.m., and awoke at 6.10 a.m., he cannot at 6.05 a.m. entertain a belief about the instant 6.05 a.m. singled out as "now"' (51). But since a non-experiencer cannot be conscious of an instant singled out as 'now', nor can such a subject be aware of a succession of 'nows' and, hence, of the passage of time. I revisit the import of time shortly.[7] For now let us remark in what sense wakeful consciousness is

[7] Interestingly, experience of the passage of time is less pertinent to an account of the phenomenology of regretting than temporal orientation is. Experience of passage does, however, seem to be central to the phenomenology of insomnia, but I leave this unexplored.

the 'parent sub-variety' of all other states of consciousness. It is the *parent* sub-variety since all other 'sub-varieties' are 'denuded' insofar as they involve privations of the powers or capacities that characterise the non-disordered wakeful state. To this extent, the non-disordered wakeful state is a perfection associated with a 'syndrome' of properties[8] (74), properties that 'travel of necessity in groups' (74).[9] For instance, when fully awake, one can perceive, think, imagine, make plans, and so on. Other sub-varieties of the conscious state are likewise 'syndromes' of powers or properties, but they are lacking insofar as they are 'denuded' of certain powers relative to the parent sub-variety: wakefulness.

Wakefulness, then, is a state that is associated with a syndrome of powers. Importantly, however, the state is more than a mere assembly or constellation of such powers or properties. O'Shaughnessy offers various considerations in support of this supposition. The most striking is the following: in removing *the state* of consciousness, say, by using an anaesthetic, one removes *all* the properties or powers. But to this extent, the properties depend on the state, for the state *explains* their presence. However, this is not all. As O'Shaughnessy also insists, modifying the properties that realise the state also involves a modification of the state thereby realised. For example, consider the effect that meditation has on one's wakeful experience. Or copious amounts of wine. Plainly, the character of one's conscious state is modified. But, as such, even while the state explains the presence of the realising properties on which it depends (remove consciousness and you remove the powers), the properties that realise the state are also said to *constitute* it insofar as a modification of the powers involves a modification of the state. This holism will be of some significance later. Before that O'Shaughnessy's thinking must be detailed still further.

Most, if not all, of the capacities 'marshalled' in the state of wakeful consciousness involve what philosophers have designated, obscurely in my view, as 'the will'. O'Shaughnessy is peculiar, however, in distinguishing *two* forms of willing – mental and bodily. The use of the will, says O'Shaughnessy, is *constitutive* of wakeful consciousness, though critically 'no experience utilising the *bodily* will is essential to [wakeful] consciousness' (88; my emphasis) – after all, we can be fully conscious 'though supine in a hammock' (226). But this suggests an essential role for the *mental* will

[8] This is not to say that one property of a state entails the other – some, though not all do. Rather properties necessarily occur in sets that realise unique states of consciousness (75).

[9] Note that properties of the state are powers *of the subject* in that state.

in constituting wakeful consciousness. O'Shaughnessy captures this with a necessity claim: 'The mind of one who is conscious is necessarily a mind actively governing the movement of its own attentive and thinking processes' (89). Let us understand by 'mental willing' this 'active governing'.

As might be supposed, the liminality of the 'bed-time window' is apt to throw such governance into disarray – at least when the subject is poised to surrender her will to sleep. The question is how we should understand the relation between mental activity and nocturnal regret. I begin to spell out that connection in §3. First, I explore two other features of wakeful consciousness – self-consciousness and temporal orientation – which, as I argue, may be relevant to our exploration. I then attempt an application of O'Shaughnessy's ontological reflections on the state of wakefulness to the case of regret.

2 Wakeful Consciousness: Self-Consciousness and Orientation in Time

As we have noted, for O'Shaughnessy, wakeful consciousness enables a cluster of capacities or powers in the subject, including the abilities to sense-perceive and to engage in wilful action with one's surroundings. However, not all wakefully conscious creatures are *self*-conscious – for O'Shaughnessy, a 'higher', 'more developed form' of consciousness (102). I focus here on only one feature of O'Shaughnessy's rich analysis of self-consciousness: the property of self-awareness. I will suggest that there are two broad respects in which self-awareness is explanatorily relevant to our analysis. First, regret involves awareness of the *mode* of one's cogitations – I spell this out shortly. Second, certain forms of nocturnal regretting, specifically those that are insomniacal, may be apt to have the 'self' or 'one's life' or 'occurrent existence' as one among their objects.

O'Shaughnessy supposes that the 'advent of self-awareness' brought with it a new realm of awareness and knowledge – awareness of 'the entire realm of the mental' (103). Unlike the ways in which the outer, non-mental realm comes to be known, however, the objects of the 'inner' realm are known immediately. 'Thus, I know that I am now thinking this, I know I now believe that, I know that I do so because I now observed such and such' (105).[10] What is the scope of such immediate self-knowledge? For one, the content of one's thoughts and experiences are immediately

[10] Though he also grants: 'very occasionally we discover what is here and now occurring in our own minds through inference and appeal to experience' (105).

known. Critically, one also knows their *mode* – that is, one knows that one is imagining rather than remembering, conjecturing rather than believing, and so on. O'Shaughnessy draws a comparison with the dreaming subject so as to make plain, or instruct, in what sense this is so.[11] The dreamer takes his imaginings *to be seeings* and is hence ignorant of their ultimate character – viz. that they are *imaginings*. A like failure is said to occur in mental illness (see also O'Shaughnessy 1972). A mentally ill subject may take her wakeful imaginings to be *real*. But, as such, her wakeful consciousness is thereby said to be 'disordered' or ill-formed. What is meant by this normative charge?

A subject that is self-aware of the contents of her mental states and occurrences is a subject that can encounter both the inner and outer world '*under the aspect of truth*' (111). This notion is spelt out using the idiom of 'comparison':

> (merely) animal consciousness, while it relates cognitively to the world, has nothing to do with truth. Or perhaps better expressed: animals know truths but not *their* truth. A dog knowing it is about to be fed, does not know it is true that it is about to be fed. It could do so only if it could *compare the thought* 'I am about to be fed' with the reality that makes it true (for truth arises out of the matching of thought and reality). And this in turn requires the knowledge that one has that thought, together with the capacity to contemplate its denial as a possibility that is here in fact not realised. (111; my emphasis)

This indicates the import of self-knowledge of the inner realm to the possibility of encountering the world under the aspect of truth. Those who mistake imaginings for reality are not in a position to encounter the world in this guise. Accordingly, the consciousness of such a subject is 'disordered'. I return to this supposition in §5. In what remains of this section, another feature of wakeful consciousness is sketched: temporal orientation. Again, the dreaming subject illuminates. Dream, as O'Shaughnessy vividly notes, is a 'Time Island'. The dream is created 'anew in each instant' (92), 'in experiential mid-air', 'each instant [disengaging] in certain significant ways from its predecessor instants' (91). But this being so, he insists, the dreamer cannot be genuinely cognitively orientated towards the dream past or future.

It might be asked what the status of this claim is. I take it that O'Shaughnessy means it to be a piece of descriptive phenomenology. I

[11] The dreaming subject often provides an important contrast case for O'Shaughnessy, and I use his contrastive expository method here.

hence leave to one side any kind of scepticism about the reality of dreams. My goal is only to excavate a contrast with wakeful experience and here the idea is that wakeful experience, if it is not disordered, does *not* have this character. That is to say, in wakeful experience each instant is not experienced as 'disengaging in significant ways from its predecessors'. Further, and unlike the dreamer, the wakeful subject can entertain cognitive attitudes to future and past times, including, through episodic memory, attitudes to *particular* past times.[12] Such observations then suggest an initial way in which wakefulness and regret may be linked, namely, and perhaps unsurprisingly, through the past. For if what is regretted are past events or states of affairs, and if regretting involves entertaining those events *as past*, a dreaming subject is not in the cognitive position to experience regret. It does not know the mode of its cogitations.

As might be supposed, there are different ways in which the connection between regret and the past can be spelt out. Jacobson (2013), for instance, takes it that what is regretted are bad decisions and their consequences. On this view, at least part of what is regretted is past error in deliberation. Bernard Williams' treatment of regret also makes special room for the past, albeit in a distinct way. For Williams, what are regretted are states of affairs, some of which may be past. However, the peculiar way in which the past bears on regret is not specifically due to the object of regret *being* past, rather what matters is how that past state of affairs is evaluated at the present time *when 'looking back'*. We can get a sense of how to read this notion (as we will see, the perceptual analogy is not wholly coincidental) by reflecting on one of his paradigm cases in 'Moral Luck' – his reimagining of the life of the painter Gauguin.

Williams' Gauguin deserts his family in Paris to realise his painterly ambitions on Tahiti. It might be supposed appropriate that Gauguin should regret his action, but, for Williams, this is not at all plain. He sorts among two species of regret that are relevant to a consideration of Gauguin's affective response – *agent-regret* and regret *in general*. It is worth quoting in full the paragraph that distinguishes these two:

> The constitutive thought of regret in general is something like 'how much better if it had been otherwise' and the feeling can in principle apply to anything of which one can form some conception of how it might have been otherwise, together with consciousness of how things would then have been better. In this *general* sense of regret, what are regretted are states of affairs,

[12] See Campbell (1994) for discussion of the distinction between temporal orientation with respect to phase and with respect to particular times.

> and they can be regretted in principle by anyone who knows of them. But there is a particularly important species of regret, which I shall call 'agent-regret', which a person can only feel towards his own past actions (or, at most, actions in which he regards himself as a participant). In this case, the supposed possible difference is that one might have acted otherwise, and the focus of the regret is on that possibility, the thought being formed in part by first-personal conceptions of how one might have acted otherwise. 'Agent-regret' is not distinguished from regret in general solely or simply in virtue of its subject-matter. There can be cases of regret directed towards one's own past actions which are not cases of agent-regret, because the past action is regarded purely externally, as one might regard anyone else's action. Agent-regret requires not merely a first-personal subject-matter, nor yet merely a particular kind of psychological content, *but also a particular kind of expression.* (1976: 123)

Further,

> regret *necessarily involves a wish that things had been otherwise.* But it does not necessarily involve the wish that, all things taken together, one had acted otherwise.

So, what kind of regret should we expect Gauguin to feel?

Presuming Gauguin had some awareness of the 'claims' (117) his family had on him and what neglecting them amounted to, we might suppose him prone to bouts of *general* regret. Here we might imagine him regarding his past action purely externally, and even wishing that things had been otherwise – say, that his desires had not conflicted so irrevocably. Still, he need not thereby wish that *he* had acted otherwise. In what circumstances would he wish that he had so done?

Notoriously, Williams argues that Gauguin will wish to have acted otherwise only in the event that he is unsuccessful in his ambitions as a painter. Of course, his failure as a painter might be a matter of bad luck – for example, he might have been injured on the way to Tahiti, in which case 'his decision . . . was for nothing . . . there is nothing in the outcome to set against the other people's loss' (120). But although this kind of 'external luck' renders (retroactively, for Williams) his decision unjustified, it does not serve to 'unjustify' *him*, to show that he was wrong. Rather 'what would prove him wrong in his project would not just be that it failed but that *he* failed.' To wit: his failure as a painter would *also* reveal he failed at the time of deliberation, namely in letting the dream of artistic experimentation in Polynesia override the weight of his parental obligations. For Williams, such a recognition should induce 'agent-regret'.

On Williams' understanding, agent-regret can be only experienced from a perspective or 'standpoint of assessment' that regrets the events and actions – in this case Gauguin deserting his family – that shaped *the very possibility of occupying that standpoint.* For only by leaving his family in Paris could Gauguin actually come to occupy a standpoint from which an assessment, negative in this case, *is even so much as possible.* For Williams then, the way in which the past comes to be negatively evaluated as regretful is through a concomitant evaluation of the present, the contours of which have been constitutively shaped by those past events.[13]

It is worth comparing the dream. In dream, there is no such experiential orientation in time, nor is there any constitutive connection between the dream past and dream present – the dream, recall, is created 'anew in each instant' (O'Shaughnessy 2002: 92), 'in experiential mid-air'. Further, past dreamt events are only unified with present dreamt conditions *through the continuity of content that unifies the dream* – both sectors are part of the same dream. Gauguin's past experience in Paris, however, is not related to his present experience in Polynesia merely because they are part of the same life – his. Rather, Gaugin's present experience is such that it is partly shaped by things that he did as well by things that happened to him as a matter of luck.

This invites an early attempt at isolating a connection between regret, time, and wakefulness. If the objects of regret are past states of affairs or past errors in deliberation (Jacobson), or if regret involves any kind of temporal orientation, including 'looking back' from one's current standpoint of assessment (Williams), it is unsurprising that regret necessitates wakefulness and more particularly, as we shall later see, *self-conscious* wakefulness. Why so? Dream experience precludes such temporal orientation. Still, this leaves unexplained the link between regret and *insomnia.* Granted, the 'bedtime' window may precipitate reflection on the near and distant past, but it might be wondered: why should the mere remembering that regret sometimes involves *preclude* sleep? For instance, we know that recalling past events for which one is grateful, and that so induce *positive* affect, can bring on sleep (Emmons and McCullough 2003). But this being so, neither the relevant object of regret being past, nor one's temporal orientation, pass explanatory muster in trying to elucidate a link between regret and insomnia. I try a different tack.

[13] See Wallace 2014 for a deft analysis of the shortcomings of this view.

3 Mental Activity and Wakefulness

Although wakefulness allows for temporal orientation, the mere fact of the object of regret being past, and of constitutively shaping the current standpoint of evaluation, does not yet explain why regret should induce insomnia – this is what §2 sought to establish. There is, however, another explanation. Recall O'Shaughnessy's insistence that properly formed wakeful consciousness necessitates *mental willing* – the active governance of one's own mental acts. If acute, this gestures at a second link. Earlier I quoted Zeelenberg and Pieters: regret 'both stems from and produces higher order cognitive processes' (2007: 5). But that regret may stem from cognitive activity is largely unsurprising; at least certain episodes of regretting may be preceded by *active episodic recall*, namely to provide the episode with an object. There are, however, at least two other ways in which regret and cognitive activity may be linked. This is what I spell out in this section.

As we have noted, Jacobson (2013) pits deliberative error as the proper object of regret; Bagnoli (2000) disagrees, invoking tragedy. Agamemnon sacrifices Iphigenia at Aulis, but his decision is *not* mistaken; it is grounded in what he takes to be an overriding reason – to please the gods. So is Agamemnon thereby immune to regret? Surely, he is not. Bagnoli takes her cue from Williams in explicating her alternative analysis.

In 'Ethical Consistency', Williams considers ways in which conflicts in belief and desire differ. Where two beliefs are consistent but conflicting, the discovery that one of the beliefs is not true leads to its abandonment:

> The rejected belief cannot substantially survive . . . to decide that a belief is untrue *is* to abandon, i.e. no longer to have that belief. (1973: 170)

Desires are different in this respect. When two desires conflict but where the conflict resides not merely in a contingent feature of the world, but essentially – viz. where the world is such that it is impossible that both be satisfied – the satisfaction of one desire does not always lead to an abandonment of the other as it does in the case of belief. Rather, a rejected desire may 'reappear' in another 'guise' – in particular, 'the opportunity for satisfying that desire having irrevocably gone, it may reappear in the form of a *regret* for what was missed' (170).[14]

[14] Compare the case of conflicting desires that may be contingently satisfied: someone who is lazy and thirsty may desire to remain seated while at the same time wanting to get up to get a drink. Were a drink suddenly placed in arm's reach, the conflict would dissipate.

Bagnoli is impressed by this insight. Regret, for Williams, is residual in the sense that, as Bagnoli puts it, it 'stands for a value' (174) – through the experience of regret, the subject values an opportunity forgone in deliberation. Regretting, then, is a mode of valuing. Even so, she maintains, Williams gets the moral phenomenology of regretting wrong. Specifically, he goes awry in seeing the peculiar *agency* that agent-regret involves as symptomatic of value pluralism. I explain what is meant by this charge.

For Williams, moral values are not supreme. When acting in the context of value pluralism, moral values may sometimes be overridden, precipitating regret. Consider Gauguin. In asking whether he was right to desert his family, there is, for Williams, more than one 'right' – aesthetic values may trump moral ones:

> Perhaps fewer of us than is pretended care about the existence of Gauguin's paintings, but we are supposed to care . . . the fact is that if we believe in any other values at all, then it is likely that at some point we shall have reason to be glad that moral values . . . have been treated as one value among others, and not as unquestionably supreme. (133)

Bagnoli insists that for Williams 'regret . . . is elected as a significant element of the world of values, rather than as an attitude intelligible in the perspective of the agent' (175). Whether or not we agree with the first clause of her criticism, her appeal to the first-person perspective should surely resonate. Regret is an attitude that should be intelligible from that perspective. In particular, we might wonder whether there is a phenomenological dimension to emphasising that demand for intelligibility.

As it happens, Williams *does* grant that differences in regret in general and agent-regret shore up as 'differences in the thoughts and images that enter the sentiment' (124) – a certain recognition of the phenomenological dimensions of the first-person perspective is not then absent in his account. Still, Williams does not tell us *how* we should understand this *experiential* difference between regret and agent-regret. Bagnoli's work is instructive in this respect. Bagnoli submits that regret is an emotion[15] that involves counterfactual patterns of thinking and imagining. But what kinds of differences in the counterfactual thoughts and imaginings should we suppose regret in general and agent-regret supporting?

Her thought is the following.[16] Suppose a chorus were to fictively represent the alternatives that would have been available to Agamemnon

[15] As will, of course, be clear by now, I too assume that regret is an emotion.
[16] I have adapted her example for purposes of exposition.

at Aulis – perhaps by *performing* those alternatives. The representation is *descriptive* and the full range of alternatives available is determined, as Williams would have it, by the way the world is. In contrast, the range of alternatives that *Agamemnon* would have considered – presumably in thoughts and images – *is evaluative* and is determined by what for the agent were viable alternatives at the time of deliberation. Bagnoli's idea, drawing on Williams, is that, in regret, such thoughts and images may *reappear*. What they represent in such instances, however, is not opportunities missed due to how the world is or was, *pace* Williams, but rather what *for the agent* were potentially viable and valuable alternatives not taken up. This phenomenal 'reappearance' of reasons makes plain the practical significance of regret.[17] Regret 'reminds' the subject of reasons that were supported but were not overriding. It hence 'reminds' the subject that 'some more work has to be done' (185) – for example, reparation needs to be made, an excuse offered, or forgiveness asked for, say. But to this extent, as Bagnoli explains, 'regret may have a motivational force insofar as it provides the agent with a practical reason: it calls attention to a reason for action. In calling attention to a reason for action regret can *initiate a new* deliberation' (185).[18]

This indicates a wholly different way in which mental activity and regret can be linked – regret can *precipitate* new chains of thinking. But if so, as I think seems phenomenologically plausible, and if, too, O'Shaughnessy is correct in postulating a constitutive link between wakefulness and mental activity, it is hardly any wonder that regret induces sleeplessness. Why? *For it induces thinking and thinking necessitates wakefulness.* At the same time, however, there is no reason to think that regret is special in this respect. If we are awake, we are *bound* to think – says O'Shaughnessy 'the [wakeful] conscious find themselves in the grip of a necessity to freely choose their own occupations of thought and attention' (2002: 89). But, if so, the mere fact that regret may precipitate thinking does not yet explain why regret may induce *insomnia*. We can, however, find the resources in Bagnoli's account to excavate a third link, one which, as I explain in later sections, brings us closer to an explanation.

Though Bagnoli may have reason not to explicitly invoke Nico Frijda's conception of the 'action tendency', it seems natural to wonder whether

[17] To make sense of how reasons can 'phenomenally' reappear, see Soteriou (2013).

[18] For some sleepers, the relevant chains of deliberation are neither productive nor yield closure – such subjects perceive their *minds to be 'racing'* (Schmidt, Harvey, and Van der Linden 2011), they *ruminate*. Roese et al. (2009) identify a species of regret that they call 'repetitive regret' which involves rumination.

the peculiar action tendency of regret might not simply be to so think and imagine. Jacobson's sentimentalist treatment of regret invites such speculation. Sentiments, for Jacobson, form a class of emotion types, the nature of which is open to empirical discovery. Like other emotions, sentiments are, for Jacobsen, best conceived as 'syndromes' of thought, feeling, and motivation – something that tallies with the O'Shaughnessy-inspired approach explored in this chapter (see also Soteriou, Chapter 4, this volume). Unlike other emotions, however, the sentiments are apt to display two further features. First, they exhibit stable recalcitrance – they tend not to be responsive to belief. Second, and critically, they issue in acting without thinking. In the case of regret, however, this sparks a further puzzle. For consider: if the peculiar action tendency of regret is just to counterfactually think and imagine, and if action tendencies are typically discharged *without thinking*, can we really make sense of those *mental* actions as action tendencies that can, as it were, be performed *without thinking*? Further, we might wonder: how do such putative 'mental action tendencies' compare with those of other sentiments? Someone in the grip of rage may 'lash out', stamp their feet, slam doors. Those who are fearful may tremble and flee. But in what sense could regret involve acting *without thinking* in any analogous sense, if at all?

Jacobson does not address this issue, suggesting only that regret prompts a 'policy change' for future action; it has practical significance insofar as it involves a motivation to act differently next time. It might be queried, however, just how acute this generalisation is. The notion of 'policy change' may have little traction in cases where the acts or outcomes regretted are highly idiosyncratic. Worse, it seems that regret is sometimes compatible with a complete failure of policy change, as in cases of akrasia. But if such motivation towards policy change is the peculiar 'action tendency of regret', and if sentiments are partly distinguished from emotions in having specific and even empirically discoverable action tendencies, are such episodes less 'sentimental' or less canonically episodes of 'regret' for all that? If anything, surely the regret that is experienced thereafter is even more bitterly felt?[19]

In the next section, I try to bring these twin observations into synchrony: the supposition that the peculiar action tendency of regret is to counterfactually think and imagine as well as the thought that regret can sometimes issue in 'thoughtless' thinking and imagining and so have a

[19] As Zeelenberg and Pieters (2007) report, 'inactions' – failures to act – are apt to generate even more regret than actions.

characteristic action tendency *even in cases of inaction* or where regret does not or cannot motivate 'policy change'. Here my argument harnesses aspects of Williams' account that remain unexplored in the literature but which I consider deserve further consideration – specifically his insight that agent-regret has a *peculiar mode of expression*, and that it involves a *wish*. I will claim that sometimes regret can issue in mental expressive actions that can be understood as *expressive of a wish*. And this in turn will allow me to reassert the significance of Williams' connection between regret and one's present occupation of a 'standpoint of assessment', one's *self-conscious* occupation of which, as I will argue, can sometimes preclude sleep.

4 Wishing, Reparation, and Inaction

Goldie (2000) distinguishes among expressions of emotion that are actions and those that are not – for instance, autonomic nervous responses like sweating and muscular reactions like flinching. These latter expressions are not something one *does*. Expressions of emotion that *are* actions, however, are distinguished from actions that are not expressions of emotion, and this is so even if emotion can sometimes precipitate actions that have all the hallmarks of being an emotional expressive action but that are not. For example, say in the presence of a bull, I decide to flee. Though I may feel fear in the presence of the bull, I flee *in order to* escape the bull's presence. Let us say that my fleeing is a reasoned action *out* of emotion. Though I feel fear, I was cognitively and conatively, *and not affectively*, moved to act.

Compare the following case. I flee *in* fear. In this case, the action is not adequately explained by a belief/desire pair.[20] I do not any more flee with *the aim* of removing myself from the bull's presence. I am moved by feeling. Actions that are performed *in* emotion are *genuine* expressions of emotion, says Goldie. And they are genuine since they are not done as a means to some further end. Compare a caress that is intended to demonstrate love, to one that unfolds spontaneously *in* an act of love.

We can apply this distinction to our earlier discussion. Although regret may sometimes precipitate actions that are reasoned actions performed *out* of emotion – new episodes of deliberation which may themselves involve counterfactual patterns of thinking or imagining, or even, as Williams insists, concrete acts of reparation – it may

[20] It might be queried whether the 'standard' story of action causation that appeals to belief/desire pairs is apt even to non-expressive action (see Hornsby 2010) – I assume it is, but only for expository purposes.

also, or so I am suggesting, involve actions that are performed *in* emotion, specifically the mental actions of counterfactually thinking and imagining.

It is worth noting that Bagnoli's position seems to hybridise both these forms of action – actions performed both *in* and *out* of the experience of regret. For consider: reasons 'reappear' and call for attention *and* they have a motivating force, namely to initiate new deliberations. But those reappearing reasons and imaginings are not projects *undertaken by the subject* to achieve some end. Rather, in regret, as I am claiming, the subject just tends to counterfactually think and imagine.

Let us say, then, that *in* regret the subject may sometimes engage in mental expressive actions that are not merely produced by regret – that are not merely outputs of the state regret – but *are*, in part, *the regretting*. This claim requires further clarification and indeed justification – a task for elsewhere. For now, I raise two considerations that are pertinent to a more careful delineation of the notion of a mental expressive action. First, it might be supposed that if regret does involve mental expressive action, then there ought to be some way of showing that the kinds of mental expressive actions that regret involves are continuous in kind with those expressive actions that have so far been considered in the literature – so-called arational actions; those of the grieving for example, when they embrace the garments of a loved one who has died (Hursthouse 1991). Second, if this kind of analysis is vaguely on the right track and if regret is indeed a sentiment that sometimes issues in mentally acting without thinking, then it seems there needs to be some way of explaining why regret, like other sentiments, can nonetheless be stably recalcitrant. For prima facie, if regret involves counterfactual patterns of imagining and *thinking*, then regret, surely, ought *not* to be impervious to belief.

I suggest that two features of Williams' original account should be recovered so as to make conceptual space for, and accommodate, these considerations: first, Williams' insight that agent-regret has a particular *mode of expression* and, second, his emphasis not on reasons (like Bagnoli), but wishes.[21] Williams, in recruiting the concept of 'expression' seems to have had concrete expressive acts of reparation in mind. I will instead emphasise expressive *mental actions*. Further, while Williams insists that regret may involve a wish that things had been otherwise, I shall contend

[21] Note this is a difference of emphasis: one may after all claim that reasons play the role Bagnoli thinks they play only conditional on the presence of a wish. Thanks to Fabrice Teroni for emphasising this point.

that regret may involve the wish that things be different *now*. In this, I take my inspiration from Goldie.

For Goldie, wishes that are not idle desires (like the desire to be taller, say) involve not just desiring the thing or state of affairs wished for, but imagining or being disposed to imagine that *the desire is satisfied* (2000: 28). And this helps him spell out in what sense wishes are operative in expressive actions. Such actions are, says Goldie, the imaginative expression of a wish. When a grieving subject caresses the clothes of the loved one who has died, the clothes are imaginatively invested with symbolic significance – the subject imagines that she is *really* caressing the person who has died and her imaginative act is expressive of the wish that she really *be* caressing that person. Though she is aware of what she is doing – she does not believe that by caressing their garments she caresses them – she nonetheless *imagines her wish to be satisfied*. Accordingly, she wishes that things were different *now*. As Goldie explains, 'the symbolic nature of the expression takes place as it does partly because the literal action, as it were, is not a realistic option' (29). Compare Williams on agent-regret: the agent will act in some way 'which he hopes will constitute or at least *symbolise* some kind of recompense or restitution and this will be an expression of his agent-regret (1973: 124; my emphasis).

Though Goldie considers expressive actions that involve imaginative relations to external objects – a cushion, for example, may be co-opted for the person one wants to pummel – it is not, I think, difficult to appreciate in what sense regret might involve wishes of a similar kind, and perhaps especially so in cases where the regretted situation is beyond mending or where, as Goldie puts it, 'literal action . . . is not a realistic option'. In this case the suggestion is that one may counterfactually imagine not only how things might have been, but how things could have been *now*, where such imagining is *expressive of the wish that things really be that way*.[22]

My only defence of this claim is that it strikes me as phenomenologically plausible.[23] But there are explanatory advantages to the approach too. For example, while we can allow that valued reasons can sometimes 'reappear' in the guise of regret, we need not insist that this is all there is to the phenomenology of regretting. Since wishes need not track considered

[22] On this understanding, one may even find oneself surprised by one's wishes – that is, one may be surprised to find oneself imagining as one does. To this extent, actions that are expressive of a wish need not always be intelligible from the perspective of the agent, *pace* Bagnoli. Instead, regret may provide an opportunity for insight, not just a *reminder* 'that more work has to be done'.

[23] See Gordon 1992 for descriptive phenomenological reports of experienced regret based on dialogical interviews.

reasons or desires that 'reappear', wholly hitherto unconsidered alternatives or visions of how things *now* could be may, for the first time, 'appear'. Again, this strikes me as phenomenologically resonant. Further, since such expressive actions unfold *in* regret, they are not best thought of as projects that the subject *undertakes*, which in turn preserves Jacobson's insight regarding the sentimentality of regret: since wishes are not always answerable to beliefs, such regret can be recalcitrant. In sum, this now suggests three distinct ways in which mental activity may be involved in occurrent regretting: through active episodic recall, through precipitating new chains of deliberation, or through the mental expressive actions of counterfactually imagining and thinking. But even if this much is granted – and naturally there is a great deal more to say – our original puzzle still stands. If regret and wakefulness are linked through mental action – be it reasoned action *out* of emotion or, as I am suggesting here, mental activity that is *expressive of* regret – why is it the case that regret is sometimes not merely incompatible with sleep, but may preclude falling asleep?

To get a sense of why we are left with a residual puzzle, it is instructive to consider a case that Bagnoli frames in furthering her claim that the object of regret is a valued alternative supported by good but not overriding reasons. She introduces us to Jackie. Jackie chose between two different life paths – to pursue architecture or modern dance. She chose the first and considers this decision the right one. Nonetheless, she regrets not being a dancer. As Bagnoli admits, Jackie's regret might seem odd. On many accounts, it might even come out as inappropriate or irrational. Bagnoli's account however, as well as mine, can divert this charge – through regret, Jackie may value that alternative, perhaps sometimes imagining her wish to be satisfied. Still, if Jackie's regret keeps her awake at night, then it seems to me that we might be inclined to suspect that something is, after all, amiss with Jackie's regretting. Specifically, it seems we might be disinclined to believe her when she says that she considers that she made the right decision in choosing to become an architect. So, what then is specific to those forms of nocturnal regret which are such that insomnia may result?

5 Self-Conscious Regret

In the course of this chapter, I have appealed to different properties of the wakeful state, and so properties of the subject in that state so as to motivate a link between regret and wakefulness. Since wakefulness enables in its subject the power to experience the passage of time and to relate, through episodic memory, to particular past times, and since regret constitutively involves mental activity of various sorts, including, as I have suggested, mental action that is expressive of a wish, it should be plain that regret is an affective state of the wakeful. In closing, I suggest that these twin features can be united through a further dimension of the wakeful state, one that finally allows us to resolve the difficulty of seeing how it is that occurrent regret may sometimes preclude falling asleep.

I have suggested that sometimes the regretful subject may imagine that her wish that things be otherwise is satisfied *now*. Earlier, I set out O'Shaughnessy thought that only the wakeful subject can apply the indexical 'now'. So, what capacities are involved in a subject's imagining that her wish is satisfied now?

As we have noted, only a *self-conscious*, wakeful subject can encounter the world under the aspect 'truth' – that is, only a self-conscious, wakeful subject can compare the thought 'p' with the reality that makes p true, where 'this in turn requires the knowledge that one has that thought, together with the capacity to contemplate its denial as a possibility that is here in fact not realised' (O'Shaughnessy 2002: 111). But regret, surely, involves a like capacity. The regretful subject, even while imagining that her wish is satisfied now, *is aware that she is imagining* – she is self-aware of the proper *mode* of her cogitations. But, as such, she is aware too that *what* she is now imagining is *not* now realised. This is why her imagining is an expression of her *regret*.

Return to Jackie. Suppose that Jackie's regret keeps her awake. Why might we be inclined to suppose that there is something awry with Jackie's regretting? Jackie claims that she is happy with her life as an architect and what she, on one understanding, thereby is: an architect. But surely her nocturnal regret speaks against this. Anthony Kenny expresses a similar doubt:

> If a man says that he is afraid of winning £10,000 in the pools, we want to ask him more: does he believe that money corrupts, or does he expect to lose his friends, or to be annoyed by begging letters, or what? If we can elicit from him only descriptions of the good aspects of the situation then we cannot understand why he reports his emotion as fear and not as hope. (1963: 134)

My claim is not that the case of Jackie is incoherent, but only that if her regret induces insomnia, we might have reason to query the extent to which Jackie knows her own mind. Perhaps she would prefer to dance after all. But if so, then it is plausible that the object of Jackie's regret is (some variation on) the standpoint of assessment that she now occupies, perhaps the life she now leads, or maybe the person who leads that life: herself. So why should such regretting, which has such objects, preclude sleep?

In reflecting earlier on the 'holism' that characterises states of consciousness and their properties, we noted that in removing the state of wakeful consciousness, say, by the use of anaesthesia, one removes the properties. In contrast, modifying the properties involves modifying the state. Applying this to the state of regret, itself a modification of wakeful consciousness, we might therefore expect two distinct therapeutic approaches to resolving regret-induced insomnia: those aimed at modifying the properties that constitute the state of regret (and that thereby modify the state), and those aimed at removing the state of regret directly.

There is at least some evidence for such a twofold approach. Davis and colleagues (1995) contend that those who experience regret either tend to overestimate the extent to which the alternatively imagined scenarios were possible, or the degree to which they had genuine control over the outcome of a given situation.[24] Resolving such regret involves downplaying the sense in which the relevant alternative was genuinely possible. But if what I have suggested is right, such an intervention may not resolve regret that is expressive of a wish. For such regrets may be more recalcitrant to reason.

A distinct approach aims at rationalising a discrepancy between one's values and actions, where the experience of regret may be regarded as expressive of one's evaluative perspective (see also Betzler 2004). But to this extent, the experience of regret may in fact *reassure* – despite what one has done, one's values are intact and hence, to a certain extent, oneself. Thus reassured the subject can seek to rationalise, if not justify or excuse, regretful action on other grounds.

For other subjects, however, it is clear that the experience of regret seems not to reassure at all – it may *not* 'remind' the subject of who they are precisely because who-they-are *is* the object of their regret. As Fisher and Exline explain:

> Regret can involve a sense of damage or loss focused on a person's core identity, as suggested by such statements as, 'I used to be a conscientious person before I did this act' or 'I could have been a brilliant musician if I would have made better choices.' (2010: 556)

Such may be Jackie's difficulty. But if this is so, then to resolve such regret it seems that one must remove, not the properties or powers that constitute the state – for instance, it is not merely enough to stem the flow of counterfactual thinking and imagining – but the state itself. Since,

[24] On Williams' approach, this would not preclude regret, but might allow for a transmutation of agent-regret into regret in general.

however, the *object* of regret – the subject – is *in the state*, to remove the state, one must deprive the state of its object. But how? Therapeutic approaches that focus on acceptance and self-forgiveness seem to focus on resolving regret along these lines, so that one's self, or, simply, the person one takes oneself to be, is no longer an object of regret.

This finally suggests a way in which regret may not merely be incompatible with sleep, but may preclude falling asleep. If the object of one's regret is oneself or, more minimally, one's standpoint of assessment, it is not just the case that one is awake *because* one is regretting, but rather to regret *what* one regrets – oneself and perhaps even (aspects of) one's existence – one cannot fall asleep. For what one regrets can *only* be wakefully 'given' to one: oneself.

Conclusion

I have appealed to different properties of the wakeful state so as to motivate a link between regret and wakefulness. If correct, regret is essentially an affective state of the wakeful. In particular, I have tried to motivate a position on which the cognitive activity that attends regret may sometimes occur *in* emotion and be expressive of a wish – a 'strangely enchanted' expressive mental action. Finally, I have attempted to forge a link between regret and insomnia, not just by appeal to temporal orientation or cognitive activity, which, if O'Shaughnessy is correct necessitate wakefulness, but to the self-conscious subject, something that is lost in sleep and dream.

Bibliography

Àrdal, P. S. 1989. *Passion and Value in Hume's Treatise*. Edinburgh: Edinburgh University Press.

Aristotle. 1987. *De Anima*, trans. H. Lawson-Tancred. London: Penguin Classics.

Armon-Jones, C. 1986. 'The Thesis of Constructionism', in R. Harré (ed.), *The Social Construction of the Emotions*. Oxford: Oxford University Press, pp. 32–56.

1991. *Varieties of Affect*. New York: Harvester Wheatheaf.

Armstrong, D. M. 1968. *A Materialist Theory of the Mind*. London: Routledge & Kegan Paul.

1970. 'The Nature of Mind', in C. V. Borst (ed.), *The Mind/Brain Identity Theory*. London: Macmillan, pp. 67–79.

Arnold, M. B. 1960. *Emotion and Personality*. New York: Columbia University Press.

Arpaly, N. and Schroeder, T. 2014. *In Praise of Desire*. Oxford: Oxford University Press.

Austin, J. 1956. 'A Plea for Excuses', *Proceedings of the Aristotelian Society* 57(1): 1–30.

Averill, J. 1980. 'A Constructionist View of Emotion', in R. Plutchik and H. Kellermann (eds.), *Emotion: Theory, Research and Experience*. New York: Academic Press, pp. 305–39.

Bagnoli, C. 2000. 'Value in the Guise of Regret', *Philosophical Explorations* 3(2): 169–87.

Baglioni, C., Spiegelhalder, K., Lombardo, C., and Riemann, D. 2010. 'Sleep and Emotions: A Focus on Insomnia', *Sleep Medicine Reviews* 14: 227–38.

Baier, A. 1990. 'What Emotions Are About', *Philosophical Perspective* 4: 1–29.

Barrett, L. 2006. 'Are Emotions Natural Kinds?', *Perspectives on Psychological Science* 1: 8–58.

Betzler, M. 2004. 'Sources of Practical Conflicts and Reasons for Regret', in M. Betzler and P. Baumann (eds.), *Practical Conflicts, New Philosophical Essays*. Cambridge: Cambridge University Press, pp. 197–222.

Bird, A. 2016. 'Overpowering (How the Powers Ontology Has Over-Reached Itself)', *Mind* 125(498): 341–83.

Block, N. (ed.) 1980. *Readings in Philosophy of Psychology*, 2 vols. Cambridge, MA: Harvard University Press.

Block, N. and Fodor, J. 1972. 'What Psychological States Are Not', *Philosophical Review* 80: 159–81.

Bower, G. H. 1981. 'Mood and Memory', *American Psychologist* 36: 129–48.

Brady, M. S. 2007. 'Recalcitrant Emotions and Visual Illusions', *American Philosophical Quarterly* 44(3): 273–84.

2009. 'The Irrationality of Recalcitrant Emotions', *Philosophical Studies* 145(3): 413–30.

2013. *Emotional Insight: The Epistemic Role of Emotional Experience*. Oxford: Oxford University Press.

2014. 'Emotion, Attention, and the Nature of Value', in S. Roeser and C. Todd (eds.), *Emotion and Value*. Oxford: Oxford University Press, pp. 52–71.

Broad, C. D. 1954. 'Emotion and Sentiment', in H. D. Lewis (ed.), *Broad's Critical Essays in Moral Philosophy*. London: Allen and Unwin, 1971, pp. 283–301.

Burge, T. 2010. *Origins of Objectivity*. New York: Oxford University Press.

Cacioppo, J. T. Berntson, G, Larsen, J., Poehlmann, K. and Ito, T. 2000. 'The Psychophysiology of Emotion', in M. Lewis and J. Haviland-Jones (eds.), *Handbook of Emotions*, 2nd edn. New York: Guilford pp. 173–91.

Campbell, J. 1994. *Past, Space and Self.* Cambridge, MA: MIT Press.

Campbell, K. 1990. *Abstract Particulars*. Oxford: Basil Blackwell.

Campbell, N. 1996. *Biology*, 4th edn. San Francisco: The Benjamin/Cummings Publishing Company.

Cassam, Q. 2007. *The Possibility of Knowledge*. Oxford: Oxford University Press.

Chalmers, D. J. 1996. *The Conscious Mind: In Search of a Fundamental Theory*. New York: Oxford University Press.

2002. 'Consciousness and Its Place in Nature', in D. J. Chalmers (ed.), *Philosophy of Mind*. Oxford: Oxford University Press, pp. 247–72.

Chemero, A. 2003. 'An Outline of a Theory of Affordances', *Ecological Psychology* 15: 81–195.

Chudnoff, E. 2015. *Cognitive Phenomenology*. New York: Routledge.

Churchland, P. S. 1986. *Neurophilosophy*. Cambridge, MA: MIT Press.

Cioran, E. M. 1992. *On the Heights of Despair*, trans. Ilinca Zarifopol-Johnston. Chicago: University of Chicago Press.

Clore, G. L., Schwartz, N., and Conway, M. 1994. 'Affective Causes and Consequences of Social Information Processes', in R. S. Wyer and T. K. Srull (eds.), *Handbook of Social Cognition*. Hillsdale, NJ: Erlbaum, pp. 27–62.

Cohen, J. 2010. 'Color Relationalism and Color Phenomenology', in B. Nanay (ed.), *Perceiving the World*. Oxford: Oxford University Press, pp. 13–33.

Colombetti, G. 2014. *The Feeling Body: Affective Science Meets the Enactive Mind*. Cambridge, MA: MIT Press.

Colombetti, G. and Thompson, E. (2008). 'The Feeling Body: Towards an Enactive Approach to Emotion', in W. Overton, U. Müller, and J. Newman (eds.), *Developmental Perspectives on Embodiment and Consciousness*. Hillsdale, NJ: Erlbaum, pp. 45–68.

Cosmides, L. and Tooby, J. 2000. 'Evolutionary Psychology and the Emotions', in M. Lewis and J. Haviland-Jones (eds.), *Handbook of Emotions*. New York: Guilford Press, pp. 91–115.
Cottingham, J. 1985. 'Cartesian Trilism', *Mind* 94: 218–30, reprinted in *Cartesian Reflections: Essays on Descartes's Philosophy*. Oxford: Oxford University Press, 2008, pp. 173–87.
Crane, T. 1998. 'Intentionality as the Mark of the Mental', in A. O'Hear (ed.), *Contemporary Issues in the Philosophy of Mind*. Cambridge: Cambridge University Press, pp. 229–51.
Crane, T. and Mellor, D. H. 1990. 'There Is No Question of Physicalism', *Mind* 99: 185–206.
Crowther, T. 2011. 'The Matter of Events', *Review of Metaphysics* 65(1): 1–33.
2016. 'Failures of Rationality and Self-Knowledge in Addiction', in N. Segal and G. Heather (eds.), *Addiction and Choice*. Oxford: Oxford University Press, pp. 82–96.
forthcoming. 'Experience, Dreaming and the Phenomenology of Wakeful Consciousness', in F. Dorsch, F. Macpherson, and M. Nida-Rumelin (eds.), *Phenomenal Presence*. Oxford: Oxford University Press.
Damasio, A. R. 1994. *Descartes' Error: Emotion, Reason, and the Human Brain*. New York: Putnam.
2003. *Looking for Spinoza: Joy, Sorrow, and the Feeling Brain*. Orlando, FL: Harcourt.
D'Arms, J. and Jacobson, D. 2000. 'The Moralistic Fallacy: On the "Appropriateness" of Emotion', *Philosophy and Phenomenological Research*, 61: 65–90.
2003. 'The Significance of Recalcitrant Emotion', in A. Hatzimoysis (ed.), *Philosophy and the Emotions*. New York: Cambridge University Press, pp. 127–46.
Darwin, C. 1998. *The Expression of the Emotions in Man and Animals*. Oxford: Oxford University Press.
Davidson, R. J. 1994. 'On Emotion, Mood, and Related Affective Constructs', in P. Ekman and R. J. Davidson (eds.), *The Nature of Emotion: Fundamental Questions*. Oxford: Oxford University Press, pp. 303–5.
Davis, C. G., Lehman, D. R., Wortman, C. B., Silver, R. C., and Thompson, S. C. 1995. 'The Undoing of Traumatic Life Events', *Personality and Social Psychology Bulletin* 21: 109–24.
de Sousa, R. 1987. *The Rationality of Emotions*. Cambridge, MA: MIT Press.
2014. 'Emotion', *The Stanford Encyclopedia of Philosophy* (Spring 2014 Edition), Edward N. Zalta (ed.), https://plato.stanford.edu/archives/spr2014/entries/emotion/.
Deigh, J. 1994. 'Cognitivism in the Theory of Emotions', *Ethics* 104: 824–54.
DeLancey, C. 2006. 'Basic Moods', *Philosophical Psychology* 19(4): 527–38.
Dennett, D. C. 1969. *Content and Consciousness*. New York: Routledge.
Dennett, D. C. 1993. 'Quining Qualia', in A. I. Goldman (ed.), *Readings in Philosophy and Cognitive Science*. Cambridge, MA: MIT Press, pp. 381–414.

Deonna, J. 2006. 'Emotion, Perception and Perspective', *Dialectica* 60(1): 29–46.
Deonna, J. and Teroni, F. 2009. 'Taking Affective Explanations to Heart', *Social Science Information* 48(3): 359–77.
2012a. *The Emotions: A Philosophical Introduction*. New York: Routledge.
2012b 'From Justified Emotions to Justified Evaluative Judgements', *Dialogue* 51(1): 55–77.
forthcoming. 'Emotional Experience: Affective Consciousness and Its Role in Emotion Theory', in U. Kriegel (ed.), *Oxford Handbook of the Philosophy of Consciousness*. New York: Oxford University Press.
Descartes, R. 1989. *The Passions of the Soul*, trans. S. H. Vonn. Cambridge: Hackett Publishing.
Di Paolo, E. A., Rohde M., and De Jaegher, H. 2010. 'Horizons for the Enactive Mind: Values, Social Interaction, and Play', in J. Stewart, O. Gapenne, and E. Di Paolo (eds.), *Enaction: Toward a New Paradigm for Cognitive Science*. Cambridge, MA: MIT Press, pp. 33–87.
Döring, S. A. 2003. 'Explaining Action by Emotion', *The Philosophical Quarterly* 53 (211): 214–30.
2007. 'Seeing What to Do: Affective Perception and Rational Motivation', *Dialectica* 61(3): 363–94.
Drayson, Z. 2012. 'The Uses and Abuses of the Personal/Subpersonal Distinction', *Philosophical Perspectives* 26(1): 1–18.
Dretske, F. 1969. *Seeing and Knowing*. Chicago: University of Chicago Press.
1973. 'Perception and Other Minds', *Noûs* 7(1): 34–44.
1979. 'Simple Seeing', in D. F. Gustafson and B. L. Tapscott (eds.), *Body, Mind, and Method*. Kluwer Academic Publishers, pp. 1–15.
1981. *Knowledge and the Flow of Information*. Cambridge, MA: MIT Press.
1988. *Explaining Behavior: Reasons in a World of Causes*. Cambridge, MA: MIT Press/Bradford Books.
1995. *Naturalizing the Mind*. Cambridge, MA: MIT Press.
Ekman, P. 1992. 'An Argument for Basic Emotions', *Cognition and Emotion* 6: 169–200.
1994. 'Strong Evidence for Universals in Facial Expression: A Reply to Russell's Mistaken Critique', *Psychological Bulletin* 115: 268–87.
1997. 'Basic Emotions', in T. Dalgleish and M. Power (eds.), *The Handbook of Cognition and Emotion*. New York: John Wiley and Sons.
2003. *Emotions Revealed: Recognizing Faces and Feelings to Improve Communication and Emotional Life*. New York: Henry Holt.
Ekman, P. and Davidson, R. J. (eds.) 1994. *The Nature of Emotion: Fundamental Questions*. Oxford: Oxford University Press.
Ellsworth, P. 1994. 'William James and Emotion: Is a Century of Fame Worth a Century of Misunderstanding?', *Psychological Review* 101, 222–9.
2013. 'Appraisal Theory: Old and New Questions', *Emotion Review* 5: 125–31.
Ellsworth, P. C. and Schrerer, K. R. 2003. 'Appraisal Processes in Emotion', in R. J. Davidson, H. H. Goldsmith, and K. R. Scherer (eds.), *Handbook of Affective Sciences*. Oxford: Oxford University Press, pp. 572–95.

Elster, J. 1999. *Alchemies of the Mind: Rationality and the Emotions*. Cambridge: Cambridge University Press.

Emmons, R. A. and McCullough, M. E. (2003). 'Counting Blessings versus Burdens: An Experimental Investigation of Gratitude and Subjective Well-Being in Daily Life'. *Journal of Personality and Social Psychology* 84 (2): 377–89.

Fernández-Dols, J. M. and Ruiz-Belda, M. A. 1997. 'Spontaneous Facial Behavior during Intense Emotional Episodes: Artistic Truth and Optical Truth', in J. A. Russell and J. M. Fernández-Dols (eds.), *The Psychology of Facial Expression*. Cambridge: Cambridge University Press, pp. 255–74.

Fine, K. 1999. 'Things and Their Parts', *Midwest Studies in Philosophy* 23: 61–74.

2008. 'Form and Coincidence', *Proceedings of the Aristotelian Society Supplementary* 82: 101–18.

2013. 'Guide to Ground', in F. Correia and B. Schneider (eds.), *Metaphysical Grounding*. Cambridge: Cambridge University Press, pp. 37–80.

Fish, W. 2005, 'Emotions, Moods, and Intentionality', in G. Forrai and G. Kampis (eds.), *Intentionality Past and Future*. New York: Rodopi, pp. 25–35.

Fisher, M. L. and Exline, J. 2010. 'Moving towards Self-Forgiveness: Removing Barriers Related to Shame, Guilt and Regret', *Social and Personality Psychology Compass* 4(8): 548–58.

Fodor, J. 1974. 'Special Sciences, or the Disunity of Science as a Working Hypothesis', *Synthese* 28: 97–115.

1987. *Psychosemantics: The Problem of Meaning in the Philosophy of Mind*. Cambridge, MA: MIT Press/Bradford Books.

1990. *A Theory of Content and Other Essays*. Cambridge, MA: MIT Press.

Fredrickson, B. L. and Branigan, C. 2005. 'Positive Emotions Broaden the Scope of Attention and Thought-Action Repertoires', *Cognition and Emotion* 19(3): 313–32.

Frijda, N. 1986. *The Emotions*. Cambridge: Cambridge University Press.

1994a. 'Emotions Are Functional, Most of the Time', in P. Ekman and R. J. Davidson (eds.). *The Nature of Emotion: Fundamental Questions*. Oxford University Press, pp. 197–202.

1994b. 'Varieties of Affect: Emotions and Episodes, Moods and Sentiments', in P. Ekman and R. J. Davidson (eds.), *The Nature of Emotion: Fundamental Questions*. Oxford University Press, pp. 59–67.

Gallagher, S. 2008. 'Direct Perception in the Intersubjective Context', *Consciousness and Cognition* 17: 535–43.

Geach, P. 1969. *God and the Soul*. London: Routledge and Kegan Paul.

Gibson, J. J. 1986. *The Ecological Approach to Visual Perception*. New York: Taylor and Francis.

Goldie, P. 2000. *The Emotions: A Philosophical Exploration*. Oxford: Oxford University Press.

2002. 'Emotions, Feelings and Intentionality', *Phenomenology and the Cognitive Sciences* 1: 235–54.

2004. 'Emotion, Feeling, and Knowledge of the World', in R. C. Solomon (ed.), *Thinking about Feeling: Contemporary Philosophers on Emotions*. New York: Oxford University Press, pp. 91–106.
2010. 'Love for a Reason', *Emotion Review* 2(1): 61–67.
2011. 'Grief: A Narrative Account', *Ratio* 24 (2): 119–37.
2012. *The Mess Inside: Narrative, Emotion, and the Mind*. New York: Oxford University Press.
Goldschmidt, T. (ed.) 2013. *The Puzzle of Existence: Why Is There Something Rather Than Nothing?* London: Routledge.
Gordon, D. M. 1992. The Road Not Taken: A Phenomenological Investigation of the Experience of Regret. PhD diss., University of Tennessee. http://trace.tennessee.edu/utk_graddiss/1484.
Gordon, R. 1987. *The Structure of Emotions: Investigations in Cognitive Philosophy*. New York: Cambridge University Press.
Grahek, N. 2001. *Feeling Pain and Being in Pain*. Cambridge, MA: MIT Press.
Green, M. 2007. *Self-Expression*. Oxford: Oxford University Press.
2010. 'Perceiving Emotions'. *Aristotelian Society Suppl. Vol.* 84(1): 45–61.
Green, O. H. 1992. *The Emotions: A Philosophical Theory*. Dordrecht: Kluwer.
Greenspan, P. S. 1988. *Emotions and Reasons: An Inquiry into Emotional Justification*. New York: Routledge.
Grèzes J., Tucker, M., Armony, J., Ellis, R., and Passingham R. E. 2003. 'Objects Automatically Potentiate Action: An fMRI Study of Implicit Processing', *European Journal of Neuroscience* 17: 2735–40.
Griffiths, P. E. 1997. *What Emotions Really Are: The Problem of Psychological Categories*. Chicago: University of Chicago Press.
2004.' Towards a Machiavellian Theory of Emotional Appraisal', in P. Cruse and D. Evans (eds.), *Emotion, Evolution and Rationality*. Oxford: Oxford University Press, pp. 89–105.
Griffiths, P. and Scarantino, A. 2009. 'Emotions in the Wild: The Situated Perspective on Emotion', in P. Robbins and M. Aydede (eds.), *The Cambridge Handbook of Situated Cognition*. Cambridge: Cambridge University Press, pp. 437–53.
Harré, R. and Madden, E. H. 1975. *Causal Powers: A Theory of Natural Necessity*. Oxford: Basil Blackwell.
Hatzimoysis, A. 2007. 'The Case against Unconscious Emotions', *Analysis* 67 (296): 292–9.
Heidegger, M. 1927/1962. *Being and Time*, trans. J. Macquarrie and E. Robinson. Oxford: Blackwell.
Heil, J. 1992. *The Nature of True Minds*. Cambridge: Cambridge University Press.
2003. *From an Ontological Point of View*. Oxford: Clarendon Press.
2005. 'Dispositions', *Synthese* 144: 343–56.
2012. *The Universe as We Find It*. Oxford: Clarendon Press.
2013. 'Contingency', in T. Goldschmidt (ed.), pp. 167–81.
Helm, B. 2001. *Emotional Reason: Deliberation, Motivation, and the Nature of Value*. Cambridge: Cambridge University Press.

Hinde, R. A. (1985). 'Expression and Negotiation', in G. Zivin (ed.), *The Development of Expressive Behavior*. New York: Academic Press, pp. 103–16.

Höfler, A. 1897. *Psychologie*. Wien: Tempsky.

Hofweber, T. (2014). 'Logic and Ontology', in E. Zalta (ed.), *The Stanford Encyclopedia of Philosophy* (Fall 2014 Edition) https://plato.stanford.edu/entries/logic-ontology/.

Hornsby, J. 2010. 'The Standard Story of Action: An Exchange', in J. Aguilar and A. Buckareff (eds.), *Causing Human Action: New Perspectives on the Causal Theory of Action*. Cambridge, MA: MIT Press, pp. 57–68.

Hume, D. (1739–40), *A Treatise of Human Nature*, edited by L. A. Selby-Bigge, Oxford: Clarendon Press, 1896.

(1748). *An Enquiry Concerning Human Understanding*, in L. A. Selby-Bigge (ed.), *Enquiries Concerning Human Understanding and Concerning the Principles of Morals*, 3rd edn. rev. P. H. Nidditch. Oxford: Clarendon Press, 1975.

Hursthouse, R. 1991. 'Arational Actions', *Journal of Philosophy* 88: 57–68.

Hutcheson, F. 1742/2003. *An Essay on the Nature and Conduct of the Passions and Affections, with Illustrations on the Moral Sense*. Indianapolis, IN: Liberty Fund, Inc.

Isen, A. M. 1984. 'Toward Understanding the Role of Affect in Cognition', in R. S. Wyer and T. K. Srull (eds.), *Handbook of Social Cognition*. Hillsdale, NJ: Erlbaum, pp. 179–236.

Jackson, F. 1977. *Perception: A Representative Theory*. Cambridge: Cambridge University Press.

1986. 'What Mary Didn't Know', *The Journal of Philosophy* 83: 291–5.

Jacob, P. 2011. 'The Direct-Perception Model of Empathy: A Critique', *Review of Philosophy and Psychology* 2(3): 519–40.

Jacobson, D. 2013. 'Regret, Agency and Error', in D. Shoemaker (ed.), *Oxford Studies in Agency and Responsibility Volume 1*. Oxford: Oxford University Press, pp. 95–125.

James, W. (1884). 'What Is an Emotion?', *Mind* 9(34): 188–205.

(1890) 1981. *The Principles of Psychology*. Cambridge, MA: Harvard University Press.

(1894) 1994. 'The Physical Basis of Emotion', *Psychological Review* 101, 205–10.

Jaworska, A. 2007. 'Caring and Internality', *Philosophy and Phenomenological Research* 74(3): 529–68.

Jaworski, W. 2011. *Philosophy of Mind: A Comprehensive Introduction*. Malden, MA: Wiley-Blackwell.

2012. 'Structures, Powers, and Minds', in R. Groff and J. Greco (eds.), *Powers and Capacities in Philosophy: The New Aristotelianism*. London: Routledge, pp. 145–71.

2014. 'Hylomorphism and the Metaphysics of Structure', *Res Philosophica* 91: 179–201.

2016. *Structure and the Metaphysics of Mind: How Hylomorphism Solves the Mind-Body Problem*. Oxford: Oxford University Press.

Johnston, M. 2006. 'Hylomorphism', *Journal of Philosophy* 103: 652–98.
Jones, K. 2006. 'Quick and Smart? Modularity and the Pro-emotion Consensus', in L. Faucher and C. Tappolet (eds.), *The Modularity of Emotions, Canadian Journal of Philosophy* sup. vol. 32: 3–27.
Juslin, P. and Laukka, P. 2003. 'Communication of Emotions in Vocal Expression and Music Performance: Different Channels, Same Code?', *Psychological Bulletin* 129: 770–814.
Kenny, A. 1963. *Action, Emotion and Will.* London: Routledge and Kegan Paul.
Kim, J. 1972. 'Phenomenal Properties, Psychophysical Laws, and the Identity Theory', *Monist* 56: 177–92. Selections reprinted in N. Block (ed.) 1980. *Readings in Philosophy of Psychology*, 2 vols. Cambridge, MA: Harvard University Press, pp. 234–6.
1998. *Mind in a Physical World.* Cambridge, MA: MIT Press/Bradford Books.
Kind, A. 2013. 'The Case against Representationalism about Moods', in U. Kriegel (ed.), *Current Controversies in the Philosophy of Mind.* New York: Routledge, pp. 113–34.
Kirk, R. 1974. 'Zombies versus Materialists', *Aristotelian Society Proceedings* (suppl.) 48: 135–52.
2005. *Zombies and Consciousness.* Oxford: Clarendon Press.
Koons, R. 2014. 'Staunch vs. Faint-Hearted Hylomorphism: Toward an Aristotelian Account of Composition', *Res Philosophica* 91: 151–78.
Koslicki, K. 2008. *The Structure of Objects.* Oxford: Oxford University Press.
Kreibig, S. 2010. 'Autonomic Nervous System Activity in Emotion: A Review', *Biological Psychology* 84(2): 394–421.
Kriegel, U. (ed.) 2013. *Current Controversies in the Philosophy of Mind.* New York: Routledge.
Krueger, J. 2012. 'Seeing Mind in Action', *Phenomenology and the Cognitive Sciences* 11(2): 149–73.
Lacewing, M. 2007. 'Do Unconscious Emotions Involve Unconscious Feelings?', *Philosophical Psychology* 20(1): 81–104.
Ladyman, J. and Ross, D. 2007. *Every Thing Must Go: Metaphysics Naturalized.* New York: Oxford University Press.
Laird, J. 2007. *Feelings: The Perception of Self.* New York: Oxford University Press.
Laird, J. and Lacasse, K. 2014. 'Bodily Influences on Emotional Feelings: Accumulating Evidence and Extensions of William James's Theory of Emotions', *Emotion Review* 6(1): 27–34.
Landman, J. 1993. *Regret: The Persistence of the Possible.* New York: Oxford University Press.
Lange, C. G. 1885. *Om sindsbevaegelser; et psyko-fysiologisk studie.* Kjobenhavn: Jacob Lunds Forlag.
Lazarus, R. S. 1991a. *Emotion and Adaptation.* New York: Oxford University Press.
1991b. 'Cognition and Motivation in Emotion', *American Psychologist* 46: 362–7.
1994. 'The Stable and the Unstable in Emotion', in P. Ekman and R. J. Davidson (eds.), *The Nature of Emotion: Fundamental Questions.* Oxford: Oxford University Press, pp. 79–85.

LeDoux, J. 1996. *The Emotional Brain.* New York: Simon and Shuster.
Levenson, R. W. 2003. 'Autonomic Specificity and Emotion', in R. J. Davidson, K. R. Scherer, and H. H. Goldsmith (eds.), *Handbook of Affective Sciences.* New York: Oxford University Press, pp. 212–24.
Levin, J. 2013. 'Functionalism', in E. Zalta (ed.), *Stanford Encyclopedia of Philosophy*, Fall 2013 edition, http://plato.stanford.edu/archives/fall2013/entries/functionalism/.
Lewis, D. K. 1966. 'An Argument for the Identity Theory', *Journal of Philosophy* 66: 17–25.
1972. 'Psychophysical and Theoretical Identifications', *Australasian Journal of Philosophy* 50: 249–58.
1980. 'Mad Pain and Martian Pain', in N. Block, (ed.) 1980. *Readings in Philosophy of Psychology*, 2 vols. Cambridge, MA: Harvard University Press, pp. 216–22.
1983. 'New Work for a Theory of Universals', *Australasian Journal of Philosophy* 61: 343–77.
1997. 'Finkish Dispositions', *Philosophical Quarterly* 47: 143–58.
Locke, J. 1690/1979. *An Essay Concerning Human Understanding*, P. H. Nidditch (ed.), Oxford: Clarendon Press.
Long, G. M. and Toppino, T. C. 2004. 'Enduring Interest in Perceptual Ambiguity: Alternating Views of Reversible Figures', *Psychological Bulletin* 130(5): 748.
Lormand, E. 1985. 'Toward a Theory of Moods', *Philosophical Studies* 47: 385–407.
Lyons, W. 1980. *Emotion.* Cambridge: Cambridge University Press.
Maienborn, C. 2005. 'On the Limits of the Davidsonian Approach: The Case of Copula Sentences', *Theoretical Linguistics* 31(3): 275–316.
Marmodoro, A. 2013. 'Aristotelian Hylomorphism without Reconditioning', *Philosophical Inquiry* 36: 5–22.
Martin, C. B. 1994. 'Dispositions and Conditionals', *The Philosophical Quarterly* 44: 1–8.
1996a. 'Properties and Dispositions', in T. Crane (ed.), *Dispositions: A Debate*, London: Routledge, pp. 71–87.
1996b. 'Replies to Armstrong and Place', in T. Crane (ed.), *Dispositions: A Debate*, London: Routledge, pp. 126–46.
1997. 'On the Need for Properties: the Road to Pythagoreanism and Back', *Synthese* 112: 193–231.
2007. *The Mind in Nature.* New York: Oxford University Press.
Martin, C. B. and Heil, J. 1998. 'Rules and Powers', *Philosophical Perspectives* 12: 238–312.
1999. 'The Ontological Turn', *Midwest Studies in Philosophy* 23: 34–60.
Martin, C. B. and Pfeifer, K. 1986. 'Intentionality and the Non-psychological', *Philosophy and Phenomenological Research* 46: 531–54.
Matthews, G. and Wells, A. 1994. *Attention and Emotion: A Clinical Perspective.* Hillsdale, NJ: Erlbaum.
Maund, B. 2003. *Perception.* Chesham: Acumen.

Mayer, J. D., Gaschke, Y. N., Braverman, D. L., and Evans, T. W. 1992. 'Mood-Congruent Judgement Is a General Effect', *Journal of Personality and Social Psychology* 63(1): 119–32.
Mayer, J. D. and Hanson, E. 1995. 'Mood-Congruent Judgement over Time', *Personality and Social Psychology Bulletin* 21(3): 237–44.
McDowell, J. 1982. 'Criteria, Defeasibility, and Knowledge', *Proceedings of the British Academy* 68: 455–79.
McLean, P. D. 1993. 'Cerebral Evolution of Emotion', in M. Lewis and J. Haviland (eds.), *Handbook of Emotions*. New York: The Guilford Press, pp. 67–83.
McNeill, W. E. S. 2012. 'On Seeing That Someone Is Angry', *European Journal of Philosophy* 20(4): 575–97.
Mendelovici, A. 2014. 'Pure Intentionalism about Moods and Emotions', in U. Kriegel (ed.), *Current Controversies in Philosophy of Mind*. New York: Routledge, pp. 135–57.
Michalak, J., Troje, N. F, Fischer, J., Vollmar, P., Heidenriech, T., and Schulte, D. 2009. 'Embodiment of Sadness and Depression – Gait Patterns Associated with Dysphoric Mood', *Psychosomatic Medicine* 71(5): 580–7.
Millikan, R. 1984. *Language, Thought and Other Biological Categories*. Cambridge, MA: MIT Press.
Mineka, S. and Sutton, S. K. 1992. 'Cognitive Biases and the Emotional Disorders', *Psychological Science* 3: 65–9.
Molnar, G. 2003. *Powers: A Study in Metaphysics*, ed. by S. Mumford. Oxford: Oxford University Press.
Moors, A. 2013. 'On the Causal Role of Appraisal in Emotion', *Emotion Review* 5 (2): 132–40.
Moors, A., Ellsworth, P. C., Scherer, K. R., and Frijda, N. H. 2013. 'Appraisal Theories of Emotion: State of the Art and Future Development', *Emotion Review* 5(2): 119–24.
Morris, W. N. 1989. *Mood. The Frame of Mind*. Berlin: Springer.
Morton, A. 1980. *Frames of Mind*. Oxford: Clarendon Press.
2013. *Emotion and Imagination*. Cambridge: Polity.
Mourelatos, A. 1978. 'Events, Processes and States', *Linguistics and Philosophy* 2: 415–34.
Mulhall, S. 1996. 'Can There Be an Epistemology of Moods?', in A. O'Hear (ed.), *Verstehen and Human Understanding*. Cambridge: Cambridge University Press, pp. 191–210.
Mulligan, K. 1998. 'The Spectre of Inverted Emotions and the Space of Emotions', *Acta Analytica* 18: 89–105.
Mumford, S. 1998. *Dispositions*. New York: Oxford University Press.
2009. 'Causal Powers and Capacities', in H. Beebee, C. Hitchcock, and P. Menzies (eds.), *The Oxford Handbook of Causation*. Oxford: Oxford University Press, pp. 265–78.
Naar, H. 2013. 'A Dispositional Theory of Love', *Pacific Philosophical Quarterly* 94(3): 342–57.

forthcoming. 'Love as a Disposition', in C. Grau and A. Smuts (eds.), *Oxford Handbook of Philosophy of Love*. Oxford: Oxford University Press.
Naar, H. and Tappolet, C. (ms.). 'The Possibility of Instantaneous Emotions'.
Nagel, T. 2000. 'The Psychophysical Nexus', in P. Boghossian and C. Peacocke (eds.), *New Essays on the A Priori*. Oxford: Oxford University Press, pp. 194–235.
Noë, A. 2004. *Action in Perception*. Cambridge, MA: MIT Press.
Noë, A. and O'Regan, J. K. 2002. 'On the Brain-Basis of Visual Consciousness: A Sensorimotor Account', in A. Noë and E. T. Thompson (eds.), *Vision and Mind: Selected Readings in the Philosophy of Perception*. Cambridge, MA: MIT Press, pp. 567–98.
Nussbaum, C. 2003. 'Another Look at Functionalism and the Emotions', *Brain and Mind* 4(3): 353–83.
Nussbaum, M. 2001. *Upheavals of Thought: The Intelligence of Emotions*. Cambridge: Cambridge University Press.
O'Shaughnessy, B. 1972. 'Mental Structure and Self-Consciousness', *Inquiry* 15 (1–4): 30–63.
2000. *Consciousness and the World*. Oxford: Oxford University Press.
Oakley, J. 1992. *Morality and the Emotions*. London: Routledge and Kegan Paul.
Oatley, K. and Johnson-Laird, P. N. 1990. 'Semantic Primitives for Emotions', *Cognition and Emotion* 3: 125–37.
Oderberg, D. S. 2007. *Real Essentialism*. New York: Routledge.
Öhman, A. Flykt, A. and Esteves, F. 2001. 'Emotion Drives Attention: Detecting the Snake in the Grass', *Journal of Experimental Psychology: General* 130: 466–78.
Owens, H. and Maxmen, J. S. 1979. 'Mood and Affect: A Semantic Confusion', *American Journal of Psychiatry* I 36: 97–9.
Pacherie, E. 2002. 'Emotion and Action', *European Review of Philosophy* 5: 55–90.
Panksepp, J. 1998. *Affective Neuroscience: The Foundations of Human and Animal Emotions*. New York, Oxford: Oxford University Press.
Parkinson, B. and Colman, A. M. (eds.) 1995. *Emotion and Motivation*. London: Longman.
Parsons, T. 1989. 'The Progressive in English: Events, States, and Processes', *Linguistics and Philosophy* 12(2): 213–41.
Parvizi, J. Arciniegas, D.B., Bernardini, G.L., Hoffmann, M.W., Mohr, J.P., Rapoport, M.J., Schmahmann, J.D., Silver, J.M. and Tuhrim, S. 2006. 'Diagnosis and Management of Pathological Laughter and Crying', *Mayo Clinic Proceedings* 81: 1482–6.
Phillips, I. 2010. 'Perceiving Temporal Properties', *European Journal of Philosophy* 18(2): 176–202.
Pickard, H. 2003. 'Emotions and the Problem of Other Minds', in A. Hatimoysis (ed.), *Philosophy and the Emotions: Royal Institute of Philosophy Supplement* 52. Cambridge: Cambridge University Press, pp. 87–103.
Pitcher, G. 1965. 'Emotion', *Mind* 74: 326–46.
Place, U. T. 1996a. 'Intentionality as the Mark of the Dispositional', *Dialectica* 50: 91–120.

1996b. 'Dispositions as Intentional States', in T. Crane (ed.), *Dispositions: A Debate*. London: Routledge, pp. 19–32.

Popper, K. R. and Eccles, J. (eds.) 1977. *The Self and Its Brain*. London: Routledge & Kegan Paul.

Price, C. 2006. 'Affect without Object: Moods and Objectless Emotions', *European Journal of Analytic Philosophy* 2(1): 49–68.

Prinz, J. 2004. *Gut Reactions: A Perceptual Theory of Emotion*. New York: Oxford University Press.

Prior, E. W., Pargetter, R., and Jackson, F. 1982. 'Three Theses about Dispositions', *American Philosophical Quarterly* 19: 251–7.

Pugmire, D. R. (1994). 'Real Emotion', *Philosophy and Phenomenological Research* 54(1): 105–22.

Putnam, H. 1967. 'Psychological Predicates', in W. H. Capitan and D. D. Merrill (eds.), *Art, Mind, and Religion*. Pittsburgh, PA: University of Pittsburgh Press, pp. 37–48. Reprinted as 'The Nature of Mental States', in *Mind, Language, and Reality: Philosophical Papers, vol. 2* by Hilary Putnam. Cambridge: Cambridge University Press, pp. 429–40.

Rea, M. C. 2011. 'Hylomorphism Reconditioned', *Philosophical Perspectives* 25: 341–58.

Regier, W. 2004. 'Cioran's Insomnia', *Comparative Literature* 119(5): 994–1012.

Roberts, R. C. 1999. 'Review: Emotions as Judgments: The Therapy of Desire by Martha C. Nussbaum', *Philosophy and Phenomenological Research* 59(3): 793–8.

2003. *Emotions: An Essay in Aid of Moral Psychology*. Cambridge: Cambridge University Press.

Robinson, J. 1983. 'Emotion, Judgment and Desire', *Journal of Philosophy* 80: 731–41.

1995. 'Startle', *Journal of Philosophy* 92: 53–74.

2005. *Deeper than Reason: Emotion and Its Role in Literature, Music and Art*. Oxford: Oxford University Press.

Robinson, J. 2017. "'Tú, ser abrazable': La emoción como percepción para la acción," ("Embraceable You: Emotion as Perception for Action"), in D. Pérez and D. Lawer (eds.), *The Second Person and Emotion*. Buenos Aires: SADAF. English version first presented in 2014 in Antwerp.

Roese, N., Epstude, K., Fessel, F., Morrison, M., Smallman, R., Summerville, Z., Galinsky, A., and Segerstron, S. 2009. 'Repetitive Regret, Depression and Anxiety: Findings from a Nationally Representative Survey', *Journal of Social and Clinical Psychology* 28(6): 671–88.

Roseman, I. J. 2001. 'A Model of Appraisal in the Emotion System', in K. R. Scherer, A. Schorr, and T. Johnstone et al. (eds.) *Appraisal Processes in Emotion*. New York: Oxford University Press, pp. 68–91.

Russell, B. 1921. *The Analysis of Mind*. Mineola: Dover Publications.

Russell, J. A. 2003. 'Core Affect and the Psychological Construction of Emotion', *Psychological Review* 110: 145–72.

Ryle, G. 1949. *The Concept of Mind*. London: Hutchinson & Co.

Scarantino, A. 2004. 'Affordances Explained', *Philosophy of Science* 71: 949–61.
2014. 'The Motivational Theory of Emotions', in J. D'Arms and D. Jacobson (eds.), *Moral Psychology and Human Agency*. Oxford: Oxford University Press, pp. 156–85.
Scherer, K. R. 1987. 'Toward a Dynamic Theory of Emotion', *Geneva Studies in Emotion* 1: 1–96.
2001. 'Appraisal Considered as a Process of Multilevel Sequential Checking', in K. R. Scherer, A. Schorr, and T. J. Johnstone (eds.), *Appraisal Processes in Emotion*. New York: Oxford University Press, pp. 92–120.
Scherer, K. R., Schorr, A., and Johnstone, T. (eds.) 2001. *Appraisal Processes in Emotion: Theory, Methods, Research*. Oxford: Oxford University Press.
Scherer, K. R. Banse, R. and Wallbott, H. G. 2001. 'Emotion Inferences from Vocal Expression Correlate across Languages and Cultures', *Journal of Cross-Cultural Psychology* 32: 76–92.
Schmidt, R. E. and Van der Linden, M. 2013. 'Feeling too Regretful to Fall Asleep: Experimental Activation of Regret Delays Sleep Onset', *Cognitive Therapy and Research* 37: 872–80.
2013. 'The Nocturnal Return of Neglected Regrets: Deficits in Regret Anticipation Predict Insomnia Symptoms', *Open Sleep Journal* 4: 20–5.
Schmidt, R. E., Harvey, A. G., and Van der Linden, M. 2011. 'Cognitive and Affective Control in Insomnia', *Frontiers in Psychology* 2: 349.
Searle, J. R. 1983. *Intentionality: An Essay in the Philosophy of Mind*. New York: Cambridge University Press.
Shand, A. F. 1914. *The Foundations of Character*. London: Macmillan.
Shargel, D. 2014. 'Constitutively Embodied Emotions' (Doctoral dissertation). Retrieved from http://academicworks.cuny.edu/gc_etds/472.
2015. 'Emotions without Objects', *Biology and Philosophy* 30(6): 831–44.
Shields, C. 2014. *Aristotle, 2nd Edition*. London: Routledge.
Shoemaker, D. W. 2003. 'Caring, Identification, and Agency', *Ethics* 114(1): 88–118.
Shoemaker, S. 1980. 'Causality and Properties', in P. van Inwagen (ed.), *Time and Cause*. Dordrecht: Reidel, pp. 109–35.
Siegel, S. 2011. *The Contents of Visual Experience*. New York: Oxford University Press.
2017. *The Rationality of Perception*. New York: Oxford University Press.
Siemer, M. 2009. 'Mood Experience: Implications of a Dispositional Theory of Moods', *Emotion Review* 1(3): 256–63.
Siemer, M. and Reisenzein, R. 1998. 'Effects of Mood on Evaluative Judgements: Influence of Reduced Processing Capacity and Mood Salience', *Cognition and Emotion* 12(6): 783–805.
Sizer, L. 2000. 'Towards a Computational Theory of Mood', *British Journal for the Philosophy of Science* 51: 743–69.
Smith, C. A. and Kirby, L. D. 2001. 'Toward Delivering on the Promise of Appraisal Theory', in K. R. Scherer, A. Schorr, and T. Johnstone (eds.), *Appraisal Processes in Emotion*. New York: Oxford University Press, pp. 121–38.

Smith, J. 2010. 'Seeing Other People', *Philosophy and Phenomenological Research* 81(3): 731–48.

2015. 'The Phenomenology of Face-to-Face Mindreading', *Philosophy and Phenomenological Research* 87(2): 274–93.

2016. 'Perceptual Recognition, Emotion, and Value', in J. D. Dodd (ed.), *Art, Mind, and Narrative: Themes from the Work of Peter Goldie*. Oxford: Oxford University Press, pp. 121–37.

Smith, M. 1987. 'The Humean Theory of Motivation', *Mind* 96(381): 36–61.

Solomon, R. C. 1988. 'On Emotions as Judgments', *American Philosophical Quarterly* 25: 183–91.

1993. *The Passions: Emotions and the Meaning of Life*. Indianapolis, IN: Hackett Publishing Company, originally published in 1976.

Solomon, R. and Stone, L. 2002. 'On "Positive" and "Negative" Emotions', *Journal for the Theory of Social Behaviour* 32(4): 417–35.

Soteriou, M. 2013. *The Mind's Construction: The Ontology of Mind and Mental Action*. Oxford: Oxford University Press.

Sperry, R. 1984. 'Emergence', in P. Weintraub (ed.), *The Omni Interviews*. New York: Ticknor & Fields, pp. 187–207.

Stephens, C. L., Christie, I. C., and Friedman, B. H. 2010. 'Autonomic Specificity of Basic Emotions: Evidence from Pattern Classification and Cluster Analysis', *Biological Psychiatry* 84: 463–73.

Steward, H. 1997. *The Ontology of Mind: Events, Processes and States*. Oxford: Oxford University Press.

2013. 'Processes, Continuants, and Individuals', *Mind* 122(487): 781–812.

2015. 'What Is a Continuant?', *Proceedings of the Aristotelian Society Supplementary Volume* 89: 109–23.

Stout, R. 1997. 'Processes', *Philosophy* 72: 19–27.

2003. 'The Life of a Process', in G. DeBrock (ed.), *Pragmatic Process Philosophy*. Amsterdam: Rodopi, pp. 145–58.

2010. 'Seeing the Anger in Someone's Face', *Aristotelian Society Supplementary Volume* 84(1): 29–43.

Strawson, G., 1994. *Mental Reality*. Cambridge, MA: MIT Press.

2006. 'Realistic Monism: Why Physicalism Entails Panpsychism', in A. Freeman (ed.), *Consciousness and Its Place in Nature: Does Physicalism Entail Panpsychism?* Exeter: Imprint Academic, pp. 3–31.

Tappolet, C. 2000. *Emotions et valeurs*. Paris: Presses Universitaires de France.

2010. 'Emotion, Motivation and Action: The Case of Fear', in P. Goldie (ed.), *Oxford Handbook of Philosophy of Emotion*. New York: Oxford University Press, pp. 325–45.

2016. *Emotions, Values, and Agency*. Oxford: Oxford University Press.

Teroni, F. 2007. 'Emotions and Formal Objects', *Dialectica* 61(3): 395–415.

Thalberg, I. 1964. 'Emotion and Thought', *American Philosophical Quarterly* 1: 45–55.

Thayer, R. 1989. *The Biopsychology of Mood and Arousal*. New York: Oxford University Press.

Tomkins, S. 1984. 'Affect Theory', in K. R. Scherer and P. Ekman (eds.), *Approaches to Emotion*. Hillsdale, NJ: Psychology Press, pp. 163–95.

Tormey, A. 1971. *The Concept of Expression: A Study in Philosophical Psychology and Aesthetics*. Princeton, NJ: Princeton University Press.

Toronchuk, J. A. and Ellis, G. F. R. 2007. 'Disgust: Sensory Affect or Primary Emotional System?', *Cognition & Emotion* 21: 1799–1818.

Tye, M. 2008. 'The Experience of Emotion: An Intentionalist Theory', *Revue internationale de philosophie* 243: 25–50.

Unger, P. 2006. *All the Power in the World*. New York: Oxford University Press.

Van Inwagen, P. 1990. *Material Beings*. Ithaca, NY: Cornell University Press.

Vance, J. 2014. 'Emotion and the New Epistemic Challenge from Cognitive Penetrability', *Philosophical Studies* 169(2): 257–83.

2015. 'Cognitive Penetration and the Tribunal of Experience', *Review of Philosophy and Psychology* 6(4): 641–63.

Varela, F. J. 1991. 'Whence the Origin of Perception? A Cartography of Current Ideas', in F. J. Varela and J. P. Dupuy (eds.), *Understanding Origins: Contemporary Ideas on the Origin of Life, Mind and Society*. Boston: Kluwer, pp. 235–65.

Varela, F. J., Thompson, E., and Rosch, E. 1991. *The Embodied Mind: Cognitive Science and Human Experience*. Cambridge, MA: MIT Press.

Vendler, Z. 1957. 'Verbs and Times', *Philosophical Review* 66(2): 143–60.

Wallace, J. 2014. *The View from Here*. Oxford: Oxford University Press.

Watson, J. B. 1924 *Psychology, from the Standpoint of a Behaviourist*, 2nd edn. London: J.B. Lippincott.

Whittle, A. 2008. 'A Functionalist Theory of Properties', *Philosophy and Phenomenological Research* 77(1): 59–82.

Williams, B. 1963. 'Ethical Consistency', *Proceedings of the Aristotelian Society* 39: 103–24. Reprinted in B. Williams. 1973. *Problems of the Self.* Cambridge, Cambridge University Press, pp. 166–86.

1976. 'Moral Luck', *Proceedings of the Aristotelian Society* 50: 115–35.

Williams, D. C. 1953. 'On the Elements of Being', *Review of Metaphysics* 7: 3–18. Reprinted as 'The Elements of Being', in Williams, D. C. 1966. *Principles of Empirical Realism*. Springfield: Charles C. Thomas, pp. 74–109.

1966. *Principles of Empirical Realism*. Springfield: Charles C. Thomas.

Wimsatt, W. C. 1985. 'Forms of Aggregativity', in A. Donogan, A. N. Perovich, and M. J. Wedin (eds.), *Human Nature and Natural Knowledge: Essays Presented to Marjorie Grene on the Occasion of Her 75th Birthday*, Dordrecht: Reidel, pp. 259–93.

Witasek, S. 1908. *Grundlinien der Psychologie*. Leipzig: Meiner.

Wollheim, R. 1999. *On the Emotions*. New Haven, CT: Yale University Press.

Wong, M. A. Y. 2015. 'Towards a Theory of Mood Function', *Philosophical Psychology* 29(2): 157–78.

Wyer, R. S. and Srull T. K. (eds.) 1994. *Handbook of Social Cognition*. Hillsdale, NJ: Erlbaum.

Young, J. Z. 1971. *An Introduction to the Study of Man*. Oxford: Clarendon Press.

Zajonc, R. B. 1980. 'Feeling and Thinking: Preferences Need No Inferences', *American Psychologist* 35: 151–75.

1984. 'On the Primacy of Affect', *American Psychologist* 39: 117–23.

Zeelenberg, M. and Pieters, R. 2007. 'A Theory of Regret Regulation', *Journal of Consumer Psychology* 17(1): 3–18.

Zeimbekis, J. and Raftopoulos, A. (eds.) 2015. *The Cognitive Penetrability of Perception: New Philosophical Perspectives*. Oxford: Oxford University Press.

Index

action (behavioural) tendencies, 8, 51, 57, 69, 71, 82, 84, 86, 88, 91–92, 95–96, 137, 201
action out of emotion, 202, 205
action tendencies, 79
affordances, 10, 65–66, 69–70, 110, 114–116, 118–123, 125–126, 128
appraisal theories, 73, 92, 96, 111, 113, 181
appraisals, 8, 51–52, 57, 59, 62–65, 69–70, 91, 96, 114, 137, 145, 170, 181, 184
Àrdal, P. S., 168, 209
Aristotle, 6, 25–26, 28, 33, 37, 39, 110–111, 209, 221
Armon-Jones, C., 79, 169, 172, 177, 180, 209
Armstrong, D. M., 17, 22, 209, 217
Arnold, M. B., 181, 209
Arpaly, N., 141, 209
attention, 3, 5, 25, 54, 58–59, 61, 64, 66, 68–70, 88, 97, 102, 124, 128, 147, 171, 173–175, 179, 182, 200, 203
Austin, J., 138, 209
Averill, J., 79, 209

Bagnoli, C., 188, 190, 198–200, 203–205, 209
Baier, A., 170, 209
Barrett, L., 51, 68, 209
belief, 41, 49–50, 73, 81, 98, 100, 108, 125, 131, 140, 155, 175, 177, 182, 191, 198, 201–203
Betzler, M., 207, 209
Bird, A., 166, 209
Block, N., 17–18, 209–210, 216–217
bodily changes, 6, 8, 16, 52–54, 56–59, 61–64, 67, 69, 110–111, 114–115, 118, 121, 124
Bower, G. H., 173, 210
Brady, M., 2, 88, 92, 94, 100, 107, 168, 170, 183, 210
Branigan, C., 173, 213
Broad, C. D., 170, 210
Burge, T., 98, 210
Butler, 72

Cacioppo, J. T., 51, 67, 210
Campbell, J., 195, 210
Campbell, K., 41, 210
caring, 152–153, 155–157, 162, 164
Cassam, C., 130–133, 210
causation D. J., 37–38, 44, 46, 50, 134, 202
Chalmers, 20, 23, 42, 210, 221
Chemero, A., 66, 210
Christie, I. C., 72, 222
Chudnoff E., 96
Churchland, P. S., 33, 210
Cioran, E. M., 187, 190, 210, 220
Clore, G. L., 169, 177, 210
cognitive monitoring, 68
cognitivism, 52–53
Cohen, J., 146, 210
Colman, A. M., 137, 219
Colombetti, G., 117, 123, 210
commitments, 7, 9, 33, 90, 94–95, 97, 99–101, 103–109, 122, 152, 166
component theories of emotions, 90, 92, 95
components of emotions, 8–9, 19, 51, 53, 71, 73–80, 84–85, 87, 89–92, 95–97, 101, 103, 112, 121, 128, 136, 142
consciousness, 11–12, 14–15, 25, 35, 42, 44, 54, 60, 62, 141, 169, 188–195, 198, 207
core relational themes, 10, 61–64, 122–123
Cosmides, L., 79, 211
Cottingham, J., 17, 211
Crane, T., 1, 170, 176, 211, 217, 220
Crowther, T., 79, 191, 211

D'Arms, J., 71, 92, 211, 221
Damasio, A. R., 56–58, 62–64, 71, 111, 211
Darwin, C., 57, 111, 211
Davidson, R. J., 170, 177, 211–213
Davis, C. G., 207, 211
de Sousa, R., 5, 71, 88, 125, 149, 170, 172, 181, 211
Deigh, J., 52, 211
DeLancey, C., 169, 172, 177, 211
deliberation, 195–197, 199–200, 202, 205
Dennett, D. C., 21, 97

Deonna, J., 2–3, 5, 51, 71, 91–92, 94, 98, 103, 134, 141, 148, 152, 168, 172, 177–178, 180, 183, 212
dependency relations, 73–76
Descartes, 16, 38, 44, 92, 110–111, 211–212
desires, 5, 28, 41, 49, 73, 81, 92, 110, 128, 147, 154, 168–172, 175, 196, 198, 202, 204–205
Di Paolo, E. A., 117, 212
dispositions, 4, 7, 11, 37–39, 41–43, 45–51, 165–167, 169–170, 173–176, 186
  manifestations, 11, 28, 30–32, 35, 37, 41, 45–47, 130–131, 145–146, 148, 165, 167, 174–175
Döring, S., 51, 65, 149, 181, 212
Drayson, Z., 97, 212
Dretske, F., 5, 19–21, 62, 112, 130–131, 212
dualism, 6, 16, 22, 44, 97, 123

Eccles, J., 24, 220
Ekman, P., 51, 67, 80, 137, 151, 177–178, 211–213, 223
Ellis, G. F. R., 65, 214, 223
Ellsworth, P., 51, 53, 70, 73, 212, 218
Elster, J., 71, 170, 213
embodied theories of emotion, 110
emergence, 14, 16, 22–23, 25, 33–35, 117, 189
Emmons, R. A., 197
emotional intensity, 111
enaction, 116–117, 212
enactivism, 117, 122, 129
evaluation, 1, 3, 52, 57, 61, 92, 94, 97, 99–100, 102–103, 105, 145, 197–198
evaluative possibilities, 170, 181–186
events, 3, 5–7, 9, 14, 23–24, 27–28, 30–31, 49, 52–56, 59, 64, 71, 74, 76, 78–80, 83–87, 89, 113, 127, 138, 141, 149, 153, 166, 168–169, 173, 175, 186, 191, 195, 197, 211
Exline, J., 207, 213
experiences, 2–3, 5, 9, 14–16, 20–23, 27, 31, 34–35, 42, 90–91, 93–98, 100–109, 111, 113, 133, 141, 146, 149, 153, 157, 170, 174, 181–184, 186, 193
expression of emotion, 5, 13, 57, 63, 67–68, 71, 130, 133–137, 142–145, 147, 153, 159–160, 172, 190, 196, 202–204, 206
expressive actions. *See* expressive behaviour
expressive behaviour, 134, 136, 172, 174

feelings, 3, 5, 14, 16–17, 20, 22, 35, 43, 51, 53–54, 57, 59, 69, 71, 73, 75, 77, 80, 82, 84, 87–88, 91, 104, 134, 141–142, 145, 151, 171, 177–178, 189
Fernandez-Dols, J. M., 121
Fine, K., 25, 27, 29, 134, 213
Fish, W., 3, 170, 176, 213
Fisher, M. L., 207, 213
Fodor, J., 17–19, 113, 210, 213
Fredrickson, B. L., 173, 213
Friedman, B. H., 72, 222
Frijda, N., 51, 66–67, 79, 88, 114, 169, 171–172, 174, 177, 200, 213, 218
functionalism, 18–19, 21, 41–42, 44, 146–147, 175, 217

Gallagher, S., 133, 213
Geach, P., 5, 213
Gibson, J. J., 65–66, 114–116, 119, 213
Goldie, P., 2, 4, 14, 51–52, 72–73, 76–78, 87, 89, 91, 97, 141, 150, 152, 168, 170, 172, 178–179, 190, 202, 204, 206, 213–214, 222
Gordon, D. M., 204, 214
Gordon, R., 2, 214
Grahek, N., 81, 214
Green, O. H., 92, 130–131, 134, 136–137, 214
Greenspan, P. S., 93, 214
Grèzes, J., 114, 214
grief, 72, 75–78, 89, 141, 178
Griffiths, P., 10, 50, 114, 116, 119–121, 124, 170, 172, 174–175, 214

Hanson, E., 173, 218
Harré, R., 39, 214
Hatzimoysis, A., 2, 211, 214
Heidegger, M., 181, 183, 214
Heil, J., vii, 7, 21, 28, 37–39, 41, 43, 46–47, 49–50, 83, 166, 173, 176, 214, 217
Helm, B., 9, 91, 94, 100, 103–105, 107, 151–152, 154, 156–157, 160, 163, 214
Hinde, R. A., 124–125, 215
Höfler, A., 170, 215
Hofweber, T., 4, 215
Hornsby, J., 202, 215
Hume, D., 37, 91, 165–166, 168, 209, 215
Hursthouse, R., 203, 215
Hutcheson, F., 111, 215
hylomorphism, 6, 17, 25–26, 32, 36

imagination, 13, 73, 77, 87–88, 189, 194, 199, 203–204
informational semantics, 112–113, 115
intentional action, 99–100, 172
intentionality, 14, 19–20, 28, 80, 85, 87, 126, 153–154, 163, 172–173, 177, 179, 181–182, 186
Isen, A. M., 172, 215

Jackson, F., 20, 43, 133, 136, 215, 220
Jacob, P., 133, 148, 215–216
Jacobson, D., 71, 92, 188–189, 195, 197–198, 201, 205, 211, 215, 221

Jaegher, H., 117, 212
James, W., 5, 8, 16, 20, 52–63, 65–66, 68–69, 91, 111–112, 124, 134, 212, 215–216
Jaworska, A., 152, 157, 215
Jaworski, W., vii, 6–7, 14, 17–21, 23–25, 27–28, 38, 215
Johnston, M., 25, 27, 29, 210, 216
Jones, K., 63, 210–211, 216
judgments, 62, 91, 93, 98–100, 102, 110–112, 128, 149, 151
Juslin, P., 51, 216

Kenny, A., 2, 111, 125, 138, 142, 170, 206, 216
Kim, J., 18, 21, 216
Kind, A., 171, 179–180, 216
Kirby, L. D., 51
Kirk, R., 42, 216
Koons, R., 25, 216
Koslicki, K., 25, 27, 216
Kreibig, S., 51, 67, 216
Krueger, J., 131, 136, 216

Lacasse, K., 72, 216
Lacewing, M., 2, 216
Laird, J., 59, 72, 169, 177, 216, 219
Landman, J., 188–189, 216
Lange, C. G., 53, 91, 111–112, 124, 216
Laukka, P., 51, 216
Lazarus, R. S., 51–52, 62, 80, 111, 170, 177, 181, 216
LeDoux, J., 52, 55, 217
Levenson, R. W., 51, 67, 217
Levin, J., 175, 217
Lewis, D. K., 17–18, 28, 46, 210–211, 217–218
Locke, J., 48, 123, 217
Long, G. M., 102, 217
Lormand, E., 170–173, 175, 217
love, 4, 51, 55, 60, 63, 65–66, 149, 151, 153–154, 157–164, 168, 171, 184, 202
Lyons, W., 52, 54, 170, 217

Mac Cumhaill, C., vii, 12, 187
Madden, E. H., 39, 214
Maienborn, H., 138–139, 143, 217
manifestations, 146, 167
Marmodoro, A., 25, 217
Martin, C. B., 28, 37, 46, 49, 214, 217
Matthews, G., 88, 217
Maund, B., 131, 217
Maxmen, J. S., 169, 177, 219
Mayer, J. D., 173, 218
McCullough, M. E., 197
McDowell, J., 130, 218
McLean, P. D., 80, 218
McNeill, W. E. S., 130, 132, 218
Mendelovici, A., 1, 180, 218
mental actions, 201, 203
mental activity, 13, 117, 188–190, 193, 198, 200, 205–206
Michalak, J., 172, 218
Miller, J., 29–30
Millikan, R., 183, 218
Mineka, S., 173, 218
Molnar, G., 28, 166, 218
moods, 3, 11–12, 20, 169–186
  diffuseness of, 171–173, 177, 179, 182, 186
  pervasiveness of, 172–174, 179, 182, 186
Moors, A., 92, 96, 218
Morris, W. N., 171–172, 218
Morton, A., 169–170, 172, 218
Mourelatos, A., 79, 138, 218
Mulhall, S., 181, 183, 218
Mulligan, K., 176, 218
multi-track dispositions. *See* dispositions
Mumford, S., 166, 218

Naar, H., vii, 1, 4, 11, 89, 109, 129, 148–149, 169, 173, 175, 185, 187, 218–219
Nagel, T., 24, 219
neutral monism, 22, 24
Noë, A., 21, 219
norms, 9, 90, 99, 105–109, 126, 157
Nussbaum, M., 51, 100, 146, 149, 181, 219–220

O'Regan, J. K., 21, 219
O'Shaughnessy, B., 13, 71, 141–142, 188–194, 198, 200–201, 206, 208, 219
Oakley, J., 73, 219
Oatley, K., 169, 177, 219
occurrences, 9, 14, 35, 71, 76, 78–80, 82–89, 113, 125, 140, 160, 163
Oderberg, D. S., 25, 27, 219
Öhman, A., 55, 219
Owens, H., 169, 177, 219

Pacherie, E., 3, 219
pain, 23, 42–43, 73, 80–88, 94, 134–135, 175–176
Panksepp, J., 72, 219
Pargetter, R., 43, 220
Parkinson, B., 137, 219
Parsons, T., 139, 219
Parvizi, J., 33, 219
patterns, 11, 29, 58, 62–63, 77–78, 88–89, 118, 122, 145, 151–165, 167, 172, 189, 199, 202–203
perception, 5, 11, 14, 34, 53–54, 56–63, 65–66, 68, 102, 111–112, 114–115, 118–119, 130, 132–134, 136–139, 143, 145–146, 148, 181, 183–184, 186

perceptual experiences, 3, 91, 94, 98, 150, 170, 181–184, 186
Pfeifer, K., 28, 217
phenomenology, 1–2, 12, 16, 21, 71, 80, 82–84, 86, 90, 92, 95–96, 98, 101, 168, 171, 176–177, 182, 184, 187, 191, 194, 199, 204
Phillips, I., 133, 219
physicalism, 6, 16–22, 36
physiological changes, 7, 17, 52, 65, 69–70, 91, 95–96
Pickard, H., 134, 219
Pieters, R., 189, 198, 201
Pitcher, G., 94
Place, 28, 210, 217, 219, 222
Plato, 39
Popper, K. R., 24, 220
powers, 7, 12, 27–36, 38–40, 44, 48, 56, 120, 123, 163, 165–166, 191–193, 207
predicates, 40, 43–45, 47, 50
Price, C., 3, 169–172, 181, 183–185, 220
Prinz, J., vii, 6, 8, 10, 20, 26, 51–52, 62–64, 67, 74, 77, 91, 95–96, 108–113, 118, 123, 170, 174, 176–181, 220
Prior, E. W., 43, 119–120, 220
processes, 4, 6, 8–11, 23, 39, 51–53, 55, 58–59, 63, 65–66, 68–71, 73, 76–80, 83–87, 89, 91–92, 95–96, 98, 102, 108, 117–118, 130, 135–138, 140–145, 147, 149, 169, 173–175, 186, 189, 193, 198
properties, 2, 6–7, 15–16, 22, 24, 28, 34, 37–44, 47–49, 76, 82–85, 102, 110, 116–117, 119, 123, 125, 128, 135, 138, 146, 170, 173, 176, 179–182, 184, 186, 192, 205, 207–208
psychological explanations, 75, 89, 162–163
Pugmire, D., 155, 220
Putnam, H., 17–18, 211, 220

qualia, 7, 20–21, 42–44, 176

Raftopoulos, A., 132, 224
rationality, 10, 71, 92–93, 107, 109, 111, 126
Rea, M. C., 25, 27–28, 220
reasons, 2–3, 5, 15, 21, 40, 44, 46, 50, 92, 98–99, 102, 107, 118, 126, 142, 157, 159, 166, 168, 173, 188, 200, 203–205
Regier, W., 187, 220
regret, 12, 126, 187–190, 193, 195–208
Reisenzein, R., 173, 221
representational content, 92, 113, 126
representational states, 110
Roberts, R., 2, 50, 52, 91, 93, 101–102, 220
Robinson, J., vii, 4, 8–9, 51–52, 63, 66, 68, 73, 92, 149, 214, 220
Roese, N., 200, 216, 220
Roseman, I. J., 51, 220
Ruiz-Belda, M. A., 121, 124, 213
Russell, B., 24, 220
Russell, J. A., 20, 51, 68, 169, 212–213, 220
Ryle, G., 4, 37, 43, 45, 220

Scarantino, A., 10, 87, 114–116, 119–121, 124, 214, 221
Schachter, S., 52
Scherer, K. R., 51, 73, 137, 142, 145, 181, 218, 220–221, 223
Schmidt, R. E., 187, 189, 200, 221
Schroeder, T., 141, 209
Searle, J. R., 92, 172, 221
self-consciousness, 193
sentiments, 1, 3, 11, 150–154, 156–157, 160–167, 201, 203
Shand, A. F., 170, 174, 221
Shargel, D., vii, 10, 110–113, 124, 126, 221
Shoemaker, D. W., 151–152, 164, 215, 221
Shoemaker, S., 166, 221
Siegel, S., 92, 108–109, 221
Siemer, M., 170–176, 221
Singer, J. E., 52
Sizer, L., 170, 172–173, 175, 221
sleep, 13, 121, 143, 158, 175, 178, 188–191, 193, 197, 202, 205–206, 208
Smith, vii, 10, 51, 130–131, 146, 148, 166, 168, 221–222
Solomon, R. C., 51–53, 80, 100, 149, 170, 178–179, 181, 214, 222
somatic markers, 58
Soteriou, M., vii, 8, 71, 85, 141, 144, 168, 188, 200–201, 222
Sperry, R., 32, 222
states, 1–3, 5–8, 10–12, 14, 17–23, 25–26, 28, 37, 39, 41–43, 45, 47, 49–51, 53, 57–59, 62–64, 66–67, 71, 74, 76, 78, 80, 82–89, 91–92, 95–96, 98, 110–115, 117–118, 123–128, 130, 132, 136, 138, 141–143, 145–147, 149–151, 155, 158–159, 161, 163–164, 167, 169–171, 174–176, 178, 181, 183–186, 188, 190–192, 194–195, 197, 207
Stephens, C. L., 72, 222
Steward, H., 5, 72, 79, 96, 137, 141, 144, 222
Stewart, J., 212
Stone, L., 80, 222
Stout, R., 79, 130, 222
Strawson, G., 23–24, 222
structure, 2, 5–6, 26–27, 29, 31, 33–35, 61, 70, 81, 154, 163
Sutton, S. K., 173, 218

Tappolet, C., vii, 2–5, 12, 51, 65, 67, 91, 149, 168–169, 175, 181, 183–184, 216, 219, 222
temporal extension, 149

Teroni, F., vii, 1–3, 51, 71, 79, 89, 91–92, 94, 98, 103, 109, 129, 134, 141, 148, 152, 154, 168–169, 172, 176–178, 180, 183, 187, 203, 212, 222
Thalberg, I., 172, 222
Thayer, R., 170, 222
Thompson, E. T., 117, 123, 210–211, 219, 223
Tomkins, S., 51, 223
Tooby, J., 79, 211
Toppino, T. C., 102, 217
Tormey, A., 136, 223
Toronchuk, J. A., 65, 223
tropes, 39, 138, 140
truthmakers, 40, 44, 50
Tye, M., 2, 170, 179, 181, 223

Unger, P., 48, 223

Van der Linden, M., 189, 200, 221
van Inwagen, P., 30, 221
Vance, J., vii, 9, 90, 92, 108, 223
Varela, F. J., 117, 127, 223
Vendler, Z., 5, 138, 140, 223

Wallace, J., 188, 197, 223
Watson, J. B., 55, 223
Wells, A., 88, 217
Whittle, A., 146, 148, 223
willful action, 193
Williams, B., 13, 188, 190, 195–200, 202–204, 207, 223
Williams, D. C., 29, 223
Wimsatt, W. C., 24, 223
Witasek, S., 170, 174, 223
Wollheim, R., 4, 141, 160, 223
Wong, M. A. Y., 170, 223

Young, J. Z., 29, 224

Zajonc, R. B., 52, 55, 224
Zeelenberg, M., 189, 198, 201, 224
Zeimbekis, J., 132, 224

Lightning Source UK Ltd.
Milton Keynes UK
UKHW022045030422
401046UK00015B/459

9 781107 52739